FROM SPEAKING TO WRITING
TO READING
Relating the Arts of Communication

FROM SPEAKING TO WRITING TO READING

Relating the Arts of Communication

Robert A. Wolsch

Western Connecticut State College and
Danbury Hearing, Speech, and Learning Center

and

Lois A. Cothran Wolsch

Danbury Public Schools and
Danbury Hearing, Speech, and Learning Center

Teachers College, Columbia University
New York and London   1982

In 1946 the Commission on the English Curriculum of the
National Council of Teachers of English began a study of the
relationship between the growth of language power and the pattern of the child's normal development on all school levels. The
result of the study, *The English Language Arts* (1952), showed a
consistent interrelationship of the arts of listening, speaking, writing, and reading. One spoke; another listened; one wrote; another read aloud.

The program recommended by the commission was organized around the ideas, experiences, and feelings of pupils—not
publishers. Language was to grow out of the life of the school
and the interests and activities of the children. It was strongly
recommended that the language experiences be presented as a
wholesome way to use leisure, as a useful instrument, and as a
potential art form.

Too few programs and materials have lived up to those recommendations. This book is dedicated to those who add light
along that path.

Published by Teachers College Press, 1234 Amsterdam Avenue, New York, N.Y. 10027

Library of Congress Cataloging in Publication Data

Wolsch, Robert A.
  From speaking to writing to reading.

  Rev. ed. of: Poetic composition through the grades /
by Robert A. Wolsch. 1970.
  Bibliography: p.
  Includes index.
  1. Language arts.   2.   Oral communication.   I.   Wolsch,
Lois A.   II.   Wolsch, Robert A.   Poetic composition
through the grades.   III.   Title.
LB1576.W65   1982   372.6   82-3228
                          AACR2

ISBN 0-8077-2607-9

Manufactured in the United States of America

87 86 85 84 83 82   1 2 3 4 5 6

Contents

APPENDICES
FURTHERING COMMUNICATION

Foreword

We know that speaking, listening, writing, and reading go hand in hand and that each of these language functions affects and reinforces the others. Robert and Lois Wolsch offer the reader both a sound theoretical base and a great variety of practical suggestions to guide our insights about the composing act as a way of communicating with words.

Dr. and Mrs. Wolsch offer a framework for their many practical suggestions that is revealing about the larger teaching act; they propose a way of supporting learners that not only gets results but is also sensitive to the "onlyness" of the learner. They describe communication practices that will keep the learning process humane yet rigorous, spontaneous but disciplined, enjoyable and significant.

Leland B. Jacobs
Professor Emeritus of Education
Teachers College,
Columbia University

Preface

I first developed this three-stage educational model while language arts consultant in the public schools of Mineola, Long Island. It was later submitted as part of a YMCA application for government funding during the 1960s. The proposal included a scientific method for enabling students and teachers to cope with problems skillfully and humanely, using listening, speaking, writing, and reading as means of peaceful survival. I developed and refined it, as one of three curriculum designs, while director of Curriculum Research and Development in Training Resources for Youth (TRY), an experimental program of the Urban Job Corps. The ultimate plan was to prepare coordinated vocational-academic programs that included the model's methods and materials for world-wide adoption sponsored by the United States government.

The program, variously titled "Life Skills," "Coping Skills," and "Basic Skills," has been adapted to Job Corps centers, prisons, and community adult education centers. I also used this three-stage model in my book *Poetic Composition Through the Grades*. My wife, Lois, and I have applied it to college teaching and remedial education in schools and in our private center, the Danbury Hearing, Speech and Learning Center. It also formed the structure for my graduate program, Communication Arts for Teachers, at Western Connecticut State College.

Bob Wolsch

Acknowledgments

Many people have contributed to the completion of this book. To those listed below we are particularly grateful.

Leland Jacobs, Bob's teacher, for his ideas about composition, which are found throughout this book, and for being a personal and professional model.

John Dewey and Erich Fromm, for their ideas, which have become so much a part of us that they appear unintentionally and without due credit.

Alice Miel, for her ability to recognize and willingness to implement creative ideas and guide teachers, and for encouraging continued study and writing about curriculum and teaching.

The late Kathryn Farrington, an editor, who helped us realize that the cup of creativity was never empty.

Winthrop Adkins, for encouraging this three-stage learning model and applying it to Life Skills Education.

Robert Kennedy, for his faith in the experimental language arts program of the Urban Job Corps.

Professor Adam Aitchison, Dean Gertrude Braun, President Ruth Haas, and Dean Jack Rudner, of Western Connecticut State College, for supporting Bob's program innovations, including the Master of Science Program in Communication Arts for Teachers.

Our teacher friends, colleagues, and students, for providing examples of language ways and needs and questions for which we had to seek answers.

Students from Danbury, Connecticut; Mineola, Rockville Centre, and East Meadow, Long Island; Brooklyn, New York; Grand Haven, Michigan; North York, Ontario; and the Queens College Speech and Hearing

Center; the Danbury Hearing, Speech and Learning Center; and TRY, Inc. (Training Resources for Youth), and Western Connecticut State College, for sharing the language experiences used throughout this book.

Jane Barry, a meticulous and creative editor, who taught us how to improve the book without losing our feelings of authorship.

William H. Hauer, editor of *The Elementary School Creative Writer*, for permission to use "The Sea" by Marjorie Bobbins.

Sheila Schwartz, professor of English Education at New York State University, New Paltz, for permission to include writing by and about her late daughter, Nancy Lynn Schwartz, and for caring enough about this book to recommend surgical procedures for the first one hundred pages of an earlier draft.

Edith Godel, librarian at Western Connecticut State College, for her help in preparing a list of recordings to accompany writing and reading.

Bud Mackta, for his memories of "The Furrin Lady," Bob's grandmother.

Millie and Morton Siegel, for permission to reprint their reviews and for reading the appendices and encouraging us to remain forthright.

Chris Durante, for his drawings of children, the Wolsch family readers' theatre troup, and the graphic introductions to the three levels of the program.

Peter Selgin, for permitting us to use excerpts from his journal.

Linda Jordan Torcia for her art works.

David H. Spangler for his poem about the death of John Lennon.

Marian D. Fabbio for her poem "Dictations from Paper."

Marianthi Lazos for her "Encounter" with the sea.

John Fusto, Debra Johnson, Laura E. Linden, and Susan Dugan for permission to reprint their "news items."

Kathy Chapman for her pattern poems, "Dejection" and "Hate Knows So Many Words."

The National Council of Teachers of English, for permission to use Vernon H. Smith's test of teacher judgment.

Our children, William, Jordan, and Lisa, for permission to use their compositional beginnings and for their increasing levels of understanding about our inability to be with them while we were working on this book.

Introduction

When our three-year-old awoke one night
    screaming,
    face red and salted with tears,
    we picked Billy up, put his seat on our arms, and asked,
    "What's the matter? Give us a hint."

He aimed his pointer finger
    toward his tonsils and sobbed,
    "There's a fire-breathing monster down there."
    "And," pointing next to his throbbing temple,
    "there's a little heart beating up there."

There he was,
    standing in his wooly Dr. Denton sleepers
    thinking and speaking by word painting
    to express what he did not understand
    in pictures he did understand.

People who know about the development of thinking
    and language use
    call this word painting
    analogical, says Piaget,
    nondiscursive, says Langer.

This three-year-old
    barely dry anywhere,
    without a smidgin of Latinate grammar,
    without a vocabulary list or a spelling demon list to refer to,
    without any testing as to the proper place for a predicate,
    without even declining the varieties of verbs
COMMUNICATED

under the most trying circumstances,
    feeling pain and fright,
by using what language he had
to put what he did not know in terms he did know.
He made an analogy—
    a kind of metaphor.
    Yes, he made a metaphor.
He expressed himself in poetic language
    to communicate effectively.

Language begins—poetically
    from sounds and rhythms and images.
    Repeated and varied, or varied and repeated,
    flowing and growing.
Then logical thinking begins—
    analogically.
Speaking begins—at times,
    nondiscursively.

If someone writes it down,
    the speaker becomes the writer,
    writing out of a speaking-language storehouse
    rather than from
    spelling-language limitations.

At times,
    a poetic arrangement of the page,
    like the frame of a picture,
    helps the observer focus
    appreciatively.

The message conveyed by this book is that people who paint pictures with
words are all around us, expressing themselves with words as others use
paints or music or movement or clay. Influencing our language environment, these word-crafters concentrate on the sound as well as the sight
of language and dwell on images and rhythmic phrases at least as much as
punctuated sentences. They speak to us on our streets, in our schools, and
at work. They sit with us at dinner. They speak the language of everyday
people but are often drawn first to the feelings of language and only later to
its formalities. They delight in seeking and experimenting with new ways
of communicating. Those who work with words know that, like love, the

sensitivity to communication may occur and recur and grow anywhere, anytime, and within anyone.

Since communication with words is so vital an interpersonal need, it is not surprising that other people play an important role in encouraging speakers, writers, and readers of all ages to enjoy the satisfactions known to workers in other crafts. To follow the cycle of communication, to work with words knowing the intimate relationship of speaking to writing to reading to listening to feeling and thinking, and then to take pride in their work — this is how people become word-workers.

Composing with words may begin the communication cycle, but it may also begin with listening or reading. For many, the speaking-writing-reading sequence facilitates the process. In any event, composing with words may begin at home, in public and private schools, in religious schools, in Sunday schools, in hospitals, in nursing homes, in community centers, at camp, or even in jail.

Although this book is for all sorts of beginning composers, many of the examples given are the work of children. As in a one-room schoolhouse, older people will be encouraged to attempt what youngsters have accomplished. Adults have reported their resolutions by saying, "If those kids could do that, I'll try." And they have.

And they have succeeded because, with appropriate guidance, heightened sensitivity to language can be nurtured in people of all ages and backgrounds. This handbook is a guide to increasing language sensitivity through a communication program in three stages: evoking visions through speech, fashioning revisions in writing, and sharing visions — now in the form of compositions — by reading.

The "Evoking Visions" stage includes ways of stimulating the act of painting with words, usually orally, and then uncovering and recognizing the nature and values of the language pictures evoked. Primary emphasis in this first stage is on developing an appreciation of one's own ability to think, to speak, and to compose with language.

The "Fashioning Revisions" stage covers the ways in which language may be invigorated, new composition forms created, and old forms recycled. The major goal of this stage is versatility in reorganizing language and form. Too often beginning learners have plunged — or been pushed — into this second, usually written, stage without life-preserving practice in the first, usually oral, one.

The "Sharing Visions" stage involves the search, selection, and preparation required before one can share one's compositions with others. A favorable reception by a listening or reading audience spins the communication cycle one more turn to begin again.

The evoking, fashioning, and sharing stages usually follow the speaking to writing to reading sequence. Together they form the basis for the program discussed in this handbook. The three stages, like the three modes of communication, are interdependent. One may need to repeat one stage or one mode of communicating in order to prepare for the next.

We expect the audience for this book to include teachers and teachers-to-be, students, speakers, writers and writers-to-be, parents and parents-to-be, grandparents, counselors, and friends. We urge our readers to begin to compose themselves. Teachers, like speakers and writers, do best what excites them, and so they require successful experiences in speaking, writing, and reading aloud in order to be effective in teaching these forms of communication.

The present system of certification for teachers and administrators does not stress courses, proficiency, or personal involvement in language, speaking, writing, or communication. But it is not certification that qualifies one to help another communicate. People who delight in the sound and the feel of new words and phrases and take pride in their own word pictures are the teachers we want for our children and grandchildren. These people, whether their title is parent, teacher, speaker, writer, counselor, or friend, must remain students and practitioners of the communication arts.

USING THIS BOOK

Who Might Use This Book

1. Teacher-educators who are developing courses, programs, and workshops for preservice and in-service teachers in the language arts and English.
2. Secondary, college, and graduate students of communication, speech, language, or English who are seeking alternative ways of thinking and learning.
3. Teachers personally interested in general communication, oral or written communication, language arts, remedial speech, writing, or reading, learning disabilities, basic skills, and coordinating speaking, writing, and reading.
4. Administrators, supervisors of reading, speech and language arts, school board members interested in curriculum and teaching, parents, friends, therapists, counselors — those who are helping themselves and other people communicate.
5. Authors and would-be authors, who may use it independently without a teacher.

How to Use This Book

1. Find one idea, phrase, sentence, paragraph, or section in each chapter particularly worthy of further thought or elaboration. Focus discussion, related reading, lectures, or research on your choice.
2. Prepare a short talk or paper on this item before class discussion and another after it.
3. Practice the suggestions for composition in each chapter. Ask others to read your work. Consider their opinions.
4. Collect all your work in a folder or journal. Reread it in a few weeks. Revise and share with appropriate people.
5. Review your progress. Make a plan for your next steps.
6. Try on different ways with language as you would hats in a store.
7. Work with a friend or two: Make decisions together at first, and then decide for yourself.
8. Find a section of the book that interests you: Follow the suggestions for speaking, writing, and further reading. Discuss your reactions with others.

1 Speakers and Writers All Around Us

Working with words is a craft, like shaping clay. Word crafters speak of their pleasures and their pain. They work with heightened language; they laugh, they cry, they dance with words. Composing with words is an ageless skill, like dancing, composing with music, or playing the guitar.

But composing with words is lonely, and one can become enamored of one's creation. Objectivity requires listening to the words and making sure they are written down with a soft pencil because wordcraft, like any other craft, requires reworking. It starts, ends, and begins again with listening to language. And listening, deep listening, is an expression of love and trust. An eleventh grader confides:

> I will try to show you
> pieces
> of
> my soul
> slowly
>
> If you are quiet and patient
> I will open doors
> that usually are shut tight
> and out will come
> ideas and dreams
> laughter and tears
> sounds and sights and people and places
> that have carved their way
> into my mind
> and soul
> and become me.
>
> I will show some of me to you
> If you care and wish to know
> but if you regard these parts of me lightly
> or worse

1

judge them
I will wrap them up
and lock them behind thick doors
and close myself to you.

Each of the following five selections was written by a different youngster in the same elementary school grade. They were part of a study by Vernon H. Smith that showed the variation in teacher judgments of student compositions.*

The teachers were asked to rank the five selections in order of the quality of the writing.

I. MY FAMILY

I have a dog named tawny. He is a golden retrevor, but he doesn't make a good one. When we go pheasant hunting, I shoot and Tawny goes and hides. I also have a little brother who's a bother. He thinks my modles are real neat. But, when he plays with them he throws them down the stairs. Now I won't let him in my room. I have a sister named Sara (Squara). She is a very good cook, but that's about all. Every knight she looks like a clown, because she has poka-dot pajamas, a half chewed up blue net and enough make-up for every movie star in the U.S.

II. MY FAMILY

I live in Denver. I like where I live. I go to lincoln that is the name of my school. My name is Beverly. I have one brother and no sisters. My monther works ate the Honeywell Plant and my dad workes at Dave Cooks. I am in the fifth grade. My teacher's name is Miss Jones. My princeabule is Mrs. Brown. On saterdays we clean the house and, on sundays we rest and mother and I fix the diner.

III. MY FAMILY

There are seven people in my family. My Mom and Dad my older brother Bobby and my older sister Kathy, my younger brother Tommy, and my younger sister Jill. Bobby is thirteen he plays baseball and football. Kathy is eleven Kathy and I take ballet lessons. Tommy is 9 he does not play football but he plays baseball. My Dad is a coach of Tommys team.. My Dad is a carpter contracter. Mom is a housewife she babysets the Jones four children. Jill is four and too young to go to school.

Wednesday evening we have our ballet lessons at four o'clock Kathy and I have an hour lesson with 10 other girls at six o'clock we have a half an hour of just Kathy and I alone. Every year we have a ballet recital. Kathy and I are learning a dance called Alice from Dalus.

---

*"A Do-It-Yourself Test: How Do You Rate as a Judge of Children's Writing?" *Elementary English* 47 (1970): 347. Copyright © 1970 by the National Council of Teachers of English. Used by permission.

IV. MY FAMILY

We have four people in our family counting me. We have a dog to he is brown and white. We use to have some gold fish but they died. We had them about a year and a half.

I have a brother he is 8 years old and his birthday is in March.

My dogs birthday is in March to it is 8 days after my brothers.

My father is a carpenter and is going to build us a new house but he doesn't know were to build it maybe on Pearce Street, but we don't know yet.

V. MY FAMILY

I don't come from a very large family. I have a sister, brother, mother and father. Everybody is always getting my sister and me mixed up. My sister has blue eyes and blond hair. We look pretty much alike. Down in Arkansas people are always asking if we are twins. My brother is in the army. Only six more days and he'll be coming home. He's growing a mushtas I think thats funny.

Once when we all went down to Arkansas Mama and Grandma went blue berry picken. Grandma lives out in the hills or country where it is real pretty. There is a little strem there too where all the cows get their drinks. After they got a whole bucket of berry's they sat it down by the paths side where the cows go. They decided to come back and get it when they were finished. By the time they came back for it one of the cows had eaten all the berries in the bucket. I bring in the cows every sun down. I feed the cats, chicken, and horses.

Compare your judgments with those of your friends or Smith's subjects (see his article for the results of the test). You may also want to repeat the exercise after completing this book to see if your own judgments have changed. This chapter illustrates some of the strategies that can be used in uncovering and evaluating basic writing skills. Here is an actual incident that might serve as an example.

THE UNCOVERING PROCESS

Aesthetic Awareness

The language arts consultant was asked to help Marjorie improve her composition work before she went on to junior high school. The classroom teacher reclaimed a paper from an unemptied trash basket. The discarded sample of Marjorie's composition was similar, her sixth grade teacher said, to the child's usual schoolwork. The teacher had played a recording of Debussy's *La Mer* and suggested that the children write about the sea. Each

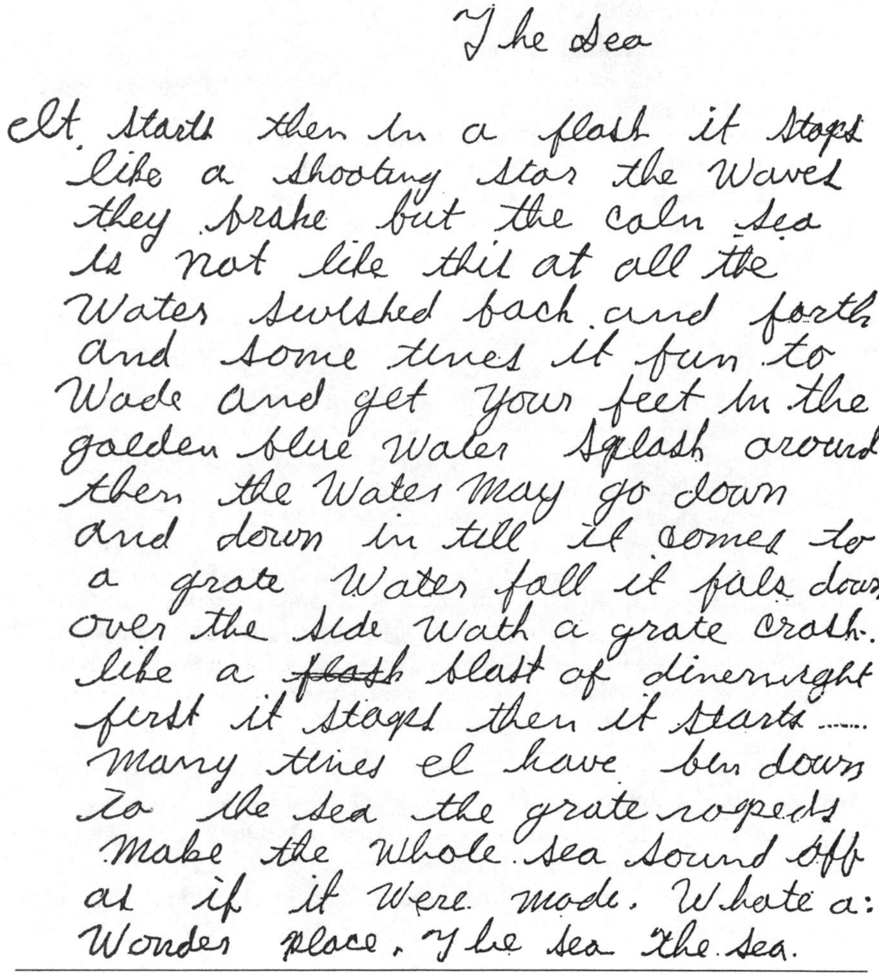

FIGURE 1.1.   "The Sea"

child was given a sheet of lined paper and a half hour to write. Marjorie's composition is reproduced in figure 1.1.

In typed form the composition looked like this.

THE SEA

It Starts then in a flash it Stops
   like a Shooting Star the Waves
   they brake but the caln Sea
   is not like this at all the

Water Swished back and forth
and Some tines it fun to
Wade and get Your feet in the
golden blue Water. Splash around
then the Water May go down
and down in till it comes to
a grate Water fall it fals down
over the Side Wath a grate crash.
like a blast of dinermight
first it Stops then it Starts
Many times I have ben down
to the Sea the grate ropeds
Make the Wholc Sea Sound off
as if it Were made. Whate a
Wonder place. The Sea The Sea

It didn't make sense to the teacher. The teacher had expected a prose essay and was disappointed with the material and the mechanics.

Ignoring mechanical errors, the language arts consultant asked the child to read her composition aloud. He arranged the selection so that the form followed the meaning and the rhythm, but maintained the same word order. Marjorie's pauses for breath and emphasis were noted with slash marks. (This is an old radio announcer's technique.) The separated phrases more clearly represented the sound, images, and rhythms of the sea.

THE SEA

It Starts/then in a flash it Stops/
like a Shooting Star/the Waves/
they brake/but the caln Sea/
is not like this at all/the
Water/Swished back and forth/
and Some tines/it fun to
Wade/and get Your feet in the/
golden blue Water/Splash around/
then the Water May go down/
and down/in till it comes to/
a grate Water fall/it fals down
over the Side/Wath a grate crash/
like a blast of dinermight/
first it Stops/then it Starts/
Many times/I have ben down
to the Sea/the grate ropeds/
Make the Whole Sea/Sound off
as if it Were made/Whate/a
Wonderplace/The Sea/The Sea/

The Pause That Expresses

In composing poems, prose fiction, and plays, (as in speech), the phrase is the unit of thought. The material must be spoken and heard. The pause — the separation between phrases — contributes to the meaning. In uncovering composition, one listens for the pauses. They mark the composer's rests for breath and signal meaning and gradations of emphasis. The pattern of pauses — the rhythmic markers — contributed to Marjorie's word painting of the sea. Some of her phrases were short; some were longer, like the great waterfall she described in her poem. Changing the arrangement from sentence form to phrase form changed what was being read as prose to nonmetrical poetry.

Next, the subtopics were noted and separated on the page. Marjorie had named and then described each of them in a logical order: the start, the waves, the water, a great waterfall, the great rapids, the wonder place. She named and described each element in a precise, topical order of increasing excitement, leading to a climax and ending with natural wonder.

Now notice the imagery. It is consistent with and appropriate to the intensity perceived by the writer. The instant flash of the shooting star helps the reader to feel the sea's heights and colorful movement. Next there is the contrast of the calm sea, where one can peacefully wade. Then one senses the sudden and multiple explosions of the great waterfall leading to the destructive rapids. Finally, there is the description of the sea as a wonder place or a place to wonder — quite different from the "wonderful" so often seen in children's writing.

Marjorie had a collection of her writings at home. Her parents had noticed her interest in describing her impressions and for several years had typed her compositions and kept a folder of her work. Much of it was similar to "The Sea." The phonograph record sparked this kind of writing at school. Apparently compositions like this had been unrecognized during Marjorie's five previous years at school.

With Marjorie's permission, the typed version of "The Sea" was included in the next issue of the school literary collection, which in turn was sent to a national magazine of elementary school children's writing.

The final version of Marjorie's work as it later appeared in the magazine looked like this:

THE SEA

It starts
    then in a flash
    it stops
    like a shooting star

The waves
    they break
    but the calm sea
    is not like this at all

The water
    swished back and forth
    and sometimes
    it's fun to wade
    and get your feet in the
    golden blue water.
    Splash around
    then the waves may go down
    and down
    until it comes to

A great waterfall
    It falls down over the side
    with a great crash
    like a blast of dynamite
    First it stops
    then it starts
    Many times
    I have been down to the sea

The great rapids
    make the whole sea
    sound off as if it were mad.

What a wonder place
    The sea
    The sea.

For five years people had tried to teach Marjorie to write in a clear, discursive style, primarily through training in the mechanics of syntax, spelling, and punctuation. They had overlooked the value of pleasurable composition in the instructional program.

The school's composition program, after years of professional effort, had been organized by the teachers into sequences of increasing difficulty to challenge students. But it had failed to interest Marjorie. No one knew of the kind of writing that she had done at home. It was not validated in school because the teachers were primarily concerned with literacy, and, in terms of curriculum proposals, this emphasis was legitimate.

The teachers did not recognize Marjorie's creative product for what it was. Their impression was that it was certainly not "good English work" if linear discourse, perfectly spelled and punctuated, was the goal. It was, however, the first draft of a nondiscursive work. Through rhythm, imagery, and analogy, Marjorie used language appropriately and precisely in expressing her feelings about the sea. She showed that she had some knowledge of the craft of composition.

Marjorie's first draft is an example of impromptu poetic composition. This type of ragamuffin writing often goes unnoticed. Teachers have to look for it, recognize it, and help "clean it up" (as one cleans sticky fingers before eating). They have to read it with their ears as well as their eyes. Similar examples of writings that reveal innate, untutored artistic abilities can be found all around us.

Alerting All Senses

Another selection (figure 1.2) was also found in a wastepaper basket, by the author's fifth-grade teacher.

In typewritten form, it read as follows:

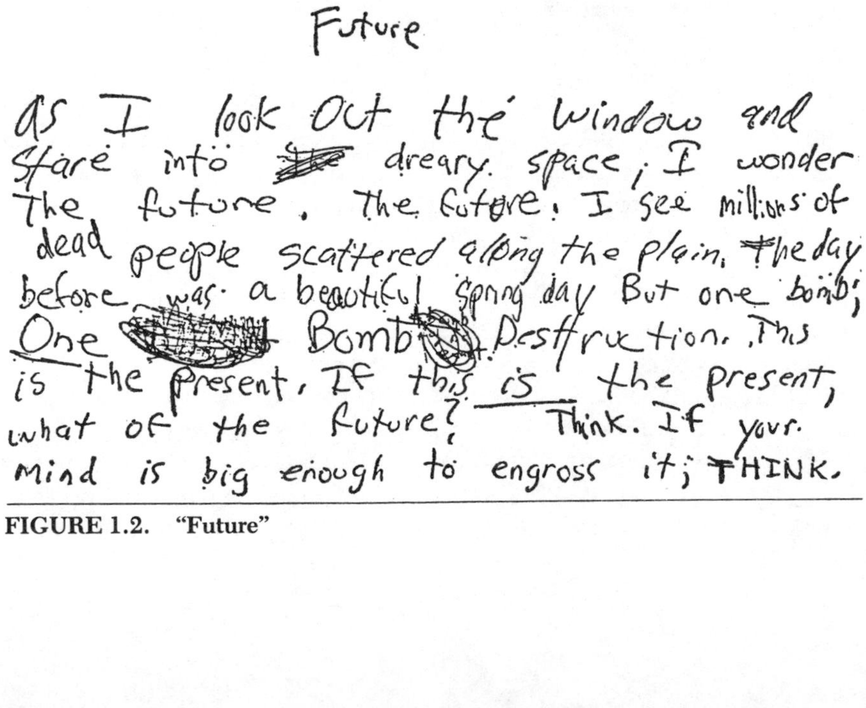

FUTURE

As I look Out the Window and
Stare into dreary space, I wonder.
The future. The future. I see millions of
dead people scattered along the plain. The day

FIGURE 1.2. "Future"

before was a beautiful spring day. But one bomb;
One Bomb Destruction. This
is the present. If this *is* the present,
what of the future? Think. If your
mind is big enough to engross it; THINK.

David, the author, was asked to read his composition aloud. While he read, the language arts consultant listened and rearranged, using David's pauses and phrases as a guide for a new form. Then the composition was typed.

FUTURE

As I looked out the window
    and stare into the dreary space
I wonder.
The future,
the future.
I see millions of dead people
    scattered along the plain.
The day before
    was a beautiful spring day
    but
    one bomb
    ONE BOMB
    destruction.
If this is the present,
    WHAT OF THE FUTURE?
        think
    If your mind is big enough
        to engross it;
    THINK.

Aided by the arrangement of words on the page according to meaningful phrases, the selection demands thought from the reader. We may think about the future, but we are reminded of the past. Was the reference to the Japanese dead of 1945? Is this a prediction of the future? Is the poem in cause-and-effect or effect-to-cause order, or both? Whatever, the composer's idea or age, it is exciting to observe someone thinking in this way.

WHY COMPOSITION IS NOT UNCOVERED

We have seen two examples of children's clear thinking on serious subjects in creative modes. Both Marjorie and David accepted the standard of evaluation that is held by many parents and teachers. David was a top student; he threw his work in the wastepaper basket. Marjorie was a poorer student; teachers saw her selection as an example of unacceptable writing. Implicit in the behavior of many teachers and in its acceptance by their students is the idea that the importance of poetic writing has a very low academic place in the elementary school.

There are several reasons why good compositions are overlooked or unappreciated. Some are difficult to decipher because of handwriting, spelling, or form. Others are never shown to the teacher or read aloud. Others are judged too casually, too early, too harshly or according to inappropriate criteria. This chapter examines each of these reasons.

The Teacher Wears a Cryptographer's Hat

Handwriting and spelling are often difficult to decipher. They depend upon personal differences, purpose, time, and other factors. One of the many hats the teacher or parent must wear is that of cryptographer. Reproduced in figure 1.3 is the attempt of Jordan, a three-year-old, to make a personal shopping list. The written expressions of school-age children or the elderly may at first be equally difficult to decipher, but they are easy to understand when the writer's private code is known.

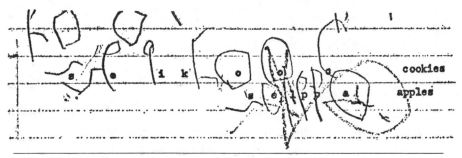

FIGURE 1.3.   Shopping list

The Teacher Wears the Cloak of a Secret Agent.

Louis, an eighth grader, had refused to hand in written work or speak in class. His encounter with the topic "Skies Unlimited" helped him to "make the scene" one day in his English class. His teacher had to resort to decoding in order to get at the real worth of the boy's first offering; reading it (figure 1.4) was as difficult as reading the three-year-old's shopping list. But one look at the thoughts beneath Louis's tough shell was revealing. His composition, in typewritten form, appears below.

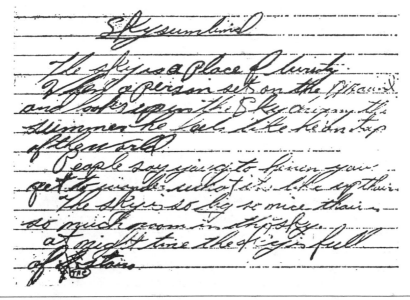

FIGURE 1.4. "Skies Unlimited"

SKIES UNLIMITED

The sky is a place of beauty.
When a person sits on the ground
And looks up in the sky
During the summer,
He feels like he's on top of the world.

People say
  You go to heaven
You get to wonder
  What's it like up there?

The sky is so big
So nice.
There is so much room in the sky.
At night time
The sky is full of stars.

Although Louis then began to write his assignments, he never handed in written work with the other pupils. He would slip it to the teacher in the hall or in the teachers' parking lot, or he would place it in the teacher's jacket pocket so that it would be discovered at home. This cloak-and-dag-

ger atmosphere added just the right amount of stimulation for Louis to continue to compose.

The Teacher Wears the Robe of Judge

Judgments of compositions are often made too early. Many compositions
have been hastily judged merely on the basis of their neatness or the mechanics. If superficially judged, what is shallow, rather than profound,
may be the object of praise; what is "correct" in sentence structure will get
more credit than what is compositionally well crafted or what reflects
honest feelings.

Language is meant for the ear and the eye. Many compositions, however, are only read silently. Primitive feelings expressed in language may
often be better caught by a comprehensive ear than by a highly selective eye.
The rhythms and other musical aspects of word compositions are more
readily absorbed through listening and movement than through silent
readings. Teachers who have overlooked reading aloud their pupils' compositions are probably out of touch with the insight of the oral reader. It is
possible that the silent reading and writing tradition of the school has contributed to the lesser popularity of speaking, oral reading, and composition.

There now seems to be some movement toward an oral-aural renais-
sance. The importance of listening is becoming obvious to writers,
speakers, and readers. Authors need to hear their work. How else can one
compose with words? How else can one fully comprehend language?

RECOGNIZING THE COMPOSERS ALL AROUND US

Criteria for recognizing and evaluating creative works include integrity
of feeling, unity of form, and appropriateness of language. Knowledge of
one or more of these ingredients of composition and the ability to use them
may be intuitive in rather large numbers of people. Such people need only
be drawn out. For others, feeling, form, and language must be learned by
observation and experimentation.

Basic composition can be taught by having the composers, together with
friends, parents, or teachers, evaluate their own work. These teams can
look for the ingredients of the composition and the ways in which they were
put together, and they can help the author ask and respond to such questions as: What is the feeling here? Is there a picture? What is the mood?

Those who desire to uncover composition may ask themselves the following questions:

1. Is the classroom (or home) atmosphere conducive to composition?
2. Am I perceived as the kind of person beginning writers and speakers would entrust with their secret thoughts?
3. Have I allowed sufficient time for each composition?
4. Have I read the compositions aloud?
5. Have I made it clear that ideas come first and mechanics last?
6. Have I tried marking the pauses instead of using standard punctuation?
7. Have I tried appropriate line arrangements?
8. Have I stressed the good work and minimized the weaknesses?
9. Have I helped authors prepare their compositions for others to appreciate?
10. Are we progressing from speaking to writing to reading to listening and speaking again?

There are three guideposts along the educational route from speaking to writing to reading. First, be on the alert for thoughtful and picturesque language. It may occur at the most unlikely times and in the most unlikely places. When listening to oral work, get such language down on paper. Second, assist the authors in making their works more recognizable as crafted compositions and thus more worthy of attention. Look and listen for ways to arrange the language so that the creative qualities are more apparent. Edit the mechanics. Third, help authors find acceptable ways of sharing their work. Composition may be shared by performance, display, or publication, in or out of the classroom. Every occasion of sharing work may add to interest, vigor, and pride in composition. It may start another cycle of communication.

There are other ways that we can uncover and nurture language ability. We can learn more about the nature of language and the qualities of good composition. We can prepare a classroom climate that encourages composition. We ourselves can learn to speak and write from personal experience, use language with greater precision, capture fleeting images, invent original language patterns, and work within appropriate predesigned forms. We can help beginning writers and speakers polish and dignify their work and then share their products. It is the express purpose of the succeeding chapters of this handbook to provide suggestions that will make composition and communication stimulating and fruitful experiences throughout life.

SUGGESTED READING

Bobbins, Marjorie. "The Sea." *Elementary School Creative Writer Magazine* (Spring 1963): 27.

Day, Robert, ed., and Weaver, Gail Cohen, assoc. ed. *Creative Writing in the Classroom: An Annotated Bibliography of Selected Resources (K–12)*. Urbana, Ill.: National Council of Teachers of English, 1978.

Forsdale, Louis. *Perspectives in Communication*. Reading, Mass.: Addison-Wesley, 1981.

Goodman, Yetta. "The Roots of Literacy." In *Claremont Reading Conference Forty-Fourth Yearbook*, edited by M. P. Douglas. Claremont, Cal.: Claremont College Library, 1980.

Martin, Nancy; D'Arcy, Pat; Newton, Bryan; and Parker, Robert. *Writing and Learning Across the Curriculum, 11–16*. London: Ward Lock Educational, distributed by Hayden Book Company, Rochelle Park, N.J., 1976.

Mearns, Hughes. *Creative Power: The Education of Youth in the Creative Arts*. New York: Dover, 1958.

Phillips, Gerald; Butt, David E.; and Metzger, Nancy J. *Communication in Education*. New York: Holt, Rinehart and Winston, 1974.

Sloan, Glenna Davis. *The Child as Critic: Teaching Literature in the Elementary School*. New York: Teachers College Press, 1975.

Smith, Frank. "Demonstrations, Engagement and Sensitivity: The Choice Between People and Programs." *Language Arts* 58 (1981): 634–42.

Smith, Vernon H. "A Do-It-Yourself Test: How Do You Rate as a Judge of Children's Writing?" *Elementary English* 47 (1970): 346–48.

2 Organizing Conditions for Composition

Optimum conditions for composition begin with stimulation, are aided by success, and result in confidence. As Alice Miel says, in designing opportunities for creative teaching, "using the 'raw' materials of teaching — time, space, things, and people — a teacher creates his designs, arranging, ordering and reordering those ingredients of education in a constant flow and in an intermingling way."* This section discusses how to organize those raw materials of teaching to prepare the conditions for stimulating and nurturing successful composition.

STIMULATING CONDITIONS

The following incident illustrates some of the conditions that stimulate in people their own motivation for composition. Diane was in a junior high school class for the mentally retarded. She was usually sullen and verbally hostile. The language arts consultant had been working with the "special" class one hour each week. Choral speaking, puppetry, role playing, and television shows were each explored for two weeks. Class dictation had been tried the previous week. This week, Diane saw four classmates leave the room with the language arts consultant. After about five minutes each returned smiling, carrying his or her dictated composition. She volunteered to take a turn sitting on the stairway outside the room with the consultant. She sat on the top step. Her "secretary" sat three steps below. He asked her just to talk as he took down her words, which follow.

ON SUNDAY IS EASTER

On Sunday
    is Easter;
I received.

---

*Creativity in Teaching (Belmont, Cal.: Wadsworth, 1961), p. 71.

I love my Lord,
    because
    my mother and father died.

I pray for them.

I wish they were back.

Now
    I am with another parent
    and I spend my happy Easter
        with them.

God Bless
    my mother and father
    and my little sisters.

Happy Easter
    to you all.
                                    —*Diane, grade 7*

Diane's composition catches glimpses of the meaning of a child's long-ing and loneliness. Unreserved acceptance of foster parents and a sense of equilibrium and concern for others are evidenced in this work by a child who otherwise appeared mentally and emotionally retarded.

After this experience Diane seemed to change. Her teacher reported that she acted more friendly and even volunteered for activities that re-quired face-to-face responses. She continued dictating to the language arts consultant once a week for a month. Then the classroom teacher be-came her secretary. Within two months, she had begun writing by herself. She wrote:

THE FLOWERS BEGAN TO PUFF

The summer was pretty,
    The flowers
        began to puff
And the birds
    began to sing
And the bees
    began to buzz
    around the flowers.
Then,
When it got warm enough
    the children
    started to play in the sun
And then
    they went to the beach
    and had fun.

THE NEED FOR TIME

Time is vital to composition. There are three kinds of time to consider: composer time, helper time, and institutional time. Each influences the result of a composition program.

Composer Time

Composers need time. They need time to think secret dreams and offbeat ideas and to organize, reorganize, or discard them and start all over again. They need time to play with ideas, to catch hold of fleeting ones, to incubate young ones, and to tend to old ones. They need time to help ideas grow, to nourish them, to clean them up, and to present them, finally, in Sunday clothes.

Composers need talking time and listening time. Talking and listening were essential to ancient Greek writers. Greek generals argued about the writing of poetry in the hours before battles, and Socrates and other philosophers discussed their ideas hour upon hour as Plato and others took notes.

Everyone needs to talk — to hear and play with language, to exercise the mind and emotions and tongue together. Out of this spirited speech can come meaningful, flavorful language worth the time and effort of writing and rewriting, phrasing, rehearsing, and reading aloud.

Composers need time to decide on a topic, gather material, organize it, and wait for ideas to simmer. Just as some foods taste better a day or two after preparation, time adds flavor to ideas. Time affords speakers and writers an opportunity to bathe in and be saturated with a subject.

Time is needed to gather and work out ideas. Composition requires time to experiment, try out, think over, practice. Learning any craft requires hours of practice and coaching by someone who knows some of the rules and techniques for developing the desired product. Composition also requires time to collect and recollect, to compose and recompose, and to present and represent.

Helper Time

Time is the same for everyone, but everyone organizes time differently. Some teachers and counselors say, "I do not have time for composition." This means simply that they are not convinced that it is worthwhile to sacrifice other activities to spend time on composition. Others do not allow themselves or the authors enough flexibility in scheduling, and perhaps in thinking, to explore new paths. But teachers, parents, and other helpers who believe that composition is one of the most basic and meaningful language arts activities consider the time well spent.

Time for composition need not be forced into a rigid schedule. One has to make a mental commitment. Counselors and teachers who are interested in composition find time: large blocks and little bits of it, quiet time and prime time. They find time for students and campers and retired people to do their own writing and time for them to read the work of others. They know that the moment of writing is a reciprocal moment of reading, so they share the reading time. They know that beginners need time to be good composers as well as readers and that helpers need time to plan and prepare, encourage, stimulate, read aloud, discuss, and enjoy processes and accomplishments.

Organization Time

School, camp, and retirement time comes in various forms. Regularly scheduled periods may be needed. Some authors get to school, work, or the community center early and compose best before the others arrive. Some use flexibly scheduled free time during the day. Some wish to stay after hours. For some, these are their only truly quiet moments. Early or late time may offer a refuge from the sometimes overpowering din of family or classmates and the cultural noises that interfere with concentration. Times that are appropriate for individuals to reflect, meditate, and compose — before, during, or after regularly scheduled activities — can be discussed and made a part of the planning of organization time.

Composition time is available when a person cannot participate in physical activities for reasons of health or forgotten sneakers. In many places state law forbids assigning new work when some of the students have left the classroom for religious education. These periods are certainly a good time for completing compositions. Time may also be found during the second half of a lunch period, especially if pupils are otherwise left to shift for themselves. Story hours, reading times, and the periods immediately after them may also be profitably reserved for composition. Since the creative moment is also a moment of recreation, recreation time should be shared with composition. Communication is fun too.

THE NEED FOR SPACE

Space is another requirement for composition. The place and the amount of space needed are individual matters. Some composers need to sit on the floor, and some on the window sill. Some pace up and down.

Some may have to put their heads down for a while. Others may have to stare out the window. Still others work best at the chalkboard.

A room where the desks are always arranged in rows is often a sign of an outmoded concept of the teaching-learning process. Sitting in rows is fine for watching a movie, but it is not a practical arrangement for interacting with anyone but the teacher, although some composers find sitting in rows secure, private, and just right. Authors who are allowed to move their desks into various helpful arrangements for small or large group discussions and appraisals of their compositions may do more effective work that way. Finally, some people are not able to compose well in the presence of others, and movable chairs enable such people to find some privacy within the classroom or out in the hall.

Space and the use of space must be appropriate to the work at hand. Some writers and speakers may at different times prefer to work in the hall, the cafeteria, or the library. The empty auditorium, with its aura of mystery, the great quiet, the comfortable seats, and the opportunity for isolation, may aid some people in composing. Colored stage lights may be used to set the mood for composition; turning on only the amber or the blue lights has been known to stimulate some writers (figure 2.1). The

FIGURE 2.1.   The empty auditorium

auditorium is also a good space for choral readings or the oral reading of compositions.

There are teachers, counselors, and parents who, unhappy with ordinary institutional surroundings, have tried to make spaces more conducive to learning. Composers in these places are allowed to stretch out, like their pets, on soft rugs. A large easy chair or a rocking chair is best for others. Portable screens that can create some quiet and privacy are sometimes available.

The libraries in some schools, community centers, condominiums, and hospitals are equipped with comfortable living room furniture and rugs. As at home, children are found reading and writing in every possible position: on the floor, under the library tables, and in easy chairs. Some school libraries have on their shelves collections of original poetry and prose. Many of the materials were first composed in those rooms.

In such libraries, storage space must be provided for each person's composition folder. The usual method is to allow each class one drawer of a standard four-drawer file cabinet, from which people may take their folders at appropriate times during the day. Many counselors and teachers restrict access to the drawer to certain times. Some maintain complete control of the file; others appoint a librarian.

Competent helpers are alert to the space needs of their student-composers, as they are alert to other needs. Just as they can develop rubber time budgets, they can stretch the space for composing, in and out of the classroom or center.

THE NEED FOR THINGS

Materials for composition are not as bulky and expensive as the equipment needed in a science laboratory or art studio. Although many things may be considered appropriate materials for composition, none of them are restricted to this aspect of the language program. The basics are paper, writing instruments, manila folders, and language reference books. Paper for first drafts may be newsprint, old ditto sheets, waste paper from the mimeograph room, or rejects from print shops and offices. The use of scrap paper or colored newsprint helps writers relax because it reminds them that they are about to compose a draft and not a final copy. A variety of pens and soft pencils and a pencil sharpener are needed, but not erasers, because scratching out and writing over is quicker than erasing. Scissors and staplers help in editing. Manila folders are useful for filing each writer's accumulation of compositions and his or her ideas for future compositions. A variety of dictionaries, including rhyming dictionaries and a thesaurus, are essential if the writers are to learn to get the right word in the right place.

Typewriters are useful in composition. Many enjoy using them and are able to read typed copy more easily than their own handwriting. Teachers may save a step by taking dictation directly on the typewriter. When working with primary school children or with the elderly, one can use large primer type face that resembles print or manuscript writing and can be read easily by young and old.

Teachers and counselors find it advantageous to have available a variety of art supplies for displaying composition: felt pens, colored inks, colored papers, double-stick plastic tape, materials for mounting, framing, lettering, and fastening, T-squares, press-on letters in several styles and sizes, a wax-coating machine, wax-coated sheets, and glue sticks, which are safer to use than inflammable rubber cement. Paste-up sheets, used in producing newspapers and yearbooks, will prove helpful; they have vertical and horizontal rules preprinted in blue ink that does not photograph. Also valuable are materials and equipment for reproducing compositions, such as spirit duplicators, mimeograph or photocopy machines, and book-binding equipment.

Audiovisual materials are also assets in the composition program, especially cameras, macrolenses, overhead projectors, tape recorders, and special translucent screens for rear screen projection. Bookcases and cabinets in which writers can keep their favorite compositions or personal collections contribute to pride in composition.

Other potentially useful materials are sound-effects records, records of songs, historical events, regional music, and mood music, flags, banners, slides, movies, tape recordings, and such artifacts as pottery, woven goods, and sculpture. Furniture and stage scenery may be borrowed from the school district prop room to enhance composition as well as dramatics. Music stands and lecterns will be helpful for reading aloud.

Several excellent old and new anthologies should be available in the classroom. Collections of published works by and for peers and copies of single pieces from books, magazines, and newspapers are also valuable resources. Materials composed by other pupils are useful stimuli. These works will often be in need of replacement because of their constant use.

The school media specialist and public librarian should alert the teacher to the availability of new materials for the classroom, the library, or personal use. They may also suggest ways to improve the use of space for storing or displaying books and materials.

Materials for composition may be simple and inexpensive or complex and costly. Whatever is used, the prime consideration is that it be appropriate and readily available to the composers.

THE NEED FOR PEOPLE

A variety of people may be helpful as composition develops: people in or out of the class, older pupils, family, friends, neighbors next door or across the hall or down the street, colleagues from other levels of education, student teachers, aides, special resource personnel, and pen or tape pals. Taking dictation, helping with artwork, binding booklets, bringing together composers from different classrooms or neighborhoods — all may be helpful. Authors often help themselves, as well as the others, when they assist in the composition program.

Additional ways in which neighbors, student teachers, or aides can be helpful include working with part of a group while the teacher takes private dictation from a composer or edits or types a composition. Teachers will commonly cover a class for a colleague with bus duty. Composition duties deserve at least the same cooperation.

Visiting high school and college teachers of English and speech as well as artists, writers, and poets may serve as consultants or resource persons. By reading aloud stimulating material, listening, commenting, and answering technical questions, they contribute not only information but also a sense of importance and dignity to the written work.

Some teachers work along with their students, describing their thoughts, their feelings, their previous experiences, their reasons for suggesting changes in wording or arrangement. They think of new ways to paint pictures with words. After observing the teacher's progress, the youngsters can address the same topic.

Members of a fifth-grade class wrote the following selections, suggested by the rain outside.

RAIN

Gentle rain
   falling on the branches
   hanging low
   heavy with new leaves.

The children play
   unaware of dark clouds
   unaware of the coming storm.
          — *John (the teacher)*

RAIN

When I think of rain
   I think of music.

The howling
of the wind and the rain
remind me of rhythms.

The drops
on a window pane
remind me of notes on a sheet.
— *Ralph*

RAIN

Rain
drops when it rains.
I think of people
about men and boys
that don't have any shelter.

I wish
they were in a house
where they have heat and food and clothes
for them.

And I wish
that it will never happen.

— *Phillip*

Composing along with one's students is frightening to some teachers and natural to others. It does change the relationship and the classroom atmosphere, though Ruth Whitman, director of Poets Who Teach, Inc., in Newton, Massachusetts, assures teachers that "it need not destroy the teacher's position of authority when authority is needed."*

Decisions about the allocation of time, space, materials, and people as discussed here require that teachers and administrators ask themselves and one another: What are the most important things to be taught? How can we consider the individual students first, then the teacher, and then the institution? When they encourage flexible scheduling, have available a variety of appropriate materials, and arrange for team teaching, consultants, and resource people, they have added new dimensions to professional decision making. When teachers and counselors think through, preferably with administrative support, what composition can mean to language and personal development, suddenly time, space, materials, people, and words become available.

---

*Ruth Whitman and Harriet Feinberg, *Poemmaking: Poets in Classrooms.* (Lawrence, Mass.: Massachusetts Council of Teachers of English, 1975), p. viii.

SUGGESTED READING

Deutsch, Babette. *Poetry Handbook: A Dictionary of Terms.* New York: Funk and Wagnalls, 1976.

Elbow, Peter. *Writing Without Teachers.* New York: Oxford University Press, 1973.

Hennings, Dorothy Grant, and Grant, Barbara Moll. *Written Expression in the Language Arts: Ideas and Skills.* New York: Teachers College Press, 1981.

Herrick, Virgil E., and Jacobs, Leland B., eds. *Children and the Language Arts.* Englewood Cliffs, N.J.: Prentice-Hall, 1955.

Jones, Margaret, and Nessel, Denise. *The Language-Experience Approach to Reading: A Handbook for Teachers.* New York: Teachers College Press, 1981.

Kamler, Barbara. "One Child, One Teacher, One Classroom: The Story of One Piece of Writing." *Language Arts* 57 (1980): 680–93.

Miel, Alice, ed. *Creativity in Teaching.* Belmont, Cal.: Wadsworth, 1961.

Whitman, Ruth, and Feinberg, Harriet, eds. *Poemmaking: Poets in Classrooms.* Lawrence, Mass.: Massachusetts Council of Teachers of English, 1975.

Stage One
EVOKING VISIONS
THROUGH SPEAKING

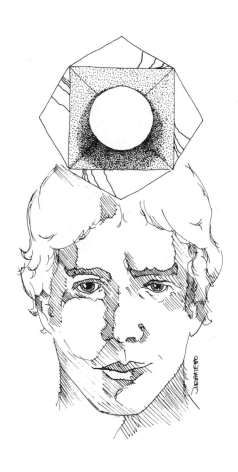

The first of the three cyclical communication stages, "Evoking Visions," is covered in the following three chapters. Stage One includes ways of uncovering and recognizing feelings through speech and stimulating the act of composition. Primary emphasis in this first stage is on oral stimulation and the appreciation of one's own language ability. Thus, learners begin to speak and think positively about themselves as thinkers, speakers, and composers. They become caught up in the romance of language, learning, and composing with words.

3   Starting the Composing Process

Beginning composition requires answers to two questions. First, how can people be encouraged to begin to use language in skillful, communicative ways? Second, what can helpers do to ensure speakers and writers of a warm reception for their products? These are the professional challenges to which this chapter turns.

STARTING DEVICES

Starting devices are basic in teaching. They include sensory spurs, first-hand observation and recall, pump priming, literary launchers, and block breakers.

Sensory Spurs

Sensory spurs may stir one or more of the five senses. Music and movement are common spurs; so are materials read, said, or acted, pictures and films. A few teachers have on their desks special jars of puffed rice or wheat, candy, nuts, gum, or fruit marked "Rx Imagination. Dosage: One each day before writing." Others, possibly inspired by Peter Pan, use magic wands or "Inspirational Powder." Talcum powder or confetti is sprinkled on a beginning writer's head or shoulder. "Magical potions" brewed by teachers help conjure up previous thrills from books, plays, storytellers, and story readers. All spurs are used to focus attention and start the compositional flow.

The stage can be set for composition with talking, singing, rhythm, or physical exercise. All types of creative expression—storytelling, creative dramatics, role playing, puppetry, music, movement, and artwork—have turned people to composition. Stimulating conversation alternated with listening to the reading of poetry, prose, and plays is helpful. Some helpers

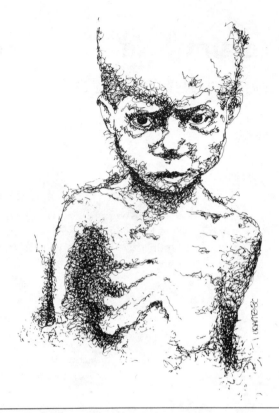

FIGURE 3.1.   Hungry child (drawn by Chris Durante, 1980)

focus composers' attention on a picture. They may look at a picture of a child—figure 3.1, for example. The composers might talk to one or two friends about the picture, or to the youngster in the picture. What would they say to him?

Rob, a teacher, wrote as he would speak:

> What's your name?
> What's your name?
> Tell me your name
>   so I can talk to you
>   and know you
>   and help you.
> What's your name?
> Will you forgive me?

Will you ever forgive me?
You do blame me, don't you?
Don't you?
Don't you?
What can I do?
Tell me what I can do.
What's your name?

Alan, another teacher-writer, remembering the boy's eyes, wrote:

Almonds of hate

Those almonds of hate
Like
Smoldering cinders

Branding my soul.

Observation and Recall

Direct observation and recall of sensory experience, prompted, if necessary, by questions from the teacher, may help composers point their artistic antennas. They may be stimulated to collect impressions in a variety of places and times. During a walk, for example, authors should be alert to what they see, touch, smell, hear, or feel. They may pick up leaves, twigs, stones, and insects, and so items may be brought back to the classroom to be displayed, studied or used to stimulate ideas for composition. The teacher may also suggest that composers observe similarities and differences in various environments. They can compare the noises of the parks with the noises of the streets, or they may consider the unique inhabitants, movements, smells, colors, patterns, dangers, and delights of each environment.

Acting and speech teachers, as well as composition teachers, sometimes have students keep a sense notebook and every day add something that stimulated one of their senses. It may be the smell of bathroom cleanser or the smell of fresh-cut grass. Then they add the setting, their feelings, and anything else that helps them to recall the experience.

Open-ended questions also help to begin and to broaden sensory awareness. For example, exactly how does it feel to be hit with a snowball, or get your socks wet, or slide on ice or on skis? What are snowmen like? Describe what breath looks like in the cold.

The playground may stimulate composition. An hour in the park or school playground can be as helpful to word-painters as to picture artists. Artists of any age may take turns on the sliding pond and the school's athletic equipment after being asked such questions as: What does it look like from way up high? How does it feel to slide down fast? What is it like when you're up in the swing and come down toward the ground? How does it feel to use the athletic equipment? to run fast? to lose or win a race? to fall down? What do you see when you lie on your back in the grass and look up at the sky?

Observing busses may be interesting to others. Their shapes, the exhaust fumes, the driver's and the passengers' rudeness or courtesies, the sudden starts and jarring stops, what people say about the wrong bus, the horns, the conversations, the standing up for adults, the holding on to poles and straps, are a few of the sensory experiences that may lead to composing with words.

Trains may also offer sensory impressions for composition. The sounds of the wheels on the tracks and the variations in the sound of the horn or whistle as the train approaches and disappears can be recorded by tape, memory, or notebook. The wave to the engineer and the passengers and their waves back, the different kinds of cars, the tracks converging to infinity, the possible destinations, the feeling of riding and looking backward at what you have passed compared with that of looking forward to what you have not seen — these are some of the experiences that help artists discover sensory impressions about which they might compose.

Declaring the train his favorite means of transportation, Paul Theroux, in *The Great Railway Bazaar*, states:

> Ever since childhood, when I lived within earshot of the Boston and Maine, I have seldom heard a train go by and not wished I was on it. Those whistles sing bewitchment: railways are irresistible bazaars, snaking along perfectly level no matter what the landscape, improving your mood with speed, and never upsetting your drink.*

Pump Priming

Walking by a classroom while visiting a new school, I paused to read some children's writing displayed outside. Each composition was a prize. Inside the classroom several children were writing; others were reading; a few were drawing. I approached the teacher. "Yes, the material was done by the children here," she replied in answer to my inquiry. "My technique? Pump priming.

"When the youngsters come in, in the morning and after lunch, I read to them for about a half-hour. It settles them down; it begins the day's work in a quiet and friendly way. Then I allow them to do whatever they want for

---

*(Boston: Houghton Mifflin, 1975), p. 1.

about the same length of time. Mostly they talk for a while and then write. Sometimes it sounds a little like the literature I have just read; often it doesn't, but I'm sure some rubbed off in little ways. I read to my class about five hours a week."

Few people can read aloud effectively without preparation and oral practice. Many professional readers mark their scripts for pauses, emphasized words and phrases, volume, and rate. They also make note of ideas in the text for further discussion or reading. Teachers should do this for themselves when planning to read aloud to their pupils.

Many teachers prepare for important occasions by collecting calendars with holidays marked on them, courses of study, anthologies, and topics that are of interest to students. When this material is ready, they prepare a manila folder for each season, holiday, subject, and category of curricular content or personal concern. Selections from newspapers, books, or magazines, found by the teacher or the students, are placed in the appropriate folders.

Thus, the teacher and students are ready to read aloud about snow when the snow falls. In February they can read about Lincoln and Washington, the Revolutionary War, taxation, the colonies, the Civil War, slavery, assassinations, freedom, and brotherhood. As spring and summer approach, they can read about friendship, birth, growth, life, death, preparing for the future, planting, and caring. When the temperature is high, they can read about cold things to escape from the heat: cool drinks, cold streams, ice skating, Eskimos, ice cream, and sliding in the snow. They may read at any time about people's feelings. Teachers may also supply materials related to science and social studies: their feelings about the universe, the meanings, mysteries, and wonders of nature, the ways of people, and journeys to both common and unusual places. People's concerns for themselves and one another, their social actions and their self-control, their burdens and their brotherhood — the teacher may turn to all or any of these subjects for classroom reading and discussion.

Exposure to material that deals with both everyday and unusual experiences helps listeners recognize apt expressions and develop a sense of the power of words helpful in both speaking and writing.

LITERARY LAUNCHERS. When priming the pump with the works of well-known authors or other pupils, it is both interesting and helpful to the beginner to note their ways of introducing their subjects. Mark Twain, in *The Mysterious Stranger*, set the scene with time and place.

> It was in 1590 — winter. Austria was far away from the world, and asleep; it was still the Middle Ages in Austria, and promised to remain so forever.

Stephen Crane, in *The Red Badge of Courage*, used fog as an opening curtain.

> The cold passed reluctantly from the earth, and the retiring fogs revealed an army stretched out on the hills, resting. As the landscape changed from brown to green, the army awakened, and began to tremble with eagerness at the noise of rumors.

Thomas Mann, in *Tonio Kröger*, establishes a dreary, cold, and wet scene in winter.

> The winter sun, poor ghost of itself, hung milky and wan behind layers of cloud above the huddled roofs of the town. In the gabled streets it was wet and windy and there came in gusts a sort of soft hail, not ice, not snow.
> School was out.

James Baldwin's *Notes of a Native Son*, notes the end of his father and other memorable events of the day.

> On the 29th of July, in 1943 my father died. On the same day, a few hours later, his last child was born.

Franz Kafka, in *Metamorphosis*, shocks the reader into attention and gets right to the point — his protagonists' affliction.

> As Gregor Samsa awoke one morning from a troubled dream, he found himself changed in his bed to some monstrous kind of vermin.

A student began his story:

> I wanted a baby brother. From the very start I detested that newly arrived drooling little butterball whom everyone fussed over. That was nine years ago. It's funny how first impressions are sometimes lasting.

Teachers, parents, and other helpers can point out other opening lines as memorable as the six passages quoted here.* Some helpers use traditional starting phrases as well — "Once upon a time, . . . " "One dark and stormy night, . . . " and "And it came to pass. . . . "

BLOCK BREAKERS. Consider also the following starters commonly used in speech. Try using one, in conversation with a friend, to introduce a topic you wnat to get off your chest or a newspaper or magazine article you read or a picture you found in some publication. As you find yourself speaking,

*Mark Twain, *The Mysterious Stranger* (New York: Harper and Bros., 1944); Stephen Crane, *The Red Badge of Courage* (New York: Appleton, 1895); Thomas Mann, *Tonio Kröger* (New York: Alfred A. Knopf, 1936); James Baldwin, *Notes of a Native Son* (Boston: Beacon Press, 1955), p. 76; Franz Kafka, *Metamorphosis* (New York: Schocken, 1968); Robert Wolsch.

write down your comments with a soft pencil. Keep writing until you've told all you've got to tell.

1. Did you know that . . .
2. Incidentally . . .
3. Really . . .
4. Before I forget, will you . . .
5. I don't care who . . .
6. Am I right? I ask you . . .
7. Naturally I wouldn't want . . .
8. You ought to know that . . .
9. Its none of my business, but . . .
10. I simply can't tell you how much I . . .
11. I think . . .
12. That's nothing, compared to . . .
13. As you may remember, we talked about . . .
14. Believe me, I know . . .
15. So she said . . .
16. I want to ask you something . . .
17. Ya know . . .
18. You won't believe this, but . . .
19. I swear . . .
20. Don't tell a soul, but . . .

Canopy Topics

The secret in artistic stimulation is to find a subject that interests the potential speaker or writer. Leland Jacobs has characterized broad, appropriate, open-ended topics that are big enough for all potential authors to fit under as "canopy topics," as opposed to "umbrella topics," which cover only one or two. Canopy topics are similar to the subjects used to start conversations. The weather is often chosen by strangers because it is something they have in common; from this beginning they may go on to other topics according to their experiences or imaginations. In composition, too, the leader seeks topics to which all may relate, but to which all will have unique reactions: for example, sky, cloud, water, sun, home, school, tears, joys, and sorrows, places to go to, ways to travel, pleasure, concern and love, progress and action.

The teacher must also find ways to help students approach these conventional themes in a unique and individualized way. Helping a person learn how to think without telling him or her what to think is a rewarding experience. The following incident illustrates how two teachers helped a child with his composition.

"I think I've got a poem," reported a second grader to the language arts consultant as they met in the school lunchroom. "Fine — write it and then show it to me later." Billy returned to the consultant's office later that afternoon with this:

> The air is high.
> The ground is low.
> The astronauts
> are blasting off below.

"That's very good, Bill. Listen to it, children." Billy turned and read to the small group assembled for special help. They listened, smiled, and congratulated him. At this point Billy's teacher came by and asked, "Did you hear Bill's poem?"

"Yes, did you help him with it?" asked the consultant.

"In a way."

"How?"

"He came to my desk and said, 'I'm writing a poem, but I'm stuck; all I've got is: 'The air is high./The ground is low.' I said, 'Think of where you are in the picture.' He did, and finished it."

Collecting Notes

It was suggested above that students keep a sense notebook. They should also learn to carry notebooks, small pads, or suitable scraps of paper to collect impressions, ideas, questions, words, phrases, or lines at any time. Covering one subject on a page is a handy arrangement. The notes will help them recall a fleeting feeling about a mood, character, experience, sound, or word. They will seldom use all they collect or all they know, but what they collect and know will show up in their writing and speaking. Later they may put their notes into some suitable order. If these jottings are on separate slips of paper, they can be ordered and reordered as new ideas appear and new arrangements become necessary. Collecting notes for composition can begin at any age. Parents, brothers and sisters, children, and friends can help by collecting interesting comparisons and contrasts. Anyone can point out the well-turned phrases that creep into everyday talk or copy them down and put them on a bulletin board for others to enjoy.

Many artists, speakers, and writers keep practice journals. We all enjoy reading what we have said at a certain age, or rereading what we have written, much as we enjoy our early pictures. Like collecting notes for writing, collecting compositions and keeping a journal are ways of dignifying our language. They also help people to remember the positive aspects of their lives and build a sense of themselves as authors.

Composition Plans

Learning to use the right arrangements is part of learning to express emotions through language and artistry of form. The following arrangements can be used by teachers and writers to organize thoughts for composition. Everyone can look at a picture — figure 3.1, for example, talk about it with one or two friends, and then write quickly, without stopping, for about ten minutes following one of the plans listed below. At another time, they may try another arrangement and write again for ten minutes without stopping. These composition plans often help break through that difficult starting time.

1. *Cause-to-effect order*. Point to the cause and then to the result.
2. *Topical sequence*. Arrange ideas according to subtopics.
3. *Elimination*. All possible alternatives are discarded except one.
4. *Effect-to-cause order*. A situation or feeling is described by stating the cause — a flashback.
5. *Spatial order*. Set the scene. Describe where things are, usually in relation to other things.
6. *Chronology*. List events in the order in which they occurred.
7. *Catalogue verse*. Describe something through a sequence of images.
8. *Litanies*. Repeat a verbal formula to cover many aspects of an emotion: "We are grateful for ____. We are grateful for ____. We are grateful for _____." Or "I'm angry about _____. I'm angry about _____. I'm angry about _____."

Starting Rituals

For some, sensory spurs, pump priming, and similar techniques are not enough. Anxiety may block communication. Several starting devices are helpful in breaking through, going around, or avoiding tension in starting.

Many composers, amateur and professional, follow a starting ritual at home that may be adapted for use in a classroom. They are capable of writing and speaking but find it difficualt to start — particularly the writing part of speechmaking. Instead of adjusting their ties and clearing their throats like speakers, fluffing their pillows like some sleepers, or readying their nest like birds, they have their own personal devices for starting. Some must clean off the desk; some must borrow something. Some scratch, sharpen pencils, or blow their noses. Others pick lint off their clothes. Some pace. A few tell others to keep quiet because people are working. Many composers chew gum, bite their nails, nibble on pencils, or drum on the desk. One composer ceremoniously dips his pen into the ink, which is his way of saying to himself, "Get started."

Teachers and friends can be helpful to beginning writers and speakers by turning away from the old idea that starting rituals signify a desire to procrastinate or a lack of ability. Instead, they might allow people to find their own starting rituals and get on with their composing.

Meditation — to dwell in thought, to muse, or to reflect — is a helpful starting device for some. One sits comfortably on a chair, closes one's eyes, and repeats silently a sound or group of sounds that ends with a nasal sound like "one." It may be a nonsense word like "danung." Some repeat the word slowly and silently, think it, and keep thinking it over and over for about twenty minutes. When thoughts bubble to the surface, they write down a word or phrase and repeat it several times while waiting for the next line to reach their consciousness. Then that phrase is repeated, as they wait for the next one, and so on.

Group Starting

Group singing and choral speaking often help people take the first step in music more readily than a solo performance. Teachers find that group writing likewise frees many to begin. There is psychological safety in this method. Some teachers start with discussion, during which a topic is decided, and then take dictation from a group. The teacher picks up one idea from this person, another idea from that one, and writes each comment on the board as received. Further ordering and reordering can be done by the students for one another.

Teachers who have continued this technique into the high school years and beyond have found it valuable in evoking composition and maintaining pupil involvement. Some cooperative or chain compositions are started by one person and continued by another. In the following poem, for example, each of the lines was contributed by a different kindergarten youngster.

CHRISTMAS

Christmas is:
A christmas tree
A candle
A Christmas cake
A ball
Snow falling
A decoration
A present with a bow on it
The Christmas bulbs
Different sized cookies

My mother looking at my toys
    while I am asleep
A chimney
Snow and some faces
Reindeer
Santa Claus
A Christmas tree, a bulb, a
    cookie
All the presents packed
A star
A present all wrapped up with
    pretty bows
Me and my dog, presents, cookies
    and a fire
A lovely day and a Christmas tree
Santa Claus day.

Cooperative compositions can be started in one school or home and taken up by others. An itinerant teacher, interschool mail carrier, or friend may bring them around to schools or homes for additional verses. Each stanza of the following poem, "The Dinosaur," was written by a different group because the speech teacher traveled to six schools each week. (Note how this poem is arranged for choral speaking.)

THE DINOSAUR

Sing: Once there was a dinosaur
Sing or say: A great big ugly dinosaur,
                 Once there were some dinosaurs
                    One or two or three or more.

Say: One day a tremendous dinosaur
                 Saw a tree he'd like to gnaw,
                 Leaves and branches disappeared
                 Into that creature that looked so weird.
                 Then he walked along the grass
                 Not letting other animals pass.

                 When along came a Brontosaurus;
                 And because the dinosaur wouldn't let him pass
                    on the grass,
                 They began to fight — in fact,
                    there was a terrible battle there.

Sing or say: And the dinosaur swung his tail,
                 And all we heard was a horrible wail.
                 mmm-m.
Say together: This is a whale of a tail.

Sing: And the dinosaur swung his tail
                  And again we heard that horrible wail.
                  mmm-m.

                  It was a wail like a shout
                  Because the dinosaur knocked the
                          Brontosaurus out
                  And this is the end of our tale.

Say (solo):   What sort of tale?
Say together: A dinosaur tail!
                  — *Children in a speech improvement program*

Assuring Anonymity

For some writers, anonymity is a prerequisite for composition. Young, hesitant writers, like some speakers, are often able to think more clearly and speak more easily when they use puppets. Some need to participate in role playing. Others, as noted in the last section, feel more at ease when they sing or speak in a chorus. Some may choose to use pseudonyms.

Many authors have used pen names, including Lewis Carroll, Mark Twain, and Golden McDonald. Pseudonyms may help free some people from their own or other people's habits and expectations. Like makeup, masks, costumes, and puppets, they relieve the fear of exposure and ridicule. Beginning composers may be offered the same privilege. They may assume a name for one composition, check people's reactions to their work, and either reveal their real identity then or keep it secret for a while longer, or perhaps maintain a pen name throughout a lifetime.

Turn on any citizens' band radio channel and you will hear people assured of anonymity. Big Bird, Yellow Rabbit, Babe in the Woods — CB handles offer a new kind of anonymity for beginning broadcasters. Some, like the educable retarded children in one school district who use the CB in their teacher's car, would never have the courage to speak out as they do if they had to use their real names. So too with beginning authors. Their CB handle may also serve as their pen name: ten-four.

CB HANDLES

CB

The citizens' band
The people's band
People who
know the joy,
the usefulness,

the power
of
the people's language.

Hear
People reaching out to people
Using language
In times of
distress,
concern
loneliness.

Breaker six
This is Yellow Rabbit
Hey good buddy
Got your ears on?
I'm at your back door
Holding on to
Your mud flaps
Wall to wall
And treetop tall.

Hey good buddy
I'm waiting for a Tijuana Taxi,
    a smokey, or a plain wrapper
To zap
    that cotton-picking,
    wall-banging, Willie Weaver
    in the red cowboy Cadillac.

Hey good buddy
I'm wishing you threes
So you and your seatcovers
Can get to your home twenty
And cut some zs
ten-four, Good Buddy,
ten-four.

Turn on any channel
You'll find
companionship
helpfulness
concern,
humor,
anonymity.

Hear
People reaching out to people

Trying on new language
Trying on new roles.

Now a friendless
retarded child
can ready her message
in the classroom
then deliver it
from her teacher's car
in the parking lot
to the new friends
she might never have had.

CB
The citizens' band
The people's band.
                                    — Big Bird

Dictation: Speak Up, Write Down

Business executives, principals, college presidents, and some successful authors dictate letters to their secretaries. They may never touch the paper until they sign the letter, but they are still considered the writers. Everyone may be afforded the same opportunity to dictate thoughts and feelings to a secretary — a teacher, a friend, a teaching aide, an older student, or even a machine. Dictating helps authors to focus and to say whatever comes to mind. Writing requires freedom, like singing in the shower or whistling. Dictating is one way to achieve that freedom to start writing.

Some teachers invite the composers to their desk, exchange chairs, and act as the secretary. Or the authors may be taken to the rear of the room, a quiet corner, a stairway, or anywhere a feeling of complete concentration on the part of both pupil and teacher can be established. When the secretary sits lower than the composer, making sure to write down every word, the composer is provided with a sense of instant power. The following example shows how well this system can work.

Exactly one week had passed since George dictated to the language arts consultant. The special class teacher observed George's mounting excitement as the hour approached for the consultant's next visit. George paced up and down talking to himself and the teacher. "I feel like I'm blowing up. I got so much in me. I don't know how it's going to get out. I have so much to say. Boy, it's real dynamite. I got to see that guy."

To his secretary, the language arts consultant, George prefaced his dictation with "What I'm thinking is way far out, man." The invitation to begin was "Go man, go."

A SPRING NIGHT

It was a spring night
  and on the beach
    there walked a boy and girl
    along the beach.
There was a soft wind
  coming off the ocean.
They stopped
  and watched the ocean
    for a little while.
Then birds
  began to fly overhead
  singing a sweet tune to them.
                    — *George, grade 8*

Upon returning to the room, George informed his teacher, "I feel better now. I feel great. I'm all played out. I'm cool again."

COMPOSING FOR A SYMPATHETIC AUDIENCE

Drafts: The Soft-Pencil Stage of Writing

Most speech is off the tip of the tongue, improvised, impromptu. People reading aloud require a similar freedom to let go, to read fully — substituting "teakettle" or "padoodle" for unfamiliar or unpronounceable words. The meaning will emerge from the context, just as in listening we fill in the pieces of what we don't understand. The same is true in writing. Meandering with a soft pencil, after one has been stimulated by speaking, is an enjoyable experience as long as one is not worried about being published or judged.

Some people block when facing a blank page armed only with a pencil. Like stutterers, we anticipate problems and seek to avoid the struggle. The starting devices outlined above will help. Another secret is to address a particular person or group and tell them how you experience or experienced something. Don't worry about judgment or criticism; just talk it out on paper. Maybe no one will ever read it. Who cares? You're just playing — like someone hitting a tennis ball against the wall. You're not playing at Wimbledon or Madison Square Garden. Get the pencil to do what you tell it to. This sort of impromptu practice writing is like what artists call sketching.

Practice begins to be fun as the writer finds more words. The composer learns to make corrections, sharpening his or her focus and therefore enjoying the results more.

One of the most effective starting devices is an announcement by the teacher, after discussion, that "spelling, grammar, punctuation, and hand-writing do *not* count on the early drafts — just get the feelings and ideas you discussed down on the paper." Another device that often works is to use newsprint, yellow practice paper, or a supply of old, used ditto paper, or have the writers wrinkle the paper before writing on it or divide each sheet into three parts and put only one idea on each piece. All these devices underline the fact that this is a first draft.

In the beginning stages of composition, the mechanics should not get in the way. Spelling, grammar, punctuation, and neatness are not, at this point, important. Suggest to students that they cross out words instead of erasing them. Erasing takes too long and may tear the paper. Tell them, "Keep going; get the feelings and ideas down; don't wait; don't change; don't interrupt the flow of the ideas. You can get to the mechanical skills later, but you can't get back into the flow." Reporters can call in a story to a rewriter. Professional speakers and writers are allowed several drafts and a time for proofreading later. Why not beginners?

Some teachers spread on a bulletin board or table separate slips of paper with all the ideas the class has discussed. The group arranges them in a meaningful order, like a puzzle, and staples them to a master sheet. Not on-ly does this process make the ideas more accessible, but it adds importance to each idea and encourages the class as well: "See how many ideas we have!" "Look at all the possibilities for writing!"

Assuring composers that they are not completing a final copy helps to re-lease bottled-up imagination. The habit of making rough drafts encourages composers and their helpers to probe until something touches a deep, pri-mary experience. Helpers require a friendly, firm, confident, and persever-ing manner. There has to be lots of talk.

Simplified Spelling

Forty million people read Will Rogers's column every day. Many thought him profound; some thought him quaint; few thought him ignorant. Will Rogers never succeeded at spelling, but he never let his spelling interfere with his communicating. He probably never advocated poor spelling; neither did his publisher, the McNaught Syndicate; but they both under-stood the relative importance of spelling and communicating. What would have happened if Will or his publisher had equated the mechanics and composition?

Our private shopping lists include "O.J." (orange juice), "brd" (bread), "egz" (eggs), "letis" (lettuce), "apls" (apples), "tom" (tomatoes), and "mlk" (milk). First drafts are private too, like artists' sketch pads or photogra-phers' proof sheets. First drafts are meant to capture the essence, not to perfect the mechanics. Only final copy may (or may not) be for public view and therefore require strict attention to spelling and other mechanical matters.

George Bernard Shaw used his friend Pitman's phonetic shorthand and campaigned for a simplified English spelling, which he believed would help balance the monetary budget of the English-speaking world. No more spelling books and tests; no more secretaries wasting time and stationery because of misspellings. Fewer students who believe themselves incapable of writing because of their poor spelling.

Most kuntryz hav a speling that soundz just liek its riten. We cuud have it too. Children, adults, and forin stoodents cuud reed and riet quikly and with no fus, no frustraeshun frum memoriezing, no geses. Wee can feel free to riet watever wee can sae withaut avoiding words becauz ov speling. Simplified speling tacks th woree out of rieting and reeding. Soundspel, a pradukt ov th Typographic Council for Spelling Reform, iz wun wae to spel it liek it iz.

The Initial Teaching Alphabet and the International Phonetic Alphabet are other simplified spelling systems. Teachers should at least remember that there are variant spellings in modern American dictionaries. Concern for correct spelling in first drafts is inhibiting. First things first.

Composing for Specific Audiences

Encourage composing for a specific receptive audience — friends or younger people, for example. Some speakers and writers feel most at ease with grandparents, grandchildren, pets, animals, shy people, or imaginary ones. (Composers can role-play these parts.) Too many try to compose for and please the teacher who grades the work instead of those who are most accepting. They lose the intensity of sharing their strong emotions, their senses, and their personal experiences with someone who will respond personally to their compostions. When shared with people who have similar interests, the compositions can be as spontaneous and genuine as the conversations of friends speaking enthusiastically face to face.

Composition begins when composers allow themselves to consider and capture their own personal expressions of thought about feelings. The writing moment may be quiet or noisy. Some people write quietly. Others try to disturb the group. All need to look up occasionally and see an approving face in this time of aloneness, self-doubt, and responsibility. Someone may have to protect the author from both outer and inner distractions. When the writing moment is at hand, each writer must feel free to be alone with himself or herself.

A sense of freedom — one of the most cherished goals of all people — is a basic requirement for composition. Freedom is needed to allow the senses to work, to receive and express feelings, to speak and write, and to refine later. At this stage there should be no mechanics to worry about and no negative criticism. Composers hide behind barriers when they feel their freedom is threatened; they open up to meet a challenge when they feel free and capable. The ability to compose independently of the teacher is one of the goals of the composition program. Other goals include the ability to compose with integrity, to use an appropriate variety of language forms, to express oneself with courage, clarity, and vigor, and to extract vital elements from one's own experience. These abilities are explored in the chapters that follow.

SUGGESTED READING

Applegate, Maureen. *Helping Children Write: A Thinking Together About Children's Creative Writing.* Evanston, Ill.: Row, Peterson, 1954.

Ashton-Warner, Sylvia. *Spinster.* New York: Simon and Schuster, 1959.

Elbow, Peter. *Writing Without Teachers.* London: Oxford University Press, 1973.

Emory, Donald W. *Variant Spellings in Modern American Dictionaries.* Urbana, Ill.: National Council of Teachers of English, 1975.

Goodman, Kenneth. "Effective Teachers of Reading Know Language and Children." *Elementary English* 51 (1974): 823–28.

Goodman, Yetta. "Kid-Watching: An Alternative to Testing." *National Elementary School Principal* 57 (1978): 41–45.

Graves, Donald H. "We Won't Let Them Write." *Language Arts* 55 (1978): 635–40.

Jacobs, Leland B. "Children's Experiences in Literature." In *Children and the Language Arts*, edited by Virgil E. Herrick and Leland Jacobs. Englewood Cliffs, N.J.: Prentice-Hall, 1955.

Macrorie, Ken. *Writing To Be Read.* Rochelle Park, N.J.: Hayden, 1976.

Martin, Bill, Jr., in collaboration with Peggy Brogan. Bill Martin's Instant Readers and Sounds of Language Series. New York: Holt, Rhinehart and Winston.

Reeves, James. *Teaching Poetry.* London: William Heinemann, 1958.

Rowan, Betty. *Learning Through Movement.* New York: Bureau of Publications, Teachers College, Columbia University, 1963.

Shanahan, Timothy. "A Conical Correlational Analysis of the Reading-Writing Relationship: An Exploratory Investigation." Ed. D. dissertation, University of Delaware, 1980.

Tauber, Abraham, ed. *George Bernard Shaw on Language.* New York: Philosophical Library, 1963.

4 Speaking and Writing out of Experience

This chapter is about using experiences, real or imagined, as a springboard for composition. One may use both external experiences, including relationships with other people, incidents, episodes, happenings, escapades, observations, and tribulations, and internal ones, including wishes, daydreams, reflections, wonders, whimsies, and nonsense. Both kinds of experiences are grist for the composing mill.

EXTERNAL EXPERIENCES

Urban, suburban, and rural worlds overflow with subjects for composition. Too often we are led to believe that appropriate subjects are only found in the woods or in outer space. In other words, we may have come to believe that creative subjects must be romantic or "pretty." If encouraged to examine closely our own environment and our personal experiences in it, we will find waiting an infinite number of subjects for composition.

Relationships

Like other successful songwriter-entertainers, Jim Croce wrote about real incidents involving real people he had known: the Roller Derby Queen, Big Jim Walker, and Big Bad Leroy Brown. He even described a memorable dog in the line "meaner than a junk-yard dog." To be that mean is to be unforgettable. Love, loneliness, and pain can also be unforgettable and worth writing about.

Nancy Lynn Schwartz, in "The Mother Daughter Act," recounts her own experiences and those of her mother, the writer Sheila Schwartz, and reveals how similar they were.

> It's rare that a daughter who is a screenwriter gets the chance to adapt a novel for television which just happens to have been written by her mother. It's even more rare when that novel is her mother's first novel,

when there is more than a touch of autobiography involved. But that's the story of *Like Mom, Like Me,* and it's the sort of experience that happens once and is not likely to recur. . . .

I was in California, a fledgling screenwriter, and my brother and sister were both in college. I remember calling her from my L.A. apartment and asking, "So what're you up to?" and my mother said, very timidly, "I'm writing a novel, I think." I thought that was terrific and she sent me the manuscript as soon as she'd finished. We'd been each other's writing critics for years.

When I read the first draft of what was to become *Like Mom, Like Me,* I was stunned. My mother had taken the painful trauma of her divorce and turned it into a warm, loving story of how a mother and daughter cope with and survive the breaking up of the family and how they help each other to learn and to understand. . . .

I thought to myself, "This would make a terrific movie for television." There was never, of course, any question of who would write that movie.

Nancy Malone, who produced *Like Mom, Like Me,* is an extremely warm sensitive lady who had been very close to her own mother. During our first meeting, we barely spoke about the project. Instead, we told loving stories about our mothers. And I knew that I had found somebody who cared about *Like Mom, Like Me* as if her own mother had written it.

The first day of rehearsals for *Like Mom, Like Me,* happened to fall on March 15, 1978, my mother's birthday. My mother happened to be in L.A. visiting me, so we went to the reading. We sat together listening to Linda Lavin, Kristy McNichol, and the rest of the cast reading the script and it was like a resurrected memory, listening to a portion of our past unfolding. There was so much of both of us in it that, even though the book and script are fictional, it felt true. The sad moments and the funny moments felt like they'd just happened. By the end of the reading, holding each other's hand, we were as moved and drained as if we had just lived through the entire experience.

I was, I must confess, moved to tears. "Have you got a tissue?" I snuffled quietly.

"You can have half of mine," my mother snuffled back, and at the sight of each other's tears we just couldn't help laughing. Like Mom, like me.

Incidents

Incidents, or chance occurrences, often seem to be of minor importance, but they may lead to serious consequences. The happiness or unhappiness of a remembrance is not crucial to composition; either way, the incident may be memorable and worth preserving and sharing.

The following selections were gleaned from the work of one classroom.

The assignment was to attempt to recall and compress one unforgettable incident into seventeen syllables. We talked for quite a while and then wrote. These moments were preserved.

> There was a sharp knock
> My soaking wet aunt came in
> She brought us sad news.
> — *Stefanie, grade 5*

> When I dug his grave
> I saw my old dead turtle.
> And ran through the dew.
> — *John, grade 5*

Though the language and form were simple, the children achieved what they set out to do — report an incident nonjudgmentally and compress the report into seventeen syllables.

Episodes

Episodes are events that occur in connection with something else — a milestone in a series of experiences, one battle in a campaign, or one campaign in a war. These three unrhymed, dispassionate pieces were written by a Jewish parochial school seventh grader. Each selection was suggested by his previous reading of an episode in the history of the Jewish people.

About the plague of locusts in Exodus:

> The beetle flew high
> Fearing that he would be prey
> And then it all came.

The story of Lot and his wife:

> The soldier looked back
> To see the burning ashes
> As they disappeared.

The ship *Exodus*:

> The time came too soon
> Time to leave our beloved
> As the anchor raised.
> — *Phillip, grade 7*

Group Happenings

Happenings are occurrences or events that often involve group participation. Discussions and projects frequently provide memorable experiences. Some happenings involve interaction between performers and an audience. In one sixth-grade classroom, children moved around while listening to the first part of Tchaikovsky's *Swan Lake* and then wrote down their reactions. One child wrote:

THE SWAN

Over the waters of the silent lake
Glides the swan.
Peacefully she floats along the tranquil
    surface.
How elegantly she fluffs her cloud-like wings,
    Sweet Swan.

—Jill, grade 6

Excitement filled the air in one elementary school when a fifth-grade class held a pet day to which the entire school was invited. Three children wrote the following selections.

IF I WERE

If I were, a puppy new,
    I'd chew and ruin my master's
       shoe!

If I were, a rabbit white,
    I'd eat the farmer's lettuce,
    in the night.

If I were, a scared little cat,
    I'd climb a tree, and spit and
       spat!

If I were, a little mouse,
    I'd eat all the cheese,
    In my master's house!

But, after all,
Can't you see,
I'm rather glad,
That I'm just me!

—Kathleen, grade 5

Barbara's selection contained unexpected information and a pretty rhyme.

I have two turtles
Who don't wear girdles.

—Barbara, grade 2

Nancy wrote about the owls she had seen pictured in the class.

Ooooo Ooooo, says the owl.
On a dark and dreary night.
Will he ever stop?
—*Nancy, grade 5*

In another class, a discussion about the threat of nuclear warfare was followed within an hour by the composition of the following poems. Note that each is limited to seventeen syllables—an additional challenge the composers met.

WINTER

Winter was coming.
   The last bird flew out of sight
   Then the snow fell
      fast.
        —*Denise, grade 6*

ROSES

I remember spring
   When the roses were blooming
   But the roses just died.
        —*Denise, grade 6*

THE U.S.

I love the U.S.
It would look better
   without
   Nuclear Weapons.
     —*Michael and*
     Phillip, grade 6

EMPTY WORLD

There were no people
Just the water
And the ships
   in the cool fall air.
     —*Penny, grade 6*

A LONELY MOMENT

When the last leaf fell
   And there were no birds
     in sight

I felt
  so
Lonely.
     —*Carol, grade 6*

WAR'S END

The bomb had fallen
   the dew glistened on the grass
   No one was alive.
                    — Leslie, grade 6

A display of these selections on the bulletin board outside the school cafeteria captured a somber moment in national life and renewed students' interest in social studies.

Escapades

Escapades are reckless adventures, larks, sprees, antics, or wild pranks.
They are amusing and often represent an escape from confinement or restraint. Anthony remembered his escapades of the last Halloween evening, when he had played ghosts.

GHOSTS

Ghosts have fun at night
They scream
   when the moon is full
I hide
   and scream too.
                — Anthony, grade 4

Beatrice wrote about the escapade of others.

BY THE SEA

By the sea,
   by the beautiful sea in the evening
   you see parties being held
   near the foam.

At night
   the seagulls crowd around
   and make a big fuss
   over the whiskey bottles.

And the sea is churning
   in the ocean
   beneath the foaming brine.
                — Beatrice, grade 6

A teenage boy described the escapades of two little hellions — Archibald
and Cheryl (figures 4.1 and 4.2).

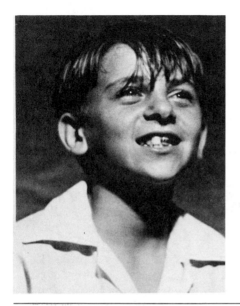
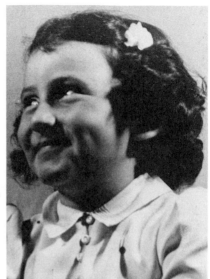

FIGURE 4.1.   Archibald   FIGURE 4.2.   Cheryl

Dragons of similar plumage tend to be gregarious. Of all the twenty-six children residing on West Eleventh Street, Cheryl had to choose, as her guide, philosopher, and friend, a terrifying little boy irrelevantly named Archibald. Archibald is wiry, agile, and undersized, even shorter than Cheryl, though he is almost three years her senior. He has a small, alert face, with a ? in each of his eyes and a grin that exhibits millions of teeth. His pet diversion is hiding behind trees and flinging snowballs or squirting his water pistol at passers-by; if you chase him, he sics his dog (an odious mongrel) after you. Among his other accomplishments is an expert kleptomania: he filches fruit and candy from neighborhood stores with a nonchalance and efficiency that would shame Fagin. At first he's a bit suspicious, but as he warms to you, he will show you his ill-gotten plunder with sparkling eyes, a wide grin, and a bubbling elation over his technique that is second only to his pride in his new Boy Scout uniform. And it seems that whenever I turn around, this miniature ogre is under foot, usually in close conspiracy with Cheryl. Trying to decide who abets whom in mischief is like attempting to choose between Hitler and Tojo.

Every Friday night, the Ebanees, my basketball team, meet at my home. Since we are all growing rather too mature to be concerned wholly with basketball, the conversation imperceptibly veers into other channels, some of which the Hays office would frown upon. During this part of the meeting, Sidney, the thirteenth man on our starting five, acts as chairman and inserts many savory autobiographical details. (The fact that Sidney has irresistibly wavy orange hair has contributed much to his career as a Casanova, though it hasn't improved his basketball playing any.) After the boys leave and I go about straightening up the living room, I usually hear suppressed giggling behind the bookcase. There crouches Cheryl, her eyes aglow at our lusty male talk. As I drag her forth and begin to strangle her, Archibald dashes out from behind the sofa and escapes through the front door. The next night, Mother and Father, with long, serious faces, lecture to me about Life and the problems of emergent manhood. (Mother once attended some courses in adolescent psychology at N.Y.U. and takes her parental responsibilities very seriously.)*

Observations

Observations may be based on momentary impressions or on attentive investigation, watching, listening, studying, interviewing, searching, and researching. After hearing a program by black gospel singers, one white listener was moved to write:

> It was a powerful gospel
> Listen to them sing
> Listen to them sing
> Listen to them sing them gospels.
>
> Oh didn't they sing
> Oh didn't they sing
> Oh didn't they sing
> HALLELUJAH.
>
> Talk about singing
> Talk about singing
> Talk about singing all night long.
> —Robert, grade 7

A kindergarten class observed the signs of winter, and the teacher wrote each child's observation on the board in the form of a poem.

> Bare trees
> Birds flying South
> Grey outdoors.

---

*Robert Wolsch, "Life with Sister," Lafayette High School *Marquis*, 1943.

A youngster in another class summarized the transition from winter to spring.

SPRING

It was snowing
Now winds are blowing.
I was in
Now I'm out.
— *Sheree, grade 2*

A third-grade teacher asked, "What are the signs of spring?"

When the birds are
   singing —
And the children are
   swinging —
The frogs are hopping —
And ladies are mopping —
We know it is spring!
— *Bonnie, grade 3*

Nancy, a fifth grader, wrote about an exciting moment.

A frog in the pond
Jumping at a small green fly,
Garoompf, then silence.

Life is full of thrilling moments. Watching someone blow up a balloon and waiting for the balloon to pop can become an exciting experience (figure 4.3).

Carol Larsen described what she saw during a morning drive near Windsor Castle: "The ground was completely white with frost, and the daylight was all pink and purple. The castle and the 500-year-old oak trees were opalescent. I just gasped."

Observations may be generic and timeless, or timely and very specific. Greg, a fourth grader, described the shark he saw at the beach as "the size of a foreign car." Dick Gregory's autobiography contains a picture of himself as a young man watching a pretty girl walk down the street:

Everybody's got a Helene Tucker, a symbol of everything you want. I loved her for her goodness, her cleanliness, her popularity. She'd walk down the street and my brothers and sisters would yell, "Here comes Helene" and I'd rub my tennis sneakers on the back of my pants and wish my hair wasn't so nappy and the white folks' shirt fit me better.*

---

*Dick Gregory, with Robert Lipsyte, *Nigger: An Autobiography* (New York: E. P. Dutton, 1964), p. 43.

FIGURE 4.3.   Waiting for the balloon to pop

Tribulations

Tribulations are unpleasant trials, tests, or ordeals; they are not fun, like escapades. One girl recalled what happened to her on Halloween.

HALLOWEEN'S GARDEN

Halloween's garden
Pumpkins in the fields.
Eyes glaring from them,
With a weird look.
A rustle in the bushes
A flapping sound of birds
In the moonless night
Ghostly trees bending over you,
As you walk along
The wind is playing windy tunes,
As you run along.
When you get home,

> Your mother will ask,
> Why do you shudder so?
> — *Sue, grade 4*

Some tribulations may be extended. Revealing the tribulation and declaring that one has survived it sometimes creates a sense of relief. Before the following poem was written, the topic of class discussion and subsequent role playing had been race relations. The role playing turned the observation of another's ordeal into a shared experience for June.

UNWANTED

I am ashamed of what I had shown
To one so frightened, one so alone;
No one wanted to be his friend,
I had to make matters worse in the end.
He wanted friends and warm affection,
To this my back was turned
I made no correction.

His color I laughed at,
T'was black not white;
His hair was dark
His eyes were bright.
Restlessly shifting, first here, then there,
He seemed to sense that none of us cared.

When treated rough, not like he should
He never fought back as I'm sure he could,
He'd take it all, made never a fuss,
He was always kinder than the rest of us.

I know now — I should have known before —
That by giving kindness you'll receive so
much more.
> — *June, grade 6*

INNER EXPERIENCES

Inner experiences are also ready subjects for composition. Feelings, daydreams, wishes, reflections, and whimsies may be caught and formed compositionally. The distinction between actual and imaginary experiences is not always absolute. There are solid lines and intermittent lines on both real and imagined roads. The storyteller or writer may be allowed to cross back and forth, just as a motorist does on the highway, depending on the circumstances. A person can derive a deep personal satisfaction from communing with his or her own world, real or imagined. Such moments afford inexhaustible subject matter for creative work.

Feelings

Feelings are our primary communication system. Inner computers, reacting to each new situation, convert our reactions into energy, which is reconverted into words. Writing without feelings often becomes merely an exercise. The following rainbow of universal feelings can be harnessed by beginning speakers and writers and other artists (figure 4.4). The painful feelings are anger, anxiety, hurt, guilt, and loss. The pleasurable feelings are love, joy, satisfaction, and well-being.

FIGURE 4.4.   Capturing feelings

Composition, like all aspects of education, starts with the stimulation of some kind of feeling or thought. Some may think about subjects like rats, dope pushers, filth, and garbage. For others, the subject matter may be a little red wagon or ice cream cones, museums, or concerts. Teachers can help composers capture their feelings of love, hate, enthusiasm, boredom, pity, respect, or pleasure. Whatever they write about, they should be encouraged to call upon their own feelings first. Once they can capture their own feelings or the feelings of others, their writing and speaking will seldom be dull.

Nevertheless, writing or speaking about our feelings has not always been encouraged; our culture has more commonly emphasized restraint and self-control. So often we hear:

> "Cheer up,things will get better tomorrow."
> "You're acting like a baby."
> "Control yourself."
> "Temper, temper."
> "Shame on you."
> "Sticks and stones will break your bones, but names will never harm you."

But names *can* hurt when they evoke feelings that hurt. Just sitting down and putting one's feelings on paper may help one feel better; it certainly makes one's speaking and writing better. The following pages suggest some of the many alternatives to just keeping feelings bottled up or denying that they exist.

ANGER.   Anger ranges from mild irritation to wild rage. It needs release or it festers. A story about a person's venting his anger over a perceived injustice was in the news. A sixth grader tried to describe anger.

> Anger is—
> A furious boiling sea of foam
> A burning, white hot furnace of fire
> An erupting volcano of molten rock
> An exploding atom bomb
> The door to Satan's drain
> A roaring, thundering, crashing waterfall,
> Violent,
> A pile of silent,
>   glowing,
>   embers,
> An ugly mar on happiness.
>
> — *Hugh, grade 6*

Anger, whether it follows frustration, a hurt, or a loss, summons forth strong
emotions and language. To be angry is to be human. To recognize one's
anger and express it appropriately is a sign of maturity. Some need coax-
ing; others need restraint. Composing may lead to feeling composed. Billy
provides an example of frustration followed by anger.

> I FELT ANGRY WHEN . . .
>
> When Howard, Tom, and my friend David went to a football game and
> my brother came along. He was yelling and yelling at home, and I final-
> ly let him go "but on one condition," I said. Howard, Tom and David
> and I answered him, "SHUT UP."
>
> *— Billy, grade 3*

Anger toward others may sometimes be triggered by hurt feelings.

> HE'S NOTHIN'
>
> He's nothin'!
> He's a nobody!
> He can't read or write;
> He can't even fight.
> He's like no light at night.
> He's nothin'!
> *— Althea, grade 5*

Perhaps reading through table 4.1 will help composers begin to describe their anger. Ask who was responsible for their anger. Talk about
these people. Put the feeling on paper: the paper will not answer back, no
matter how angry they get. They can start with the feeling, the person, or
the situation:

> I feel angry as an open blister because _____.
> Harry took my _____.
> While walking down Main Street _____.

TABLE 4.1. Anger

agitated	callous	fierce	irritated	severe
aggravated	combative	furious	mad	spiteful
aggressive	contrary	hard	mean	vicious
angry	cool	harsh	nasty	vindictive
annoyed	cranky	hateful	obstinate	violent
arrogant	cross	hostile	outraged	wrathful
belligerent	cruel	impatient	resentful	
biting	disagreeable	inconsiderate	rough	
blunt	enraged	insensitive	rude	
bullying	envious	intolerant	savage	

At times, it is easier to write about someone else's anger: "Alice turned rage red because ____." Or they can imagine wild things happening to the person, place, or thing responsible for their anger: "His ears wiggle when he lies."

Carlyle used his imagination and his anger in telling the language arts consultant and then writing:

> Teacher put me down
> I got no bumps on me
> It don't show outside.
> I'll sic my dog on her
> He'll run her all around the town.
> — *Carlyle, grade 6*

ANXIETY. As the dark sky and sudden wind signal a coming storm, anxiety is a feeling of impending danger, loss, or hurt (figure 4.5). Like a per-

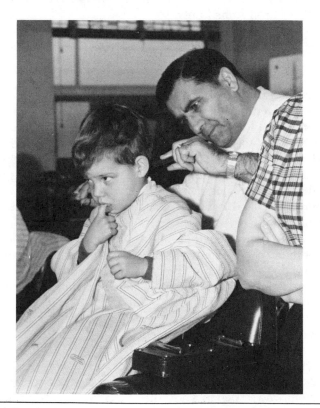

FIGURE 4.5.   Anxiety

sonal alarm system, anxiety is easily triggered. It may be a helpful emotion, alerting us to potential danger and the need for positive action.

Too many people misinterpret the normal and helpful body changes associated with anxiety as a danger from inside themselves rather than a response to a threat of loss or hurt from outside. It is necessary to decide whether a particular anxious feeling comes from people, from a situation, or from nature itself. Eight-year-old Jordan managed to express his anxiety and identify its source at the same time: "All those guys start hanging around and its like I'm in a forest."

In the television play based on *The Diary of Anne Frank*, the author Albert Hackett, conveyed anxiety through the stage directions and the dialogue. In one scene Anne's father has just said the prayer over the Hanukkah candles and is about to blow them out when there is a crash in the house above which they are hiding. Can anyone who saw the play ever forget how they all stood, paralyzed, fearing that they had been discovered by the Nazis? As they listen, anxiety about the unknown intruders builds in all the characters until Anne faints.

Grace, a part-time graduate student, interviewed her husband, who, at fifty-two, suffered two heart attacks and a stroke. The interview vividly conveys the anxiety he felt.

Q. What did you experience within yourself when you went into intensive care the first time?

A. At that time I didn't feel anything wrong and wondered what all the fuss was about. I thought I had the flu.

Q. When did you have the heart attack?

A. I was in intensive care when everyone came running up to my bed. I had been looking at all the gadgets, and I asked what was going on. Then I felt it and I was scared. I was scared.

Q. What did it feel like?

A. I couldn't get my breath. I felt I couldn't breathe anymore. Had a knot in my chest. I hung onto the nurse for dear life — afraid to let go. I didn't want to die. They gave me a needle, but I was so excited I don't know what went on. There were four or five nurses and doctors.

Q. Did you know what had happened to you?

A. I knew I had had a heart attack . . .

Bud Mackta, in an unpublished manuscript, writes of the anxiety experienced long ago by his family, early twentieth-century refugees from a Russian pogrom who settled in Knoxville, Tennessee, and describes how it proved to be a premonition of coming events.

My mother became quite a "furrin lady." She provided the mill workers with food, coal for their fires, and most of their worldly needs; she helped to deliver the babies and helped to bury the dead. . . .

There was a beautiful relationship between the former hill people and Sara's family, but we never felt 100% secure. There was always an unspoken undercurrent of almost silent proportions. We were foreign and nothing could change that.

It was nothing unusual to see my mother, the "furrin lady," holding court on her large veranda, chatting with the sun-bonneted ladies, serving lemonade, talking and gossiping. During slack times the men often joined these "veranda gatherings," talking about their cockfights, their hatred for mill work, their brawls at the railroad crossing, their prison sojourns at the old brushy mountain prison. The fact that my mother spoke little English seemed to matter little; she always made herself understood. The men did not partake of my mother's lemonade — they always had their bottle of "white lightning" in their hip pocket.

These "veranda gatherings" seemed normal. What was not normal was the fact that the friendly neighbors who gathered by day for lemonade, gossip, groceries, and the like donned white sheets and rode through the area at night terrorizing and setting fire to piles of straw they had banked around the "furrin lady's" house.

But one night my mother and us five young children were alone. She was the sole protector as the white-robed neighbors riding by under the Ku Klux Klan banner — earlier that day her friends and neighbors, by night her enemies — were now threatening her and her family. She thought fast. She took her broom handle and thrust it out the second-story window and shouted the equivalent of "Come closer and I'll blow your stupid heads off," and, indeed, in the moonlight it surely did look like a rifle. Off went the riders. They had met their match.

A grade-school student summarized her worries:

> I worry about:
>   Failing a test,
>   The chair falling back,
>   The stain on my bedspread,
> If I am going to move away,
> My rabbits dying.
>   — *Suzanne, grade 5*

The following formulas may help composers begin to speak or write about anxiety.

ANXIETY CAUSED BY PEOPLE

I fear my friend.
I fear my teacher.
I fear —

TABLE 4.2.   Anxiety

afraid	dread	insecure	overwhelmed	tense
agitated	embarrassed	intimidated	panicky	terrified
alarmed	fearful	jealous	restless	timid
anxious	fidgety	jittery	scared	uncomfortable
apprehensive	frightened	jumpy	shaky	uneasy
bashful	hesitant	nervous	shy	worrying
desperate	mortified	on edge	strained	

ANXIETY CAUSED BY SITUATIONS

I fear tests.
I fear school.
I fear playing —

ANXIETY CAUSED BY NATURE

I fear lightning.
I fear the dark.
I fear snakes.
I fear —

After they have added some fears of their own to each category, they can write some more about the possible loss, hurt, or danger that lies behind the feeling of anxiety.

The word list in table 4.2 may be helpful in beginning.

HURT.   To hurt is to feel a loss. Everyone must lose from time to time; therefore, everyone must at one time or another have felt hurt, abandoned, betrayed, disappointed, or rejected.

Disappointment stings. James Joyce, in "Araby," writes of experiencing an unfulfilled promise.

> At nine o'clock I heard my uncle's latchkey in the halldoor. I heard him talking to himself and heard the hallstand rocking when it had received the weight of his overcoat. . . . When he was midway through his dinner I asked him to give me the money to go to the bazaar. He had forgotten.*

The word list in table 4.3 and the following open-ended sentences may help composers to describe disappointment or hurt feelings.

You disappointed me when ____.
I hurt when ____.
I miss the good times when ____.

---

*In *Dubliners* (New York: Viking, 1967), p. 33.

TABLE 4.3. Hurt

ache	displace	injure	resentful	twinge
affliction	disservice	lament	rile	unforgettable
agony	distress	maim	ruffle	unhappy
ailing	disturb	malevolent	shock	vex
bear	endure	malice	smart	victimize
bitter	evildoer	maltreatment	sicken	violence
bother	fret	misery	sore	waste
brutality	gall	molest	sorrowful	woe
collide	grate	nettle	spoil	worry
crack	grave	offend	sting	wound
crush	grievance	outrage	suffer	
damage	harm	pain	torment	
despair	inflict	prejudice	torture	
deplore	impair	punish	trouble	

GUILT. Guilt is feeling angry at oneself, perhaps for hurting someone unfairly. Composers should look at the situation as they would observe a movie and start simply: "I hurt you (them, her, etc.) when ____.

The words in table 4.4 may be signals that a feeling of guilt is being described.

LOSS. A loss is often followed by a feeling of deprivation. Roberta found that time helps to ease the pain of various kinds of loss.

I LOST MY BALLOON

I lost my balloon
I lost my balloon
I lost it yesterday.

I lost my balloon
I lost my balloon
I saw it blow away.

TABLE 4.4. Guilt

accuse	contrite	illegal	naughty	sheepish
ashamed	corrupt	indictment	nefarious	villainy
atrocity	criminality	infamy	rebuked	wicked
blame	delinquent	injury	redhanded	worthless
caught	felony	malefactor	regretful	wrong
censure	foul	mischief	remorse	
confess	harm	misconduct	repentance	
convict	hurt	misdemeanor	shame	

I lost my balloon
I miss it still today
But not as much as yesterday.
                    —*Roberta, grade 2*

In contrast, death is the ultimate loss; death touches feelings and memories with disbelief. Emotion and language, in spoken and written forms, aid in weathering the deprivation until time and the acceptance of reality can help us miss the dead today—but not as much as yesterday.

Sheila Schwartz, the author of *Like Mom, Like Me*, shared with us her pain following the incomprehensible loss of her daughter Nancy.

My daughter, Nancy Lynn Schwartz, died on September 3, 1978. It is now September 17, two weeks after her death, and I am still unable to comprehend this tragedy. She was twenty-six years old.

Nancy was an extraordinary girl. Many people thought she had everything: beauty, brains, figure, sweetness, integrity, compassion, social and political conscience, and amazing success at a very young age. Friends called her a golden girl. She was generous and had a vast army of friends at every age level. People of like tendencies immediately recognized her as an exceptional, superior kind of human being, vital, vibrant, totally devoid of malice, someone good to be with. . . .

Nancy once said to me, "There has to be one intelligence in the world that each person writes for, and you are that intelligence to me." And she was that intelligence to me.

Five weeks ago she came to New York to assist in the selection of actors for *Charleston*, an exceptional honor for a writer. She looked as beautiful as ever, healthy, joyous, creative, successful, and happy. She had a lovely humility.

"I can't believe how successful I am, Mom," she said before she left.

She returned to Hollywood and two days later she called. "I'm not feeling well. Maybe a virus, so they're hospitalizing me overnight."

"Should I come?"

"Don't worry. It's nothing serious."

The next day she called, "Mom, come quick, it's a brain tumor."

Out of nowhere, the holocaust again.

She lingered for two and a half weeks after the operation. She was lucid, intelligent, humorous, and completely functioning in the hospital. . . .

In all the time we had in the hospital she never complained, cried, or bemoaned her fate. She kept me from crying. . . .

The only bad night was the night she died. The last things she said to me were, "Mom, are you getting enough sleep?"; and "*Like Mom, Like Me* is going to be a big success. It's the most beautiful mother-daughter relationship ever depicted in television."

The doctor came in then. "Nancy," he asked, "are you awake or asleep?"

"I must be awake," she joked, "or why would I be feeling all this pain?"

And then she was gone.

People try to find things for me to feel good about. "She was always a joy to you." "You have the memory of a beautiful relationship." "She had more success than people have in their entire lives."

But there is no consolation. All that I can do is to endure and to survive and to wait. Nancy was working on a phenomenal book about the Hollywood Blacklist. I will try to finish her work. I have lost my beloved daughter, my dearest friend. There is no consolation.

Neil Simon's *Chapter Two* is an account of his feelings after the death of his wife. In the first act of the play, George, the widower, experiences a grief that turns into nonacceptance and denial, and then into anger at the dead wife for leaving him. A similar connection between grief and anger is made in a child's three-line poem. Following the loss of a beloved grandfather, Tommy wrote:

> The phone rang loudly;
> My grandfather died last night;
> I punched the couch *hard*.
> — *Tommy, grade 5*

The words in table 4.5 may help composers capture a sense of loss. Table 4.6 lists words associated with death. These words and the feelings they evoke or represent may assist writers and speakers in moving from the shock and denial that so often precede an acceptance of death.

Composers can start with a painful situation that they have overcome or one that they avoided. Once it is spoken of or written down, they can relive it or share it with a friend. It is interesting to share pleasurable as well as painful feelings. Seeking pleasure is instinctual, but how does one describe it? Is it love, joy, satisfaction, or well-being? Is it all of them? The following are cherished thoughts and expressions from our children's early years.

TABLE 4.5. Loss

abandoned	cut	drop	lapsed	stray
absence	damaged	failure	lost	toll
alone	decrease	forfeit	misfortune	undoing
astray	defeat	frittered	mislaid	vanished
bereaved	depressed	grief	missing	wanting
bereft	deprived	harm	obscured	wasted
bewildered	destroy	injury	penalty	without
casualty	disappear	inattention	ruin	
cost	dispossess	irreclaimable	squander	

TABLE 4.6.   Death

ancestry	dying	interred	reincarnation	transitory
bemoan	dissolution	karma	remains	unveiling
bereave	everlasting	kill	rest	undertaker
bury	expire	loss	sacrifice	vault
cease	extinct	mortality	sadness	wash
coffin	funeral	nirvana	service	will
cremate	grieve	passing	sleep	yonder
cry	heaven	perish	shroud	
deceased	hell	procession	stone	
demise	home	quiet	tomb	
depart	immortal	regeneration	tragedy	

LOVE, AFFECTION, AND CONCERN.   One way to remember pleasant times is to record them as children grow. These language snapshots are pictures of their development.

Billy expressed concern at two years and eight months: "You hurt? Dat's a shame." Indoors, warm and dry, he reflected while watching the rain: "When rains, birdies shake water from dere wings." About the same time, he expressed his love and affection.

> I miss you Daddy;
> I wove you Daddy;
> I wove you a bushel and a heck.

At three years, six months, Billy told us of his concern for his little brother:

> And then I grew up to be a great, big, handsome
>   and wonderful boy.
> I hugged Jordy,
>   and that made him feel very, very proud.

At four, Billy introduced his brother:

> This is my little brother, Jordan Andrew.
> He's a nice little fellow;
> Pat him on the head.

Jordan, at two and a half, was certain that everyone loved his grandma: "The airplane can't go without grandma. She's a friend." At four he showed concern for various items. Once he opened the ice box and said: "Those little ice cubes are freezing to death." At six Jordan announced:

> When we go by the home of the old people,
> I'm going to say, "Hi kids," and make them feel good.

Nine-year-old Jordy reported his concern about the embarrassment of another boy at school.

> I was in the boys' bathroom and a little kid came in.
> He musta seen my long hair and thought he was in the girls' room.
> You could hear his teacher calling,
> "Doo-wayne, Doo-wayne,
> What's the matter, Doo-wayne?"

JOY.   There are moments of great joy in remembering, experiencing, or anticipating some events or pleasures (figure 4.6). Lisa, at three and a half, took time to share the experience while swimming at the beach: "I've been

FIGURE 4.6.   Joy

under water visiting fish." Another time she shared some joyous news with
her brothers: "Mom's parking nuts in the cookies."

Jordan, age five, was so happy to lend his turtles to his seven-year-old
uniformed brother.

> When you show my turtles to the Boy Scouts,
> tell them they're your little brother's,
> and he's the kid right here in the audience,
> and I'll stand up and take a bow.

SATISFACTION AND WELL-BEING.   Satisfaction and well-being are the feelings we yearn for all our lives. Billy, at two years, six months, verbalized a
macho sense of well-being and used a kind of syllogistic reasoning in comparing himself to his six-month-old brother.

> Jordy is little folks;
> Little folks no eat grapes;
> I'm a tough kid.

At three, he awoke and announced:

> I have a little story to tell you this morning.
> I'm dry.
> That's all.

Three-year-old Billy announced after dinner:

> I'm going to bed and sleep soundly till spring.
> This saves me a trouble of storing food and nuts for the winter.

At four he described how he got ready to sleep:

> I put my ear up, my thumb in my mouth,
> And my feet under the covers.
> Then I'm ready to go to sleep.

Lisa, at four, in her new snowsuit, said: "I feel like the president of the Teddy Bears of the World." Later, putting on her socks: "My toes are going in
their little sleeping bags." At five, she confided:

> I'll always remember
> You're my Daddy with loving fingers.

Feeling particularly good one day, three-year-old Jordan evaluated
himself: "I'm so cuddly."

In some ways pleasurable feelings are harder to separate out and analyze
than painful ones. Closeness, contentment, and pride in the father of
whom he had once felt so ashamed are all represented in Sherwood Anderson's "I Discover My Father."

I climbed the stairs to my own room, undressed in the darkness and got into bed. I couldn't sleep and did not want to sleep. For the first time I knew that I was the son of my father. He was a story teller as I was to be.*

Table 4.7 on p. 70 lists adjectives that may be used to describe pleasurable feelings.

Wishes

Wishes, wants, or desires suggest a lack and a longing for various types of fulfillment. John had been suspended from school for several weeks. He had found life at home terribly unsatisfying, too, and wrote down his thoughts on his first day back in the seventh-grade special class.

THE BIRD AND THE BOY

A beautiful bird
   flew in the sky
     and
A sad little boy
   sitting in the sand.
     then
The beautiful bird
   flew on his shoulder
     and
   sang to him
     and
   the sad little boy
   happy again
     and
   they both walk
   on the dirt road.
             —*John, grade 7*

Muhammad Ali, in *The Greatest: My Own Story,* tells how he wished for his own boxing equipment:

I may have been the best fighter, but I was also the poorest. I owned one T-shirt, two pairs of pants, several pairs of shoes with holes in them. My jackets were torn and patched, and hardly a day went by when my pants didn't split somewhere. And although I had won nearly all my fights, and was on the verge of turning professional, I had never been able to af-

---

*In *Memories of Sherwood Anderson,* ed. A. Ray Lewis (Chapel Hill: University of North Carolina Press, 1969), p. 85.

TABLE 4.7.   Pleasurable feelings

Love, Affection, Concern

admired	considerate	good	mild	respectful
adorable	cooperative	helpful	moral	sensitive
affectionate	cordial	honest	neighborly	sympathetic
agreeable	courteous	honorable	nice	sweet
altruistic	dedicated	hospitable	obliging	tender
amiable	devoted	humane	open	thoughtful
benevolent	empathetic	interested	optimistic	tolerant
benign	fair	just	patient	truthful
brotherly	faithful	kind	peaceful	trustworthy
caring	forgiving	kindly	pleasant	understanding
charitable	friendly	lenient	polite	unselfish
comforting	generous	lovable	reasonable	warm
congenial	genuine	loving	receptive	
conscientious	giving	mellow	reliable	

Elation, Joy

amused	elevated	glorious	jubilant	splendid
blissful	enchanted	good	magnificent	superb
brilliant	enthusiastic	grand	majestic	terrific
calm	exalted	gratified	marvelous	thrilled
cheerful	excellent	great	overjoyed	tremendous
comical	excited	happy	pleased	triumphant
contented	fantastic	humorous	pleasant	vivacious
delighted	fit	inspired	proud	wonderful
ecstatic	gay	jovial	satisfied	
elated	glad	joyful	sorrow	

Satisfaction, Well-being

able	confident	fearless	important	sharp
adequate	courageous	firm	influential	skillful
assured	daring	forceful	intense	spirited
authoritative	determined	gallant	manly	stouthearted
bold	durable	heroic	powerful	strong
brave	dynamic	hardy	robust	sure
capable	effective	healthy	stable	tough
competent	energetic	mighty	secure	virile

ford a first-class mouthpiece to protect my teeth. I had to wait until the other fighters finished so I could borrow their headgear, or their trunks or bandages. I wanted my own training gloves, my own gear.*

Ellie had been wishing for something more than just "hand-me-down" clothes.

> I wish I had a pretty blue dress
>   a pretty blue dress
>   a pretty blue dress
> I wish I had a pretty blue dress
>   that I could wear to school.
> — *Ellie, grade 4*

Richie often missed the school bus. He dreamed of a way to solve his problem.

> I wish that I could fly
>   around the block
> Then I could fly
>   to school
> I'd sleep till about eight o'clock
> Then flap my wings — like cool!
> — *Richie, grade 4*

Writing about wishes gave Bobby a chance to express something he had never before discussed in school.

> I wish I had wishes
>   for the rest of my life
> I wish they would all come true.
> I'd wish and I'd wish
>   and I'd wish and I'd wish
>   for a dog and a daddy to play with too.
> — *Bobby, grade 2*

Daydreams

Daydreams provide an unending supply of topics for composition. Daydreams, or reveries, are often looked upon unfavorably by teachers. Soon forgotten, they seem to be wasteful of time. When written down, however, they become a prime source of inner experiences for composition. John daydreamed about the surf.

---

*Muhammad Ali, with Richard Durham, *The Greatest: My Own Story* (New York: Random House, 1975), p. 55.

surf
water swirls around rocks
frothy
swirling around nooks and crannies in
the rocky shore line
falling in miniature Niagaras
from
pools filled from the surf
eating away the rocks
crashing against solid rock
then a loud roar
then quietly retreating
battering again and again
and again
eating away the ancient stone
turning mountains to sand.
                                    —John, grade 8

John, who was failing English, was asked how he happened to write this selection. His answer was in the following form.

I write mostly in the evening
but this was done in study hall,
second period
I don't know how I got the idea
Maybe because time passed so slowly,
reminding me of an eternity,
eternity maybe reminds me of
tide, tide-surf etc. I was bored.

Debbie, in grade 5, thought about war. She wrote:

The sun was shining
The trees were quiet and still
Then the rains came down.

William, a fourth grader, thought about sprockets.

Sprockets
    are making my wheels spin
Sprockets
    are making them go
Sprockets
    go into the chain and round
    and faster and faster
    the pedals go
Wow, do I have velocity!

Helen, in grade 3, daydreamed about a delicious treat.

> Three straws in a milkshake
> Burgers and buns
> French fries and catsup
> Umm, tastes like fun.

Andy wrote about the "big fellow" down the street.

> Kenny down the street
>   can't get hurt
> He's ten!
> He does "wheelies" in the street
>   Never wears a hat
>   and never catches cold.
> Ten's old!
>   —*Andy, grade 2*

Buzzy thought about scouting.

> You wanna know
> Why I wanna go
>   and join the scouts?
> Cause on the rugged trail
> I might find frogs and toads.
>   —*Buzzy, grade 2*

Lisa thought about a day with Dad.

> Dad can take us to the movies
>   and buy us popcorn, and candy, and gum.
> And Mom
>   can stay home and clean the house
>   like Cinderella.
>   —*Lisa, kindergarten*

An anonymous piece, "The Me Nobody Knows," communicates a kind of universal daydream.

THE ME NOBODY KNOWS

Nobody knows what I'm really like inside. My parents, my neighbors, or my friends don't really know. I act cheerful and try to look that way, but inside I'm lonely. In the night I lay in bed, thinking, just thinking, how it would be if I really had friends. Most of all, I'd like to have something more than friends, more than people. I'd like to have a pony — any pony. If I had a pony, I could gallop into the fields and jump streams and trees. Then after that I could lie on the grass and be free from all trouble. I'd be free from my brother's talk and the radio.

>   —*Unnamed author, grade 5*

FIGURE 4.7.   Reflections

Reflections

Reflections are thoughts one meditates on or ponders about (figure 4.7). There are infinite varieties of images upon which to reflect. They include embarrassing things, like running out of ink during a test; frustrating things, like remembering the answers after the papers are collected; things that are disliked, like being kissed by a particular relative; and things that are exciting, like passing the hospital where one was born, watching cats wash their kittens, or seeing the first snowflake of the winter.

Looking out the kitchen window one cloudy Saturday morning, Nancy, a fifth grader, picked up her pad and pencil and wrote:

Clouds are proud
    to be allowed
to crowd a rainy day.

Andy, a third grader, considered the sky and wrote:

The way I think of the sky
It seems so beautiful
I don't think
God could have made it any beautifuler.

Pamela was in a junior high school class for the mentally retarded. When the program turned toward composition, she wrote these selections in class.

SPRING HEART

My heart
    is full of sadness
    as I
    skip along the dew.

My heart
    needs lots of gladness
    but that
    will come with you.

Your love
    is so enchanting
    that ne'er a dove
    could fly

Without your sweet
    and tender love
    my heart
    will surely die.

'TWAS AN EARLY MORN

'Twas an early morn
    and the sun was shining
    on the breast of the beach.

The birds
    were singing their merry
    spring songs.
And the boys
    were sailing
    in their little green boat.

Then
    all at once
    there was silence.
A boy screamed,
    'Tis spring
    'Tis spring
    'Tis spring.

Wonder

Wonder — the natural sense of interest, astonishment, and awe that is vital to living — often leads to composition. It inspires people to look life's problems and pleasures straight in the eye, to be honest with words and with themselves. This intimate, personal, internal experience may at times be verbalized, and these times, when wonder is captured on paper, are naturally creative.

A composer must learn to value his wonderings and intuitions as well as his intellect and senses. If he is to take responsibility for his future, he must have opportunities to wonder about it, and about his past and present as well.

Some writers and speakers need experience in grasping or coming to grips with their own wonderings, which are as difficult for them to hold and work with as a soaped puppy. Others are already quite conscious of their wonderings. They are curious and concerned and in touch with their impressions. Jenny held on to her wonderings about the unknown, beautiful sky at night:

THE UNKNOWN

Bright-eyed stars on a crystal night,
Shine in the smooth, dark sky,
What beauties rare are hidden there?
What secrets old but strangely new,
Are waiting . . . waiting?
— *Jenny, grade 6*

Speakers and writers who hold on to their wonderings may need help in retaining or directing them. The teacher may remind them:

some people wonder about people
some people wonder about people's opinions
some people wonder about things
some people wonder about experiences
some people wonder about feelings
some people wonder about values
some people wonder about ideas
some people wonder about themselves
some people wonder about nature.

Four-year-old Billy observed skywriting and wondered: "Why is that airplane scraping the sky?" Our other children wondered:

Why do my tears dry up when
you hold me in your arms, Mummy? — *Lisa, age 3*

When someone gets hurt,
Why do I feel sorry for myself? — *Lisa, age 5*

How come I don't have any warts?
So many other people do. — *Jordy, age 7*

Teachers may encourage older children to keep pad and pencil handy at home, in school, wherever they go. They can never tell when they will wonder a winner. The selections that follow were written by children who took this advice for a day or two. Susan, a fourth grader, wondered:

How the birds fly in storms and rain
How men have courage to go to space
How the planets stay in the air
How big the stars are
    and
What will happen in the future.

Tom's grandfather had recently died. Tom, a fifth grader, wrote:

DEATH

Death is an endless sleep.
Death is the beginning of
    peace.
Death is many things in
    many ways.
Death is the beginning of
    the Judgement day.
Death is a time to moan and
    cry
Why do so many people die?

Suzanne, a fifth grader, wondered about those close to her:

As a child I thought:
    God was Santa Claus,
    My friend was a goddess,
    My house was a palace,
    My dad was the smartest man,
    Eight-year-olds were sooo tall,
    My cat was a rag doll.

Composition may also be a way to celebrate the wonders of the world.
Anne rambled through her garden and wondered:

I see two trees,

    One is a slender, young white birch;
    The other a gnarled, old, ugly tree.
    But they both sway together harmoniously.
    How could that be?

I see two birds,

    One is an oriole, swift and free;
    The other a work-worn chickadee.
    But they both sway together harmoniously.
    How could that be?

I see two flowers,

> One is a blood-red tulip;
> The other a pale-white lily.
> But they both sprout from a seed.
> How could that be?
>
> *—Anne, grade 4*

To be enthusiastic and open to wonder is to be childlike. The joy of wonder need not diminish with age. It should be nurtured. In the Orient it is not uncommon to invite friends to a party to watch the birth of roses or of a full moon.

Whimsies

Whimsies are the product of playful and sudden fancy. Whimsies begin and flower in the observations of young children. Billy, a three-year-old, observed: "Minnesota. That's a yummy name." He asked:

> If a cowboy wears a star
>   He's a sheriff.
> What is he
>   If he wears a moon?

At four he asked:

> If my bedroom was pink
>   would I wake up in the morning
>   and smile at the pinkness of it?

And he observed that something was "as good as a mountain full of raisin bread," and that

> When you drink something
>   it goes into your boilers
>   and you go ZOOM.

A fifth-grade girl returned from visiting a friend whose family cat had produced another litter. The sudden thought of her friend's future suggested the following selection.

> There is an old lady,
> On top of Mount Splats,
> She has one million and sixty-four
>   cats!
> She feeds them pickles, frogs, and fats,
> The little old lady with so many cats.
> She's one hundred years old,
> She has silver and gold,
> But she lives in a little wood shack!

This little old lady
On top of Mount Splats
That has one million and sixty-four
      cats!
                    — *Kathleen, grade 5*

Concentrating on ways to trap a pesty fly led Keith to compose this whimsical selection:

THE SHY FLY

There once was a fly,
A terrible fly,
I hated that fly,
I wanted him to die.

I swatted and swatted,
Until I was red
But that sly fly
Was still not dead.

I used a spray
But the fly walked away,
And all that day,
My efforts were grey.

Then I thought to myself,
"How can he give me so much trouble?"
So I set out some soap,
And he got caught in a bubble.

And all through the days,
I just sit and gaze,
At that so very sly fly,
Floating so high
In the blue sky.
                    — *Keith, grade 6*

Nonsense

From whimsies, one may go on to nonsense verse, with funny names and impossible events that exercise the logic of artists. The infant's first peek-a-boo game signals delight in recognizing his or her separation from other people and other things. Playful distortions of language, too, are a way of sharing a tongue-in-cheek attitude toward language and logic. The teacher can join in the fun or stand back and act as recorder.

Some authors invent names like "Nanoon," "Crazyville," or "Inkadink." Others invent strange actions for well-known companions: "kittens bark" and "teachers stand in the corner." They know what's upside down and what's right side up; they know others know it too. Whatever the form, nonsense is one path to composition. Bill and his friends enjoyed "Riding a Frog to Alaska."

RIDING A FROG TO ALASKA

"Riding a frog to Alaska
Is hard to do."
Said the Snake-Headed-Noo
"Especially in fog,"
Said the Non-a-jog,
Yes-a-roo
It's hard to do —
Riding a frog to Alaska.
                    — *Bill, grade 4*

The following five selections were written with tongue in cheek. Notice how meter and rhyme added to the fun for the writer, the reader, and the listener.

Wink your eye
Wiggle your toe
Stick out your tongue
And your ears will grow.
          — *Mark, grade 4*

Uncle Maxie
Drives a taxi.
He drives so fast
His paint won't last.
     — *Rebecca, grade 3*

Mister Fester
Had a son Lester
Lester Fester was his name.
Lester Fester
was a class jester
Classroom jester was his fame.
What a name
What a fame
What a shame
Was that Fester
By the name of Lester.
               — *Ruthie, grade 6*

Rip raa ree
Hit them in the knee
Rip raa rose

Hit them in the nose
Fight team Fight.
— *Robin, grade 7*

Riddle-D-Diddle-D-Dee
What number do I see?
It ends with the *r* sound
And follows number three.
— *Lois, grade 5*

We are never really without material for composition, for we may speak or write out of actual or imaginary experiences. Some people require only a signal or a hint to begin; some need to read or hear the work of others. Some merely need to capture their experiences; others need time to shape them. Once people have captured their feelings and preserved them in written form, experiences are at least as secure as beetles in a bottle.

Experience with real or imaginary beetles may lead to writing. The word "beetle" itself may start a chain of events leading to the next approach to composition: speaking and writing into experience.

SUGGESTED READING

Cazden, C. J. "Play and Metalinguistic Awareness: One Dimension of Language Experience." *The Urban Review* 7(1974): 29–39.

Chukovsky, Kornei. *From Two to Five.* Translated and edited by Miriam Morton. Berkeley: University of California Press, 1963.

Clark, Ann Nolan. *Little Herder in Spring, Summer, Fall, Winter.* Phoenix, Ariz.: U.S. Indian Service Printing Department, Phoenix Indian School, 1950.

Geller, Linda Gibson. "Riddling: A Playful Way to Explore Language." *Language Arts* 58 (1981): 669–74.

Kohl, Herbert. *36 Children.* New York: Signet, New American Library, 1968.

McDowell, H. J. *Children's Riddling.* Bloomington: Indiana University Press, 1979.

Marzollo, Jean, and Lloyd, Janice. *Learning Through Play.* New York: Harper and Row, 1972.

Shonagon, Sei. *The Pillow Book of Sei Shonagon.* New York: Columbia University Press, 1967.

Viscott, David. *The Language of Feelings.* New York: Arbor House, 1976.

5 Speaking and Writing into Experience

Many compositions begin with the stimulation of language, images, or the senses; others start from a combination of them — an impregnation of one by another. Sometimes a message from one of the senses stirs other sense perceptions, as sight sometimes stirs taste. A word may come to mind that invites other words. One image may be the first link in a chain of images. When collected, these sensations, words, and images begin to multiply and take shape. Conception has occurred. A new life is forming. This is writing into experience.

Sharing the beautiful clouds seen through a skylight, Anne Frank shared her secret way of thinking herself out of captivity. She told her friend Peter of being able to transport herself to friendlier times and places, including parties and gardens. To ease the pain, she used a kind of self-hypnosis.

There are several ways of beginning composition by speaking and writing into experience. Composers may stimulate one or more of the senses. They may experiment with a point of view new to them. They may recognize analogous relationships and evoke word associations. Some writers begin by enlarging a melodic line. Others imitate someone else's format. Many start with function-centered definitions, startling statements, and evocative questions. At times, teachers may prescribe a form: a play, story, a poetic form, or one of the playful distortions of language. Prescribed forms relieve writers and speakers of certain mechanical decisions, enabling them to compose more readily. Others find free choice of topic, form, and opening helpful. Any one of these approaches may be used to start composition.

STIMULATING THE SENSES

Stimulating the senses to increase awareness is a way to begin to speak and then write into experience. Our senses are often taken for granted until something happens to help us appreciate them. Teachers have helped people become more aware of their natural powers by using only one sense at a

82

time. For example, artists might examine an object first with their eyes, then with their hands. Next, they may taste it, smell it, and try to bounce it. Then they discuss their sensations. Increased sensory awareness helps some people to examine, describe, collect, and order their perceptions. The following sections include suggestions for stimulating the various senses in preparation for composition.

Sight

Some teachers display pictures as an aid to composition. Pictures are most useful if the artist has not said all that can be said. One may work with the whole picture or zoom in on one part while blocking out the rest. A real or imaginary circle may be drawn around part of the picture, exposing a part at a time.

Using this aid, the writer may ignore the ship that is sailing in the background and concentrate on the plight of the man rowing the small dinghy. Or he or she may choose to concentrate on the dinghy itself, or the freshly caught fish lying together in it, the dark clouds threatening to unleash a storm. The writer may think only of the sound of the water, the wind, the oarlocks, or the labored breathing of the man rowing. Each aspect may evoke questions. Each question may begin another composition.

The same concept is practiced by a science teacher who has his or her students toss plastic hoops onto the ground and tells them to concentrate on what exists and what happens within that circle for fifteen minutes. They then talk and write about their observations. The papers are collected and read aloud, and everyone is amazed by the varied scientific and compositional experiences in that one field (figure 5.1).

Teachers can also use a picture like that of the child in chapter 3 (figure 3.1). First, have composers cover all but the eyes. They can study those eyes, listen to themselves, and write. Next, they cover all but the face. Finally, they expose the entire picture, studying it as carefully as they did the other two times. They may wish to talk about it with one or two people. They should do so, and then write together or alone.

Some writers need to frame the picture, which adds another dimension. Others are inspired by changing the color of the frame or directing lights of different kinds and colors onto the picture. Each change evokes different sensations, words, and images.

Hearing

Sounds are all around us (figure 5.2). Many of the sounds in a room or just outside it can be tuned in one at a time. The roar heard might consist of human, animal, and mechanical sounds. They may be the sounds of chil-

FIGURE 5.1.   Sight

dren or adults, the city or the country. Various conditions determine how fully they can be tuned in. Walking sounds, for example, vary according to the walker's footwear, condition, and proximity to the hearer.

Packaged music environments are used to control people's moods and behavior on the job, while shopping, loving, skating, marching, typing, telephoning, riding in elevators, watching movies, exercising, worshiping, driving, or eating. Music can be used as a type of controlled substance arousing one and making one alert and energetic. We react strongly to our own kind of music—the kind we enjoy—and reject the music of another generation or culture. It feels so good when we turn off music we don't like. Music we enjoy helps us in times of loneliness and depression, just as it establishes the appropriate mood for production lines, romance, weddings, and funerals. It can also be used before and during writing and speaking to

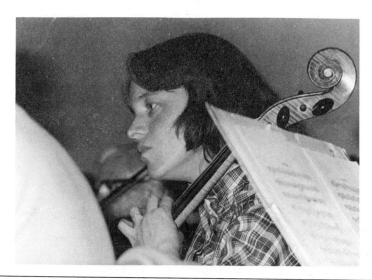

FIGURE 5.2.   Sound

stimulate composition. (See chapter 11 for a list of musical selections that may be used for this purpose.) Some teachers use sound effects records to help focus composers' attention. Others recommend attention to sounds oc-curing naturally in the environment.

Some places have their own special sounds. Authors may listen atten-tively in particular areas of the school or home. They may focus on the sounds of the schoolyard or the principal's office, the basement, the kit-chen, or the living room. Such community institutions as stores, churches, and ball fields all have interesting sounds. Sounds also vary with time of the year, and one can certainly tell a holiday by its sounds.

As composers become more sophisticated, they may be helped to notice the sounds of emotion: grief, gaiety, anger, or fear. These are the kinds of sound writers and speakers frequently use to add depth to their work. They may add them or begin with them.

Marcel Proust clung to his memories of hearing his mother climb the stairs to his room.

> My sole consolation when I went upstairs for the night was that Mamma would come in and kiss me after I was in bed. But this good night lasted for so short a time: she went down again so soon that the moment in which I heard her climb the stairs, and then caught the sound of her garden dress of blue muslin, from which hung little tassels of plaited

straw, rustling along the double-doored corridor, was for me a moment of the keenest sorrow.*

The following cooperative selections about sounds are well within the capabilities of all school-age children — or any beginner.

IT'S AS QUIET AS . . .

An empty house
A kitten purring
A dog sleeping
A picture
A piece of paper
A flag
The wind
A cat when it's walking
A bedroom at night
Somebody tip-toeing out the door
Somebody whispering
A calendar
A library
People working
A book on a shelf
Snow falling
Somebody sleeping
A tree
A raindrop
A bird flying

— Grade 2

SOUNDS THAT WAKE ME UP

My sister screaming for her
    bottle
My father's alarm clock
The birdies singing
My cat Priscilla meowing
When somebody is driving the
    car away from the house
Horns
A dog barking
The sound of my mother folding
    sheets — that's what happened to
    me last night

---

*In *Remembrance of Things Past* (New York: Random House, Modern Library, 1956), p. 10.

My mother dropping my baby's pail
Nobody wakes me up — I just wake
   up
              — *Kindergarten*

SOUNDS OF SNOW

People are shoveling
People are chopping ice

Cars slipping
Cars getting stuck.
        — *Kindergarten*

Smell

Smell is often difficult to describe (figure 5.3). There are, however, people with particular sensitivity to this sensory impression. Some people like to smell garages and gas stations and auto shops with new tires. The smells symbolize and evoke exciting images of cars and racing, and the images propel such persons further into imaginary situations involving gasoline and rubber tires. Composers should be encouraged to talk and then write about their favorite smells or smells that have strong associations — positive or negative — for them.

FIGURE 5.3.   Smell

Some teachers stimulate composition directly by spraying the classroom air with a particular aroma. Placing an item to smell in a covered food jar can also be helpful, especially if the jar is wrapped in paper to conceal the object. The teacher asks the authors to say what they think of when they first lift the cover. Different substances evoked the following responses:

> *An orange peel and juice in a jar:*
> "Reminds me of a happy morning." — *A five-year-old*
> "Like a sky full of blossoms." — *A ten-year-old*
>
> *The smell of rubber:*
> "Reminds me of the start of a drag race." — *A ten-year-old*
>
> *Alcohol:*
> "Reminds me of my tonsils." — *A six-year-old*

The precise recollection of a particular odor encountered during a field trip can be discussed and put into written form: a fish market, a dentist's office, a bakery, or the school kitchen.

George Orwell, in "Such, Such Were The Joys," shares his memories of the smell of the bathroom at school.

> It is not easy for me to think of my school days without seeming to breathe in a whiff of something cold and evil-smelling — a sort of compound of sweaty stockings, dirty towels, faecal smells blowing along corridors, forks with old food between the prongs.*

Mary McCarthy's "A Tin Butterfly" evokes the never-to-be-forgotten taste of Cracker Jacks:

> Though we sometimes had popcorn at home (Myers enjoyed popping it) and even, once or twice, homemade popcorn balls with molasses, we had never had more than a taste of this commercial Cracker Jack, with peanuts in it.†

It is possible that childhood memories of tastes are especially vivid (figure 5.4). Some teachers have tasting parties where writers are served raisins, salt, chocolate, vanilla, carrots, and other foods. Then, blindfolded and wearing clothespins on their noses, they take turns tasting and describing the same items. They then write what the aftertastes remind them of. For example:

> Salt: "Like a pretzel." — *A six-year-old*
> Sugar: "Like a birthday." — *A six-year-old*

---

*In *Collected Essays* (New York: Harcourt, Brace & World, 1953), p. 35.
†*In Memories of a Catholic Girlhood* (New York: Berkley, 1963), p. 69.

FIGURE 5.4. Taste

Bubble gum: "Like a barber shop." — *A ten-year-old*
Peppermint: "Like Christmas." — *An eleven-year-old*

Touch

William Gibson's play *The Miracle Worker* contains one of the most moving scenes of the American theatre. In it Helen Keller connects the sense of touch with language and thinking. Remember the scene where Annie Sullivan, the teacher, first forces Helen to use the handle of the water pump and feel the water splash over her hand, and then spells the word "water" into Helen's hand? That is the way of the teacher — suddenly it all makes sense to the child. The miracle of insight was stimulated by the sense of touch.

Composers can exercise their sense of touch anywhere (figure 5.5). One aid in stimulating the sense of touch is a "feelie box." This is a cardboard

FIGURE 5.5.   Touch

box with an opening for the insertion of one's hand. Inside, out of sight, a variety of common objects are attached. The objects may be chosen at random or according to categories. For example, one box may contain pieces of fabric, another various kinds of papers, another food, and so on. The box is so arranged that the teacher can see the objects but the feelers cannot. The writers try to guess the item and describe what it feels like. A pickle's skin was "as bumpy as an old dirt road" in one third grader's description. A small block of wood "feels like a dead mouse," said a ten-year-old. Another, describing the feel of velvet, wrote:

> As soft as a little white snow-
>   flake falling from the sky.
>
> As soft as a baby's hair rubbing
>   against its mother's hand.
>
> As soft as a little tissue wait-
>   ing in a box.
>   — *Hilary, grade 3*

Rhythm

Stimulating the sense of rhythm is an especially good way to start a composition. People love to note the various rhythms of pulse beats. They may examine themselves and each other before and after exercise. They may watch their pets asleep and awake. Writers can note the rhythms of their own play, including chanting, rope skipping, and ball bouncing. They can observe the rhythms of others chewing, playing, swinging, or dancing (figure 5.6). They can notice the rhythms of people at work: mothers mixing, washing, mopping; carpenters sawing, hammering; policemen waving, walking, marching.

FIGURE 5.6.   Rhythm

Older authors may also become interested in perceiving the rhythms of stressed and unstressed syllables. Using the beats of various dance patterns, writers can fit words to the rhythm. For example:

            1   2   1   2   3
            cha cha cha cha cha
            May I? Yes you may!

                1   2   3
            Watch him waltz
                on   her   toes.

Rhythm is an important part of the universe, of nature and being alive, of breathing, speaking, art, music, and certainly composition. We hear rhythms, feel rhythms, and see rhythms all around us. The wide variety of rhythmic patterns is fascinating to behold, especially when written down.

Rhythm needs to be spoken, spoken, spoken, repeated, repeated, repeated, chanted, chanted, chanted, and *then* written.

STIMULATING NEW POINTS OF VIEW

Having writers experience a new point of view can stimulate their language responses. Putting oneself in another person's shoes may mean simulating a Hindu, a Buddhist, a parent, a teacher, a member of the opposite sex, or someone of different age, color, economic level, profession, state of health, or environment. Changes in one facet have an effect on the entire scene. The thought of a peaceful scene — a pause — in the noise of the city and the classroom — led one child to whisper and then write:

NATURE

It is quiet.
I stand alone.
On a forested hilltop.
Then —
A frog croaks,
A bird soars,
And a tiny fawn leaves
Tracks in the soft mud
While trying to dodge my figure.
Then —
Everything is still,
And quiet,
Again.
                            —Lloyd, grade 6

Sheila described the plight of one creature (and all creatures) learning to walk:

> She took her first step
> With a wobble and a thump
> On the soft green grass.
> —*Sheila, grade 6*

Writers can walk into another period of time in the past or future. They can vary the angle of observation for a worm's eye view or a giant's (figure 5.7), or a view from another planet. They may try on the point of view of any form of animal, vegetable, or mineral life. Then they are free to add life or take it away, to peek at life and the absence of life from any dimension of time and space. Margaret used poetic composition to help her think about what she would do if she could fly.

FIGURE 5.7.   New points of view

IF I COULD FLY

If I could fly
I'd roar through the sky
So high! So high!! So high!!!
I'd do all kinds of tricks
I would! I would!
I'd dance in the sky with all
    the birds,
And when the day is over
I'd rest on a silver white cloud.
Wouldn't you
Do that too?
If you
Could fly?!
Fly!!!!!
                    —*Margaret, grade 4*

They can tell it like it really is (instead of how it is on television or the movie screen).

After being hit on the head
The private eye
    could not get up.
His eyes could not focus
His body twitched
    and trembled uncontrollably
Blood trickled from his ear
He could not control his bladder.
He never solved another case
He just became one.
                    —*Robbie, grade 7*

Simulating experiences can also build into writers ultra-high-frequency antennas of compassion, insight, empathy, and verve. Trying on others' shoes helps artists explore and develop and adds to their storehouse of experiences. It is a way to develop an understanding of the problems of persons and the universe.

One teacher asked her third graders to write about being sad and being sleepy. Two replies were:

As sad as a puppy in a Pet Shop.

As sleepy as a boy after a hard
    day of school.

The following youngsters wrote about the violence of nature. The teacher had asked: "What would it be like to be in the path of nature's violence?"

THE HURRICANE

The wind was cold!

The eerie darkness mingled with the forbidding
    shadows of the woods. Then all was calm as dark
    black clouds billowed forward in the sky.

The air was humid and warm.
The wind built up, a shutter banged, and then there
    was a ghastly cry.

Life was in a complete state of pandemonium as
    confusion reigned supreme.

Then it was upon us, the strong winds uprooted trees,
    smashed barns and destroyed houses!

A fence splintered to bits, a limp figure screamed
And rolled into the ditch.

Then all was quiet and calm as the unconquerable force
    passed.

—David, grade 6

STORM

The trees sway dangerously in the strong harsh wind,
The rain teems in sheets from the grey skies above.
Suddenly the sky is aflame! Then it is out.
Merely to be followed by a sharp crash, then silence.
Only the steady drumming of the rain in constant
    rhythm remains,
Wind swaying the towering trees, howling and groaning
Like a train on railway tracks,
Always the same, always the same.

—Norris, grade 6

Some people are helped to compose if they feel comfortable with the
people for whom they are composing. We compose more readily if we
speak or write for younger people or about silly people, make-believe people, talking creatures, or imaginative events. (People who stutter react very
much the same way. They sometimes verbalize more readily and fluently
when they sing, use puppets, role-play other people, and talk to pets, younger children, and others who stutter.) Composing with a younger or imaginary audience's point of view in mind can encourage composition. Speakers and writers can learn to develop new points of view in anticipation of
new kinds of listeners or readers for their compositions.

Peter looked for characters who were different from his usual playmates. He also liked the sound of "James, Jonathan, Sniper, and Twine."

THE SEA TRIP

James, Jonathan, Sniper and Twine
Went out to sea at eleven to nine.
Said they'd be back by a quarter to six.
They went out on a raft of a mast and some sticks
They took out their bait and a couple of rods,
Some flies and worms, and three half-dead frogs.
They included some candies, jubes and mints,
And that is the last I have heard of them since.
They took out my fish trap, a keepsake of mine,
James, Jonathan, Sniper and Twine.

—Peter, grade 6

STIMULATING ANALOGOUS RELATIONSHIPS

James Baldwin uses analogies in *Notes of a Native Son* to paint this word picture of his last visit with his father.

> She began to cry the moment we entered the room and she saw him lying there, all shriveled and still, like a little black monkey. The great, gleaming apparatus which fed him and would have compelled him to be still even if he had been able to move brought to mind not beneficence, but torture; the tubes entering his arm made me think of pictures I had seen when a child, of Gulliver tied down by the pygmies on that island.*

Analogous relationships may be used to stimulate perception and expression. Clouds in the sky, mountains in the distance, city and country skylines, and numerous other scenes, objects, symbols, and words evoke comparisons with other components of one's existence. Always eager to experiment with new relationships, writers can use their ability to relate familiar and unfamiliar items to start composition: for example, "the sky is as gray as my cat." A favorite game for the dinner table or short trips may easily be played anywhere. The leader asks the beginning writers questions like these:

What does____remind you of?
What do you think when you think of ____?
What is like ____?

_____
*(Boston: Beacon Press, 1955), p. 92.

What is most unlike ____ but reminds you of ____?
It looks like ____?
It sounds like ____?
It tastes like ____?
It moves like ____?
It thinks like ____?
It's as quiet as ____?

When written down, analogous relationships may be considered a kind of experience chart capturing the beginnings of composition. The following lines are typical first attempts at learning by comparing, relating, and associating language and pictures.

THE BRANCHES OF OUR TREE IN JANUARY

The branches look like
    little trees,
Like hills going up and
    down,
Like stocks and twigs.
Sometimes the branches
    look like seaweed and coral,
Like toothpicks,
Like bird nests.
The branches look like
    they have paper over them,
Like butterflies flying
    all around.
Like two hands reaching
    out.
The branches look as if
    they are about to fall off,
Like a head,
Like a V.
The tips of the little
    branches look like mosquitoes.
Like an imaginary drawing,
Like snakes,
Like a design
The branches look like
    caterpillars are going up and
    down them,
Like a thin tunnel,
Like hunks of dirt.
        — *Cooperative poem, grade 2*

STIMULATING WORD ASSOCIATIONS

The word association approach sensitizes people to language and evokes feelings about specific words. New ideas may spring from these feelings. Our ideas and our feelings come from various levels of our consciousness. The deeper the level tapped, the greater the chance that communicable feelings will emerge and be written or otherwise shared. Words evoke images, memories, and further words. When word associations can be made freely, without fear of disapproval or censorship, they may tap more images waiting to be exposed.

A junior high school teacher used word association to help stimulate composition with the following results. She used the word "fire" to start free association. (She might have used a picture of fire instead.)

Teacher: Let's take the word "fire." What other words come to your mind?
Pupils: Engine, pole, water, hydrant.
Teacher: What does a fire hydrant remind you of?
Pupils: A dog with a helmet, a space ship, mother, primitive art.

The teacher then tried to elicit descriptive words:

Teacher: Describe fires. Use only one word at a time.
Pupils: Orange, sharp, smoky, quickly, fumes, flame, spark, destroys.

The teacher suggested that the pupils decide on categories for the words about fire. They chose sight, feeling, smell, movement, and personal qualities. On the board the list looked like table 5.1. Then the teacher stimulated their perception of relationships by writing on the board sen-

Table 5.1.   Words associated with "fire"

Sight	Feeling	Smell	Movement	Personal Qualities
pointed	sharp	eggs	quickly	helper
orange	blistering	musty	sideways	grows
bright	warm	choking	up	giant
flashes	hot	smoky	licking	fighter
flame	blazing	fumes	flattening	loser
spark	intense		falling	dies
			flair	great
			hopping	helpful
			dancing	destroyer
			sweeping	

tences that required analogical thinking: "Fire is _____" and "Fire is like _____." The pupils responded with:

> a monster, destroying unmercifully
> a prayer, delicate, hopeful, pointed
> a baby, fevered and kicking
> a demon's tongue, encircling its prey
> one's dreams, gone up in smoke

The goal was to help composers collect all the raw thoughts they could, quickly, before they could begin to judge them harshly, censor them, share only the conventional ones, and lose interest. These collected scraps were the stuff that burst into a cooperative composition.

FIRE

> War, mistrust, hatred, self-hate, genocide,
>   self-destruction
> Far right, far left
> Better dead than red, better red than dead
> Our country right or wrong
> Deutschland über alles
> Banzai
> Impeach Earl Warren
> Eisenhower is a communist
> God is on our side
> We don't want to integrate
> Don't question the president
> Don't support the U.N.
> Use small atomic doses
> Use napalm
> Use blockbusters
> Use troopers
> Use boys
> Use children
> Only fire remains
> Pray for floods

— Grade 8

OTHER FORMS OF STIMULATION

Imitating a Poetic Format

Imitation and parody can help some people begin to compose. Using "Humpty Dumpty" as a model, a fourth-grade class wrote:

Billy Martin sits in his seat
Billy Martin has a good sleep

All of Bill's teachers
    and all of Bill's friends
Can't wake Bill till his dream ends.

Enlarging on a Melodic Line

Enlarging on an original or borrowed melodic line may help some bud-
ding poets begin to write. Nine-year-old Michael danced into his classroom
singing:

Up, up and away
I did all my work today.

Finishing all his work and cheerfully expressing his satisfaction were unusual experiences for Michael, who was in the class for the emotionally dis-
turbed. His teacher said, "Michael, you've written a poem. Quickly write it
down." He did, and added more.

Up, up and away
I did all my work today
I did spelling and some yelling
I did reading and some playing
Up, up and away
I did all my work today.

The youngsters in Michael's class parodied "Hickory Dickory Dock:"

Ickady, dickady, dool
The boy came late to school
    The door was locked
    The boy went home
Ickady, dickady, dool.

Later, perhaps, the writers may go on to more original forms and material.
A title may be all that is needed to remind an artist of the work of another.
Patti, remembering Carl Sandburg's description of fog moving on cat's
feet, described fog as something animated.

FOG

Enveloping the city
        crawling,
                looking, crawling,
It makes its way into the city
        shy and meek,
                fearing the crowd.

It peeks —
> it flies into the harbor.
>> — *Patti, grade 6*

Function-Centered Definitions

Function-centered definitions are common ways to stimulate composition. Taking a variety of topics, teachers may ask their students: "What does ____ do?" "What is ____ for?" This kind of thought may be stimulated with or without pictures. Using this technique, kindergarten children in one school wrote:

"Peanuts are to feed squirrels."
"Eyebrows are to keep your eyes warm."
"Roses are to bless you."
"Faces are for smiling."
"Ants are to step on."

A second-grade group cooperatively wrote these function-centered definitions about loneliness

> Loneliness is sleeping
> in your own room or
> swimming in a thousand
> foot pool and there is
> no one with you.
>
> Loneliness is falling out
> of bed and your mother
> doesn't hear you.
>
> Loneliness is not knowing
> how to play with the boys.
>
> Loneliness is getting lost
> in a deep forest.
>
> Loneliness is riding on a
> bus or reading a book.

Open-Ended Questions

The inspiration for many famous poems and songs was an evocative question: "How do I ____?" or "Why ____?" or "Where ____?" These can be the skeletons for beginners' compositions too. The teacher or the writer may choose the first line. Remember these first lines?

"How do I love you?"
"Why do robins sing in September?"
"Where, oh, where has my little dog gone?"

Selected Poetic Forms

Closely allied to the use of imitation to stimulate poetic composition is the use of standard poetic forms. There are some who feel that prescribed forms narrow the range of possible expression. Others, however, seem to require the limitations of a prescribed form in order to feel free to express their feelings. With prescribed forms, the formal rules are already established, and these restrictions seem to relieve the author of concern over what form to use. The structural narrowing helps them focus on their topic, their language, and their feelings. This need for a form may, in part, account for the popularity of such forms as the haiku:

> Tracks on the wet stone
> The little bird hops across
> After the spring rain.
> —*John, grade 8*

the couplet:

> Walk with me along the sandy shore,
> And we'll tickle our toes on a sand crab's door.
> —*Lila, grade 6*

and the limerick:

> There was a young girl named Kitty
> Who grew up and lived in the city
> To her teacher she said,
> "No books have I read,
> I must rest my eyes to stay pretty."
> —*Evelyn, grade 6*

Playful Distortions of Language

Some riddles, puns, and other plays on words have become part of everyday language. All require thinking about language. They may provide an alternative to other games, exercises, and contests. Individual and group collections provide hours of enjoyment.

Riddles are puzzling questions or statements. They exploit the multiple meanings of words and metaphors. We all remember the question, "What is black and white and red all over?" The answer—a newspaper—reveals that the questioner has exploited the homophones "red" and "read" with some humorous results. We also remember the fellow who threw his watch out of the window because he wanted to see time fly. The following are some old examples of one kind of riddle that uses homophones, exploiting both multiple meanings and distortions of language.

> Knock knock. Who's there? Boo. Boo who? Well, you don't have to cry about it.
> Knock knock. Who's there? Amos. Amos who? A mosquito bit me.
> Knock knock. Who's there? Albe. Albe who? I'll be down to get you in a taxi, honey.
> Knock knock. Who's there? Butcher. Butcher who? Put your arms around me.

Hink-pinks, hinky-pinkys, and hinkety pinketys are riddles calling for rhyming answers.

> What's a hink-pink for a long ride on a self-propelled vehicle? A hike-bike.
> What's a hink-pink for a good tree? A fine pine.
> What's an unhappy father? A sad dad.
> What's a chubby feline? A fat cat.
> A hink-pink beard. Face lace.

Notice that a hink-pink answer requires two words of one syllable each. Hinky-pinkys require words of two syllables each.

> What's a hinky-pinky mechanic? A fender mender.
> What's a hinky-pinky accident? A fender bender.

Hinkety-pinketys require three-syllable answers.

> What's an ecological decision? A pollution solution.
> What's a stay-at-home leader? A resident president.
> What's an appropriate pachyderm? A relevant elephant.

Hink-pinks are also called "ricochet words," "reduplicated words," and "Siamese-twin words." Some reduplicated words are now part of the language: Zoot suit, hanky-panky, legal beagle, mishmash, boob tube, chalk talk, claptrap, chitchat, jet set, bigwig, nitwit, and nitty-gritty.

Spoonerisms are created by the transposition or metathesis of initial sounds, letters, or syllables:

> our dear old queen — our queer old dean
> many people think so — many thinkle peep so
> one fell swoop — one swell foop
> pardon me madam — marden me padam.

A pun is the humorous use of words alike or nearly alike in sound but different in meaning. For example:

> weak — Doomsday is the last day of the weak
> avenue — we avenue baby sitter
> skid — sign on a tire store: "We skid you not"
> coincide — what to do when it starts to rain
> popular song among ghosts — "I Ain't Got No Body"
> seek — this is a seek joke
> debate — what lures de fish
> each — a minor irritation
> metaphor — it was Sunday when I metaphor the first time.

Malapropisms are words misused ridiculously:

> ransomed-rancid — "The grocer sold me a pound of ransomed butter."
> escalating-excavating — "I'm tired of the dirt and the noise of that escalating next door."

Successful experiments with forms such as these have stimulated many people to attempt further composition.

Free Choice of Topic or Form

Writers differ as greatly as Jack Sprat and his wife. Some are stimulated to write into experience by one or more of the methods suggested in this chapter. Others require only the signal to start; they react best to freedom of choice of topic, form, or way to begin. Teachers figuratively open the mail box and wait for a surprise.

The preceding chapters have been concerned with the first stage in the teaching of composition. This stage has two major purposes: to help people understand that they are capable of both imagination and composition, and to help them wish to go on to the next stage — fashioning, painting, word working, and revision.

A teacher expressed his concern about the loss, one morning, of a third grader's composition. "That's not the kind of a thing that makes me nervous," explained the boy. "I know I can always write a better one." And he did.

This child had a skill. He was also aware of that fact. This is the state of mind of one who has confidence. He knows he has a vast wellspring of thought. He knows he can share these experiences creatively, accurately, succinctly, and with some awareness of what interests others. He is ready for Stage Two of the composition program: "Fashioning Revisions."

SUGGESTED READING

Atwell, Margaret A. "The Evolution of Text: The Interrelationship of Reading and Writing in the Composing Process." Ph.D. dissertation, Indiana University, 1980.

Burrows, Alvina Treut; Jackson, Doris C.; and Saunders, Dorothy O. *They All Want to Write: Written English in the Elementary School*. New York: Holt, Rinehart and Winston, 1939.

Cane, Melville. *Making a Poem: An Inquiry into the Creative Process*. New York: Harcourt, Brace and World, A Harvest Book, 1963.

Holbrook, David. *Children's Writing: A Sampler for Student Teachers*. Cambridge: Cambridge University Press, 1967.

Mearns, Hughes. *Creative Power: The Education of Youth in the Creative Arts*. New York: Dover, 1958.

Smith, Frank, *Writing and the Writer*. New York: Holt, Rinehart and Winston, 1981.

Stage Two
FASHIONING REVISIONS IN WRITING

Stage One of this program focused primarily on helping people develop an awareness of themselves as perceivers, conceivers, thinkers, speakers, and writers. Going through the first stage is like making up your mind to get out of bed, dress appropriately, and begin the snowman, the sandcastle, the gardening, the sculpture, the painting, or the writing. A commitment is made. Sometimes getting people through Stage One is the major role of the teacher-helper.

Stage Two deals with ways of developing precision in the wordworking craft. It covers the rolling of snow, the lifting, digging, pushing, potting, swearing, pulling, smashing, and starting over. Sometimes the techniques of the second stage overlap with those of the first. In general, though, Stage Two concentrates on writing and rewriting as we move from feeling to language to form and, finally, to criticism.

6 From Feeling to Language

This chapter deals with ways of working with language. It discusses words, language symbols, and several interesting ways in which language can be used, varied, and preserved in written form.

WORD WORKING

Words are the building materials used in constructing speeches and writing. Words can be as rough and strong as cinder blocks, as smooth and colorful as stained glass, or as old and lasting as rock. Words may be alloys or pure. They may be seasonable, like blocks of ice; multipurpose, like animal hides and bamboo; or indigenous, like palm leaves and logs of maple or pine.

Words can be beautiful or ugly. Reactions to words depend on their tone or music as well as their denotative and connotative qualities. The choice of words depends on the composer's personal experience and will in turn influence his or her readers' response to a precise and artistic use of words.

Teachers may help develop an interest in words — for example, by asking questions about a specific word like "home":

When is "home" likely to be a beautiful word?
Is it more likely to be beautiful if your experience at home has been beautiful?
Do you know the difference between the word and what it stands for?
How does it feel on the tongue, the palate, the lips?
What are its sounds?
What is its meaning?
What do the dictionaries say about "home"?
What kinds of places are homes?
In what ways is the word used?

How do its neighbor words change it: hometown, Eskimo home, a bombed-out home, home of the brave, home on the range, home cooking?

Discussions growing out of these questions, coupled with the experiences of finding just the right word for a specific and relevant purpose in composition, help many people to become interested in developing more control over words and the images they evoke. "Supercalifragilisticexpialidocius" caught many people's fancy and stimulated a love for big words. They also love little words, funny words, bad words, dirty words, scientific words, and strange words. People love to sing them, chant them, say them, read them, and write them (except when spelling counts).

People genuinely interested in words could well be called "wordsters." These are the lucky ones who have been encouraged to develop the hobby of collecting, playing with, reading, saying, hearing, and feeling words. Some collect words simply because of the kinesthetic and emotional effects of saying them. Some expect to impress others with new additions to their word collection, just as a coin collector takes pride in showing each new acquisition. One of the reasons for programs like Head Start is the recognition of the need to help children to collect, use, and appreciate the kinds of words they meet in their schoolwork. School is a place filled with words and ways to learn them, a place to keep alive an interest in words. A positive interest in words can be developed by encouraging the wider use of appropriate words.

All of the words in table 6.1 came from one second-grade class where the students looked at the names of the colors of their crayons. They read them aloud to their teacher, who listed them on a chalkboard. The children then decided on the appropriate categories, which they listed on another chalkboard in random order. These categories were kept and added to throughout the school year. Newfound words met with considerable class interest, and the list sparked many a composition.

Words are thoughts' clothing. The teacher has to teach writers to dress their thoughts appropriately. Teaching styles, clothing styles, and word styles vary considerably. Although formal wear is inappropriate in the average American public school, it is expected in some private and parochial schools and in some foreign schools. Just as there are uses for sneakers, party shoes, tap shoes, and rubber boots, there are places for technical words, baseball words, courtroom words, and made-up words. The following lists may inspire word-workers to collect other special words.

Baseball jargon, words and phrases used in the game, has become part of the language:

bases loaded — there are runners on first, second, and third bases
bean ball — a ball pitched directly at the batter's head

blooper — a short fly ball that goes just past the infield
change of pace — a slow ball pitched after one or more fast balls
grand slam — a home run with three runners on base
platter — home plate
south paw — a left-handed player

Carnival or circus jargon is used by "carnie" workers who do not want to be understood by the customers:

med show — medicine show
mud show — one-night show in an area with unpaved roads
dry-weather trouper — fair-weather friend
lettuce — money
laying the note — confusing the customer by interchanging bills of
 different amounts
shill — confederates in the audience

TABLE 6.1. Color Words

Time	*Flowers*	*Metals*	*Stone*	*Woods*	*Fruits*
midnight	bittersweet	mercury	turquoise	mahogany	lime
antique	violet	gold	brick	walnut	lemon
spring	thistle	silver	coal	pine	orange
	orchid	copper	ruby	ebony	cherry
People	cornflower	gunmetal	emerald	fruit	apple
Chinese	clover	platinum	sapphire	raw	olive
baby	periwinkle	bronze	sand		apricot
royal	delphinium		pumice	*Place*	hazel
Kelly	lavender	*Holidays*	earth	sky	coffee
cadet		Easter	clay	sea	grape
	Birds	Christmas	puce	cloud	orange
Spice	bluebird	Halloween	charcoal	army	plum
cinnamon	canary	Thanks-	gold	barn	peach
ginger	cardinal	giving		air force	melon
nutmeg	teal	St. Patrick's	*Vegetables*		
mint	crow	Day	celery	*Chemicals*	*Fish*
mustard		Valentine's	corn	carbon	salmon
saffron		Day	pumpkin	iron	
sage			tomato	mercury	
		Wines	eggplant	iodine	
		champagne		gentian	
		chartreuse			
		burgundy			

marks — the unsuspecting
suckers — the general public
grinder — the barker, who urges people to participate
happy or hurt — win or lose
pitch — a game
gimmicked or gaffed — rigged to prevent winning
rubber man — the man who sells balloons or "bladders"
lot lice — townspeople who hang around watching the tent being
    put up
lumber — seats and poles
main guy — the guy rope that holds up the center pole in the big top
Joey — circus clown

A euphemism is a good or pleasant word used instead of an unpleasant or unfavorable one:

the departed — a dead person
passed on — died
plumbers — political burglars
air support — bombing

Acronyms are words formed from the initials of a group of words:

WAC — member of the Women's Army Corps
radar — radio detection and ranging
snafu — situation normal, all fouled up
mouse — minimum orbital unmanned satellite of earth
Fortran — formula plus translation
Basic — British-American Scientific International Commercial
    "English"
CREEP — Committee to Re-Elect the President
TRY — Training Resources for Youth

Generic terms are product names that have become part of the language. Examples are: Scotch tape, Cellophane, Aspirin, Escalator, Frigidare, Kleenex, Victrola, Kodak, and Coke.

CLARIFIERS

Clarifiers, or semantic word filters, make the writer's intent stand out clearly. Confusion is common when the sender and the receiver have had different experiences but use the same words. This section will discuss the following clarifiers: abstractions, time-dating, I-messages, and qualifiers. Each one is an aid in using language both precisely and interestingly.

Abstractions

Speaking the same language does not guarantee communication. Communicating on the same level of abstraction is a way of tuning in to the other person. We are conditioned by past experiences and the words that represent them. The word "dog," like the sight of a dog, can evoke fear in someone who has been bitten by one. In the following selection, Andy, who had been bitten by a large German shepherd the week before, reported a different kind of experience with another living creature — also a dog, but not the one he remembered so bitterly. The abstract word "dog" in this selection did not evoke the appropriate picture of an animal who was merely seeking a friend.

> Remembering the waist-high beast
>   That knocked me down the stairs
> And patrols the gas station
>   Like the Queen's
>   Honorguard,
>
> I ran to school today
>   Chased by fangs and tail
> And when at last
>   I saw a friend
> Who knew one dog from another
> She told me
>   that this pup
> Was only hoping
>   that I would be —
>   Her supper?
>   No,
>   Her mother.
>   — *Andy, grade 9*

Time-Dating

Time is always moving. Today's grain of sand was once a rock. Time-dating separates one frame from the ongoing reel of life.

Lois's visit from an old friend made her more aware of the necessity of adding dates to pictures, writing, and general communication.

> Have you ever met an old friend
>   different from before?
> Have you ever seen a week-old car
>   found parked with pushed-in door?
> Has your sweet little kitty cat
>   had kittens by the score?

Is your favorite big-league batter
   swinging like an old barn door?

Have you noticed that
   everything and everyone
   changes day by day?
No use avoiding it
   or confusing things.
When I have things to say
   or things to write and keep
I make a point to clear the air —
   Just mark the date somewhere
   And then go peacefully to sleep.
                 — *Lois, grade 11*

I-messages

I-messages allow the sender to focus on his or her own feelings about an interpersonal conflict without the speculation, confusion, and blame that can accompany a you-message. The receiver now has the opportunity to think about the sender's view without becoming defensive. (Thomas Gordon's *P.E.T. in Action* discusses the I-messages exchanged between parents, teachers, and children.)

Using I-messages in her college speech class helped Lori Suchejky understand her mother's objections to her apartment hunting. Accompanying herself with a guitar, Lori sang the following selection to us as we sat with tear-filled but newly understanding eyes.

I don't want to lose you.
Please don't go away.
I don't want to lose you.
It hurts me you don't want to stay.

It feels like this is the final break
When a mother must let her child go.
I realize that you must find a mate
But my pain you do not know.

I hope I've raised you well enough.
I'm not sure you can make it on your own.
And although I don't want to lose you,
My permission,
   and my blessing, is on your new home.

Qualifiers

Qualifiers help us avoid confusing facts and assumptions. Many a fight has started because someone should have used a qualifier like: "it seems," "it looks like," "I believe," "I think," "apparently," "possibly," "probably," or "maybe." Qualifiers are used by people trying to communicate their reasonableness. Without qualifiers, the same people may sound dogmatic: "I'm right; I know; you are wrong." Without qualifiers, situations become polarized into black or white, right or wrong, good or evil, friend or enemy, love or hate, hot or cold, pass or fail, prose, play, or poetry.

Roberta recalled her unhappy experience at school after an unwelcomed visitor stopped at her house. The other youngsters had not used qualifiers — they were so sure they knew what had happened to her.

> One day, in class, it seemed
>   her clothes all smelled of a skunk.
> They all laughed
>   and jeered:
> Skunk got you
> Skunk got you
> Haw, haw, haw.
>
> She cried
>   and left school early
> Went home
>   and bathed the eyes
>   of her little dog
>   nearly blinded
>   by the black and white
> Marauder
>   of the night before.
>   — *Roberta, grade 7*

LANGUAGE SYMBOLS

Another way to enrich language is through symbols. Symbols stand for other things, usually abstractions — the dove is a symbol of peace, the cross a symbol of Christianity. Aja, a sixth grader, used trees to stand for faith.

> FAITH
>
> It stands alone, its branches broken,
>   life's joy forsaken,
>   gone.
>
> But in the distance stand trees of faith,
>   grouped together,
>   strong.

Language symbols are shortcuts to feelings and serve to compress or expand the language. To the scientist the symbol "H_2O" has but one meaning, but to the artist the word "water" has a wide variety of connotations. Artists delight in the manifold uses of language symbols. Four kinds of symbols are helpful to writers and speakers: conventional, personal, cultural, and universal.

Conventional Symbols

Conventional symbols are the best known because they are used in everyday language. One knows the word "chair" when one sees it, hears it, or uses it because one has learned the convention of using the letters and the sounds of the word to refer to a certain kind of object. A national flag is an accepted conventional symbol that stands for the people, ideology, history, and honor of a country, for family, home, and future security.

Nancy used conventional symbols to describe a winter night.

WINTER AT NIGHT

Speeding cars,
Slushy streets,
People hurrying
Along to meet
Someone.

Bright lights in houses,
Trees, forlorn shadows,
Mansions, farmhouses
and their meadows,
Darkened.

Animals sensing
That something is wrong,
Run to the forest,
And through it they throng,
Somewhere.

—Nancy, grade 6

Personal Symbols

Personal symbols get their meaning from the experiences one has had. If a child had a puppy named Alice who was run over, the word "Alice" would have a special meaning, probably sadness or loss, for him or her. Whenever passing the street where Alice was struck by the car, the child would connect his or her sadness with the name of the street or the street sign or the look of the houses.

When people revisit their old classrooms or hear a school or camp song that they used to sing, they connect with the song or the school or the classroom a whole set of memories — the games they played in camp, the class projects and other events of the year, sweethearts, enemies, times when they were unhappy or enjoyed themselves. The connection between the symbol and the mood is personal. This is why personal symbols often appear in dreams, but they rarely appear in literature without an explanation.

Nan's poems refer to two places that are personal symbols for her.

> Gently she cuddles,
> In her warm arms, the baby —
> Sleep my child, sleep tight.
>
> Sadly and slowly,
> She views the desolate pain —
> Grief shows on her face.
> — *Nan, grade 7*

Cultural Symbols

Cultural symbols, shared by large groups of people, are like conventional symbols in that they are commonly used and like personal symbols in that they evoke emotional reactions. The word "flag" is a conventional symbol, but the Stars and Stripes is a cultural one. When Americans hear the words "Pearl Harbor," their reaction depends on their past group experience. The swastika, the cross, the hammer and sickle, the stars and stripes — each evokes reactions according to the age, culture, and experience of the individual. The sun is not a sumbol of warmth and protection for farmers during a drought. Warmth and life can be symbolized by a fire in a fireplace, but this is a very different fire from that feared by firemen and forest rangers.

Cultural symbols have different connotations in different countries, in different subcultures within a country, and even in different generations living under one roof. Students can discuss symbols common to their national culture and those peculiar to their region or ethnic and religious groups — Red Cross, Star of David, crescents, Hawaiian lei, white flag, great big shiny car, igloo, kilts, or oil wells. Even animals can be cultural symbols. For example, a cow is a holy symbol in Hindu India and a sign of wealth in the southwestern United States.

Writers need to remember that readers and listeners, depending on their background, may have a reaction almost exactly the opposite of the intended one. As one writer put it: "Your prison may be my cathedral, and my cathedral may be your prison." The difference lies in each culture's use of symbols.

Not everyone lives in an area with four distinct seasons. Terry, who does, wrote about them.

WINTER

Bare dark ground —
 Cold and frosty,
  Snow falls heavily.

SPRING

Bare black ground —
 A stem spurting up,
  A fat bud sprouted.

SUMMER

A hot day —
 Smell of a freshly cut lawn,
  Buzzing of insects continues.

AUTUMN

Colored leaves —
 All fall to the ground
  Only a bare tree left.
          — Terry, grade 6

Steven, a Canadian youngster, knows firsthand about the winds of the north.

THE NORTH

Vast, cold, merciless barrens,
Whipping, slashing, freezing winds,
Hungry, gaunt, ravenous animals,
These are the wilds of the north.

Resistant, repulsive, wind-swept land,
Unyielding, unanswerable, unruly,
A land far away from the man's sun world,
Raw, crude, and rough is the north.

Winds with a freezing, piercing bite,
Freeze a bleak, bitter land.
Winds of a dire strength and ferocity,
Cold, frigid, and turbulent are the winds of the north.

Famished, cold, frenzied animals
Haunt inadequate, northern food lands
Scrawny, meager, raw-boned beasts.
The inhabitants of the north.
          — Steven, grade 6

Universal Symbols

Universal symbols extend beyond the barriers of country, language, or time. All people seem to know that to cry means one is sad and that to smile means one is pleased.

Jane wrote about the "anger" of nature that all people know.

THE ANGRY SKY

The darkening clouds,
Blot out the sky,
Thunder roaring like hungry tigers,
Searching for their prey.

The animals and birds
Are helpless and afraid,
The people are in fear of it
Because it's not man-made.

The lightning bolts,
Seek out the land,
The earth with rain was soaked,
Until at last,
The storm had passed
But why was the sky provoked?
                    —*Jane, grade 6*

People have always wondered about the secrets of the stars.

THE UNKNOWN

Bright-eyed stars on a crystal night,
Shine in the smooth, dark sky,
What beauties rare are hidden there?
What secrets old but strangely new,
Are waiting—waiting?
                    —*Jenny, grade 6*

Jeff wrote about death, known to all mortals.

Crosses mark the place,
Where the victors are buried . . .
The free world mourns them.
                    —*Jeff, grade 7*

Composition requires a creative use of words and symbols. Helping composers to understand the value of symbolic shortcuts to feelings is a challenge for teachers and one of the advantages of studying and composing poetry. Working with symbols develops verbal dexterity and the ability to be both precise and economical with words.

ARTISTIC UNITY: BALANCING REPETITION AND VARIATION

Composition is a creative experience, a way of expressing feelings with beauty and precision. Composers must create a balanced synthesis of the parts of a composition. Artistic unity is based on the balance between repetition and variety. It exists when all the parts of the composition fit together while the balance is maintained. The teaching of art often starts with an examination of repetitions and variations, such as lines and spaces, straight lines and curved lines, light and dark, and roughness and smoothness and goes on to examine our reactions to them. Creative composition can also be viewed in terms of the repetition and variation of words and word symbols.

Repetition

We are used to repetition. We seem to thrive on it, as if it were our daily dose of vitamins. We use it. We understand it. We need it. We demand it. Children and many adults enjoy hearing their favorite stories read over and over again. We like to hear and repeat sounds, syllables, words, ideas, phrases, and whole lines. Repetition may add a songlike quality to feelings, impressions, and emotional reactions, or it may add a note of conviction or urgency. Sometimes repetition lulls one into acceptance by spinning a persuasive, hypnotic web around the listener. It offers numerous opportunities for adding a variety of sounds, syllables, words, phrases, and refrains within the safe limits of the familiar and the predictable. Peggy's poem repeats the initial three words of two four-word lines.

AS FUNNY AS CAN BE

Funny as a circus
Funny as a clown
Making fun of people
Making fun of sound.
　　—Peggy, grade 3

Janet repeated consonant sounds in lines 2, 3, 6, 7, 9, 11, and 12 of the following poem. Note also the (í) sound of "flying," "silently," "flight," "sky," "sighing," and "why," and the (ē̄e) sound of "eternal," "meandering," "deep," "green," "breeze," and "trees."

WHY, OH WHY?

Birds are flying,
Silently soaring,
Eternal flight to infinity.

Rivers flowing,
Gently meandering,
Deep into dark green woods.

The breeze is blowing,
Softly murmuring,
Calling the cloudless sky.

Listen to trees,
Swaying, sighing,
Why, oh why?
—*Janet, grade 6*

RHYME. Rhyme, a feature of Janet's poem, is one form of the repetition of sounds. It adds a songlike quality to language and, when effectively used, binds together the parts of a composition. The use of rhyme adds to the mood of a poem and makes it easier to remember. There are several kinds of rhyme: beginning, internal, end, and near.

Beginning rhyme appears in the first word of a line or the beginning of the first word; in the following selection, for example, listen to the first sound in the first words of each line.

Scooters are for little kids
Scooting down the hall
Skiing is for young and old
Snoopy's best of all.

Alliteration, the repetition of initial sounds, is very often found in speaking and writing. The repeated consonant sounds bind the structure together.

FAMILY AT A FAIR — GUESS WHERE

Families from everywhere
First the potbellied men
   wearing straw cowboy hats
   pointing tattooed arms
   from tattooed shirts
     from bowling leagues and little leagues
     tucked into
   red Bermuda shorts
     propelled by
     silk clock socks
     in black shiny shoes
Followed by
   blue eye-shaded
   potbellied wives and daughters

suckling pink pop
through pink-striped straws
whining their choices
for the next attraction.

Initial sound repetitions are also an aid to memory. That is why they are so common. Students find alliteration in advertising fun to collect and helpful for their own composition work. The following advertising phrases and slogans were collected by third-grade children and arranged according to the sound repeated.

B — Bright brass buttons
C — Discover the Pacific in a Caribbean cruise
      Convertible cotton cowl collar
      Quick, cool breeze
      One Crestwale all cotton corduroy
F, V — Our lobsters are flown in fighting fresh
      Breakfast is a feast of infinite variety
      First-time fliers, and veteran travelers alike,
          find . . .
L — A column of flannel, splendidly emblazoned with
          oriental scrolls will quietly steal . . .
M — Mister Mustard: flavor no ordinary mustard can match
P — Permanent press
S — Spaghetti, southern fried chicken, steaks, and
          superb salad dressing for summer salads
ST — Tenderest steamers
T — Two-toned tweeds

Sounds in any position may be repeated. Joanne used (s) sounds to impart a whispered, hushed quality to "The Jaguar." Notice her "steep," "waits," "spotted," "savage," "silent," "spry," "smell,'"innocent." These were just enough.

THE JAGUAR

On the steep rocky ledges
The spotted jaguar waits,
His savage sharp claws
His silent spry body — waiting.

Waiting for a kill,
There beyond the cliff
A smell, a whiff of animal
An innocent lamb below.
          —Joanne, grade 6

Notice the recurrence of (oo) in the following example of the repetition of middle sounds in first words.

SUPPER

Choose the best one
Do it by three
Stew it by five
Chew it at six.
— *Marc, grade 4*

Below is an example of the use of final sound rhymes ("where"-"dare" and "away"-"stay") in initial position.

Where did blond Johnny go?
Away to the sea.
Dare he return again
To stay home with me?
— *Sally, grade 5*

Internal rhyme, in which words in the same line are rhymed, can give subtle strength to the language of a composition. Mary, a second grader, spontaneously used internal and end rhyme in the following dictated selection. The end and internal rhymes tie this little word package together securely, like ribbon from two directions.

THE THINGS I LIKE

I like cats and rats;
I like toys and noise;
And most of all,
I like boys.

Near rhyme is also called related rhyme, half-rhyme, silent rhyme, and consonance. Using related rather than identical vowel and consonant sounds has a subtler effect than full rhyme but serves equally well to unify the parts of a selection. Near rhyme has several faces. One can repeat final consonant sounds without considering the preceding vowels. For example, "cost" could rhyme with "last" and "most"; "rope" with "cap" and "step"; and "froze" with "sneeze" and "ooze."

Voiced and voiceless pairs of sounds seem to be used unconsciously by some writers. The position of the lips and tongue is the same for voiced and voiceless consonants; the difference in sound is due to vocal band vibration, which is present for voiced sounds and absent for voiceless ones. When a sound is unvoiced:

(b) as in cub becomes (p) as in cup
(v) as in five becomes (f) as in fife

(d)   as in rude becomes (t)   as in root
(z)   as in eyes becomes (s)   as in ice
(g)   as in dog   becomes (k)   as in duck
(ge) as in ridge becomes (ch) as in rich

Recognition of these voiced and voiceless sounds is a matter of sound rather than spelling. Skillful use of these sound pairs is more likely to be noticed when a composition is read out loud. Other related sounds are (m), (n), and (ng). All three are produced by nasal resonance and so are commonly called nasal sounds.

The near rhyme in this poem by Pat, a second grader, was probably unintentional. Unvoicing the (d) in "reading" changed it to a (t) and made it rhyme with "eating."

SCHOOL

School is a pleasure
We learn how to measure
My best subject is reading
But at home I like eating.

In the following poem by the same girl, there are three true, or full, rhymes, and in the second stanza the (ng) in "running" nearly rhymes with the (n) in "everyone."

SHOES

Shoes are made of suede and leather.
Shoes are made for sunny weather.
Some shoes are made to keep away a bruise.
Some shoes are made for a very good news.

Some shoes are made for work and play,
and some are made for every day.
Some shoes are made for walking and running.
Shoes are made for everyone.

Note that in the following selection by Pat, "raw" rhymes with "more" because final (r) sounds are usually omitted along the east coast of the United States.

EGGS

Eggs are used for people to eat
  Some eggs are to beat

Some eggs are boiled
  Some eggs are spoiled

I love eggs to eat
  They take the place of meat

> But I don't like eggs raw
> I like them boiled more.

Internal and near rhymes may occur spontaneously in speech, but sometimes these effects are carefully planned. Winston Churchill, speaking to the British House of Commons on 13 May 1940, a time of extreme urgency as England began its war with Germany, sought unity at home. He began by reporting that he had been commissioned to form a new unified administration: "It was the evident wish and will of Parliament and the nation that this should be conceived on the broadest possible basis and that it should include all parties, both those who supported the late government and also the parties of the opposition." Unity was needed because, as Churchill admitted in short Anglo-Saxon words, "I have nothing to offer but blood, toil, tears and sweat."

> We have before us an ordeal of the most grievous kind. We have before us many, many longs months of struggle and of suffering. You ask, What is our policy? I will say: "It is to wage war, by sea, land and air, with all our might and with all the strength that God can give us, to wage war against a monstrous tyranny, never surpassed in the dark, lamentable catalogue of human crime. That is our policy." You ask, What is our aim? I can answer in one word: Victory—victory at all costs, victory in spite of all terror, victory however long and hard the road may be; for without victory there is no survival. Let that be realized; no survival for the British Empire; no survival for all that the British Empire has stood for; no survival for the urge and impulse of the ages, that mankind will move forward towards its goal. But I take up my task with buoyancy and hope. I feel sure that our cause will not be suffered to fail among men. At this time I feel entitled to claim the aid of all, and I say, "Come, then, let us go forward together with our united strength."

Notice how he brought a sense of unity to this paragraph—the final paragraph of his speech by repeating words and phrases, voiced and unvoiced sounds. Notice that the (k) in "kind" is the unvoiced partner of the (g) in "grievous." Notice the repetition of (m) in "many" and "months," the (s) and (u) in "struggle" and "suffering." He then repeats the phrase "wage war"; he repeats the (k) sound in "catalogue" and "crime"; and he repeats "victory" again and again. His famous *v* is also found twice in "survival," which is itself repeated. As a commander, he repeats the word "forward," which ends in a voiced (d) that is tied to the initial (t) in "together" and the medial (t) in "united" and "strength."

Winston Churchill was a master of both speaking and writing. We have much to learn from his life as well as his literacy.

End rhyme, though the most familiar form of sound repetition, is a rather recent addition in the long history of poetry. It was popularized during the early Middle Ages by Irish monks seeking ways to remember long passages in their rituals. Appropriate amounts of varieties of end rhyme can be fun to use and add a pleasant taste to artistic work. For example, three little pirates (complete with eye patches, cardboard cutlasses, bandannas, and boots) spent an hour stamping up and down their backyard singing:

> Yo ho ho
> and an Oreo.

Ralph, a second grader, added just two end-rhymed spoonfuls of language sugar: "habit"-"rabbit" and "stew"-"too."

LUCKY ME

> I would like to be a rabbit;
> Stealing good would be my habit.
> My lucky food will help me too
> and keep me out of rabbit stew.

Unfortunately, many people spend their time in poetic composition looking for end-rhyming words rather than words that have the most appropriate sound or meaning. The use of end rhyme is fun once in a while, but too much may hinder artistic development. The thoughts, language, and bodies of beginning writers are too supple to be limited to inhibiting poetic forms. Their composition can be improved through the use of other language devices.

Rhyme, then, is a device for repeating sounds. It can be used at the beginning, the middle, or the end of words and phrases. It is like glue. A little rhyme holds related things neatly together. Too much rhyme spills over and hides the composer's intention under a mere contrivance.

WORDS AND PHRASES.   John, an eighth grader concerned about his persistent repetition of initial words and phrases when speaking, began to write down his speech patterns. He found that these patterns, when put on paper, highlighted and dignified his strong emotions. For a while, John used only the one form — initial repetition. Soon he added others varying his emphasis, volume, rate, and phrasing. Not previously interested in writing, he learned to express himself — both orally and in writting — more easily and with greater precision. The following examples of his speech take on, when written down, a quality not usually expected in the remedial speech group.

SO HIGH

> So high in the sky, you can touch heaven
> So high in the sky, you can reach for a star

So high in the sky with the earth below you
So high can a dream go.

WATER

Water
    something cool and deep.
Water
    something wide and blue.
Water
    something alone and happy.
Water
    holding life in its hands.

From one point of view, John's language pattern may be considered dysrhythmic. Some would incorrectly call it stuttering. But there is another way to view it. Helping him see the artistic value of his word and phrase repetitions is another way of uncovering positive qualities in language. Instead of viewing his habitual language pattern as an affliction, he felt a certain pride in it and began to seek ways of varying it.

Language and ideas may be repeated in several ways, appearing side by side on the page like railroad tracks, or above and below like the steps of a ladder. John's repetition of the first and second words of each verse heightened the mood of his poem.

DEATH

Death
    something sad, cold, and unhappiness.

Death
    something strange,
    something no one can imagine.

Death
    just a term to something
    we don't understand.

A similar technique is exemplified in this selection by a nine-year-old:

Raindrops
Rainplops
Rain blows
Rain flows

Rain goes.
    — Susan, grade 4

After listening to *Brown Bear, Brown Bear,** a repetitive story for children in Bill Martin's Instant Readers series, people find themselves chanting, writing, and chanting again. Oliver, a college student, wrote the following verses.

THE STUDENT

Freshman, freshman, what do you see?
I see a sophomore looking at me.
Sophomore, sophomore, what do you see?
I see a Junior looking at me. . . .

THE POKER PLAYER

One pair, one pair, what should I do?
I think two pair is what I need too.
Two pair, two pair, what should I do?
I think a full house is what I need too.
Full house, full house, what should I do? . . .

THE SOLDIER

Private, private, what do you see?
I see a corporal looking at me.
Corporal, corporal, what do you see?
I see a sergeant looking at me.
Sergeant, sergeant, what do you see?
I see a lieutenant looking at me. . . .

Pinky, in the sixth grade, repeated the words "The Sea" at the ends of phrases to unify his description.

THE SEA

Wild, restless, ever-changing
The Sea
Destruction in its path but life in itself
The Sea
Living,
emotional
as only a vital,
powerful source can be
The Sea
We
mere grains of sand on a long
long beach dependent on one
The Sea
For life in itself

---

*(New York: Holt, Rinehart and Winston, 1971).

a burden almost too big to carry
is this independent uncontrollable mass
The Sea
It wreaks vengeance on its tormentors
robbing it of all its earthly beauties
We find ourselves victims of a raging torrent of life
giving substance which only The Sea carries in its bosom
The vibrant waves beat the defenseless shore
Until destruction is complete
and the world is left numb at its infinite power
The Sea
This masterful force
is encapturing in its beauty and glory
but vicious in its vengeful
power
The Sea

David, a sixth grader, also used repetition to tie his "Chorus Poem"
together.

CHORUS POEM

Then: All that was there were the tall, strong trees
on the rough, rugged ground.

Some very exhausted settlers
trudged toward a grove of trees that they saw ahead.
When they reached it they found that —

All that was there were the tall, strong trees
on the rough, rugged ground.

The settlers unloaded their equipment
and after quite a struggle
had their camp set up. The men in the group
wandered far and wide
in search of food and water, but —

All that was there were the tall, strong trees
on the rough, rugged ground.

The men came back to a half-starved camp
who were anxiously awaiting their supper. And the men's
only excuse was —
"All that was there were the tall, strong trees
on the rough, rugged ground."

One by one the settlers died
leaving no one trace of their existence and —

All that was there were the tall, strong trees
on the rough, rugged ground.

Patricia, a fourth grader, used beginning and ending repetition in her poem.

> I love my cats
>   my seven cats
>   that play and play and play
> I love them 'cause
>   they are my cats.
>   Hurray, Hurray, Hurray.

Parallel arrangements are common in great speaking and writing. In his address on 8 December 1941 to a joint session of Congress, President Franklin D. Roosevelt used repetition to drive home his message: a state of war existed between the United States and the Japanese empire.

> Yesterday the Japanese government also launched an attack
>   against Malaya.
> Last night Japanese forces attacked Hong Kong.
> Last night Japanese forces attacked Guam.
> Last night Japanese forces attacked the Philippine Islands.
> Last night the Japanese attacked Wake Island.
> This morning the Japanese attacked Midway Island.

The Jewish Bible rings with varieties of parallel arrangements, as the Christian New Testament does with parables. The Reverend Martin Luther King, Jr., was influenced by both and knew that repetitive arrangements of words, phrases, and ideas add interest, rhythm, and balance to compositions. We remember his most famous speech because the repetition of the phrase "I have a dream" — a dream deeply rooted in the American creed that all men are created equal; a dream that sons of former slaves and sons of former slave owners will sit together; a dream that black and white children would learn together in order to be able to communicate freely. Dr. King concluded his speech with two phrases, one from "My Country 'Tis of Thee," which ends, "let freedom ring," and the other from an old spiritual, "Free at last; free at last; thank God almighty, we are free at last." He reminded Americans that our greatness derived from the diversity of our people, land, and beliefs, and from the contributions of each.

Variation

Variety adds spice to language. Teachers and composers tire of predictable cliches and worn-out moon-June rhymes. Even the advertising media now use everyday people in their advertisements and commercials because readers and listeners tend to be suspicious of beautiful people, familiar promises, and satin-smooth voices.

The universe is filled with things that can be seen in a variety of ways. The sky, somber and uninviting from one direction, may be ribboned with rainbows from another. An apparently lusterless gem may acquire flickering light tones when the light shifts.

There are any number of ways to thrust language forward with poetic boosters. Some are easily applied in the classroom. As S. I. Hayakawa wrote:

> Metaphors are not "ornaments of discourse"; they are direct expressions of evaluations and are bound to occur whenever we have strong feelings to express. They are to be found in special abundance, therefore, in all primitive speech, in folk speech, in the speech of the unlearned, in the speech of children, and in the professional argot of the theater, of gangsters, and other lively occupations.*

Many kinds of artistic devices occur unknowingly in everyone's language. They include metaphor, simile, personification, connotation, synesthesia, onomatopoeia, contrast, metonymy, and synecdoche. The use of comparative language occurs as easily as third graders chew bubble gum. Such figures of speech as "as easy as pie" and "as tough as nails" are well known and used often. At one time original and poetic, they are now overused and trite. They are fine for everyday language, but not for creative composition.

Any creative ingredient can be varied by writers, who often do so without any formal training. Some teachers need only point to the variety of technical accomplishments already evident in the work of the composers. Others must suggest ways for pupils to add variety to their language. But whether spontaneous or learned, the following literary devices, or figures of speech, add flavor to bland speech and composition.

Caution: experiences are not universally perceived in the same way. Vegetarians, who might be repulsed by the sight, sound, smell, or taste of a sizzling steak, might be equally repulsed by a vivid description of one.

METAPHOR.   A metaphor is an implied comparison. It is a way to organize one's understanding of the new in terms of the familiar. We all use home-grown metaphors to embellish our thoughts. "He's a snake" means "He's dangerous and repulsive." "He's a bird" means "He's cute or funny." "He's two-faced" means "I don't trust him." "He's a fox" means "He's clever." Without knowing the terminology, Tony, a second grader, used a home-grown metaphor in his last line.

---

*S. I. Hayakawa, *Language in Thought and Action*, 2d ed. (New York: Harcourt, Brace and World, 1949), p. 121.

THE SNOWSHOE RABBIT

I have a snowshoe rabbit.
Its fur is white as snow.
Its tail is a pop-out pillow.

SIMILE. Similes are expressed comparisons. The words "like," "as," "as if," "resembling," or "similar" are signals for the figurative use of language. Similes are used by children, artists, and most of us to understand and explain analogous relationships — to explain what we do not know in terms of what we do know.

Louis, a fourth grader, put a new and frightening experience in terms he and his audience knew: "We were trapped like franks in buns." In October of his first year in school, Billy was chased home by the neighborhood bully. In the security of his kitchen, he sighed, "I felt like an ant on the school steps at lunchtime." During the June heat of that same school year, Billy said, "I feel like a bear wearing two fur coats." Knowing his early skill with language, it was no surprise years later to hear Bill, a college sophomore, describe his college area: "like a town that festered into a city."

Simile was also used in a poem by James, a sixth grader.

THE H-BOMB

Awe-inspiring
With uncontrollable power,
Like some huge horse,
Whose strength cannot be harnessed.

A searing flash of lights
Displays the spectrum in iridescent bands.

Violence follows —
Vegetation, like children's toys, topples.

Mushroomlike,
From tongues of fire,
Emerge the clouds,
To fuse the land.

Describing singer-pianist Nellie Lutcher for readers of the *New Yorker*, Whitney Balliett wrote:

Her hands evoke wild images. When they are low and flat on the keyboard, they look like long distance swimmers. When she suddenly lifts them from the keyboard, they become fighter planes peeling off.*

---

*17 April 1980, p. 120.

George Orwell used similes to relate how he shot an elephant:

> I fired a third time . . . He seemed to tower upwards like a huge rock toppling, his trunk reaching skywards like a tree. . . . The tortured gasps continued as steadily as the ticking of a clock.*

When will the ticking stop? Can one ever forget these word pictures?

Dylan Thomas, in "A Story," described his aunt and uncle's marriage unforgettably when he pictured his uncle as a buffalo living with a mouse. †

Composers can practice by inventing original similes to contrast with the following:

> soft as a puppy's ears, a baby's hair
> hot as a steering wheel in summer
> laster than a taxi horn behind you
> fast as a late appointment

Or they can complete these phrases:

> dirtier than ____
> confused as ____
> pretty as ____
> prettier than ____
> busier than ____
> lovable as ____
> capable as ____
> lonely as ____

PERSONIFICATION. Personification, a kind of metaphor, lends living qualities to nonliving subjects: for example, "She's a fine ship." Patricia, a fourth grader, used implied personifications when she wrote about flowers.

> I like flowers
> Those pretty flowers
> That just stand there and bloom.

Carol, a third grader, wrote:

> Pansies have monkey faces
> With pretty laces.

---

*"Shooting an Elephant," in *Shooting an Elephant and Other Essays* (New York: Harcourt, Brace, 1950), p. 192.

†In *Quite Early One Morning* (New York: New Directions, 1954).

Marjorie personified death in her poem.

DEATH

She walked slowly, her eyes
   closed.
Her hands upon mine were
   cold.
Her beauty was that of a
   rose in delicacy.
A gray mist drifted about her
   forming almost nothing but a
   shadow.
She was not a goddess, nor
   an angel. I immediately recognized,
She was death.
                   —Marjorie, grade 5

One can almost feel Thomas's excitement about spring in his imaginative language.

SPRING

In spring
     the fun and excitement
     is looking you in the eye.
     — Thomas, grade 7

Personification was also used in the following compositions:

THE LITTLE FLYER

At my feet lay the little flyer
His name was ____
He didn't have any name.
He had lived in a large family
For one summer. He had lived
First, as a young one,
Bigger, bigger.
It became very cold
Colder, colder.
He then became a flyer.
Down he came—
Looping, swirling;
He hit the ground,
Then off he took,
Finally landing at my feet.
Yes, I call him the little flyer.
You would call him a dead leaf.
                —Robbie, grade 6

FOREST FIRE

Burning up a mountain,
Down a valley,
A monster which grows through destruction,
Leaving a trail of black ashes.
The unwanted, but the inevitable.
                              — *Peter, grade 6*

Sitting on the outermost rock by the water's edge, Marianthi encountered happy memories and a new friend.

> I like it here, but I'm getting cold and a little hungry, so goodby sea grass and this particular body of water — no, no, not "water." I'm not referring to you in the third person anymore, because you're not a "third person" to me, but I said "this particular body of water" simply because I wasn't sure how to refer to you — my thoughts got in the way again. I'll refer to you as my partner along with the grass in this space and time, for you are very personal to me, water and grass, because I feel you right through the inner fibers of my being — you seep right through me and refresh and nourish me like a good friend, which you are. Perhaps we'll meet again. I now bid you so long, because I'm getting colder and colder — my body — and hence I leave, although you will live in me. I'm glad I encountered your presence.*

CONNOTATION.   Connotative figures evoke personal images. Bob observed a parent in a health food bar:

> The salesmom
>   suggesting
>   creammmmmmmmcheese
>   and date-nut bread
> to kids
>   tugging her
> to the french-fried golden arches
> "cross the way."

Old, new, foreign, technical, and descriptive words and phrases add to the flavor of the language. Third-grade children collected the following examples of connotative phrases from advertisements and window shopping:

Boston baked beans	dirt brown
Bermuda shorts	cheerful as holiday berries
Scotch plaid	you feel golden all over
holiday red	cuddly soft
soft as a soufflé	sugar white beach

---

*Marianthi Lazos, "Encounter" (manuscript, 1980), p. 2.

glen green	butter soft
loch blue	the fall countryside was aflame
scone, peat brown	pickle green

Written on the board by the children who found them, these phrases were
thus shared with classmates. These newfound ways of adding variety to
language helped people to describe their experiences, their possessions, and
other people. William, a second grader, wrote:

> I know a little boy
> Whose face was pickle green
> He is the meanest brother
> That I have ever seen.

ONOMATOPOEIA.   Onomatopoeia is the use of a word whose sound suggests its meaning, as "ommpah" describes the sound of a tuba. This fugure
strengthens the flow from sound to meaning. Examples are "bang,"
"cuckoo," "ding-dong," "hiss," "pop," "roar," "screech," "whippoorwill,"
"sizzle," and "crack." Ruthie remembered the sound of steak on a
barbecue.

> TEMPTATION!
> Steak on the barbecue,
> Sizzling and crackling,
> As orange tongues of flames
> Leap around their prize:
> The irresistible tantalizing aroma,
> Drifting with the breeze,
> Luring eager appetites.
> —*Ruthie, grade 6*

SYNESTHESIA.   Synesthesia (sin is THEE zha) is the mixing of sensations,
as when the hearing of a certain sound induces the sight of a color. Examples of this figure are: "I awoke and tasted the bright, noisy, new day,"
and "As I approached the finish, I could taste the prize money." Ralph
Ellison used this figure of speech very effectively:

> A glove landed in my mid-section and I went over again, feeling as
> though the smoke had become a knife jabbed into my guts.*

CONTRAST.   Used commonly as figures of speech, contrasts refer to
something that is the opposite of, less than, more than, or somehow different from the speaker or writer's subject. Saying the opposite of what is
meant may be classified as irony or antithesis. "You're a real beauty" may

---

Invisible Man (New York: Random House, 1952), p. 19.

be another way of saying, "You are, in fact, not beautiful or acting beautifully at all." "Yeah, Yeah" means "No, no." "I don't care" means "I care; I care." "You're a real pal" means "You're not acting like a pal; you're acting like an enemy." In speech, the tone of voice communicates the real meaning. In written work, the context must do so.

Saying less than what is meant is an understatement. "Just a second" means "Just a few minutes" or "Don't bother me." "I hardly touched him" means "Yes, we were fighting, but he doesn't seem badly hurt."

Saying more than what is meant is hyperbole. "I'm starved" means "I'm hungry." "I'll murder him" means "I'll hit him." "I could eat a horse" means "I'm hungry." "I'm dead" means "I'm tired." "I'd give a million dollars" means "I'd like it." David, a first grader, was deliberately exaggerating when he wrote:

> I like the trumpeter swans.
> They look so beautiful
> I can look at them forever.

METONYMY AND SYNECDOCHE. Metonymy (mehTAH nuh mee) is the figure of speech involved when people use a related word to suggest the one they have in mind. Here one object means or suggests another. It is an interesting way of adding variety to composition:

> "swab" means "sailor"
> "rifle" means "soldier"
> "horse" means "cavalry"
> "bottle" means "milk"
> "bread" means "food" or "money"

Thus, a poet may refer to "Forty thousand rifles marching up the hill."

Sometimes one part is used to suggest the whole. This figure is known as synecdoche (si NECK duh kee). In Ralph Ellison's *Invisible Man*, "hand" suggests the people who helped slaves escape: "On and on, passed from black hand to black hand and some white hands, and all the hands molding the Founder's freedom and our own freedom like voices shaping a deep-felt song."*

Other examples of synecdoche:

> "leaf" means the tree
> "slice" means the pie
> "ivory" the elephant
> "point" means the sword
> "chimney" means the house

---

*Ibid., p. 95.

Synecdoche is often used in "jive" talk:

give me some skin (shake hands)
weaver (tailor)
threads (clothes)

Once we have learned to recognize these, we can look at many ethnic expressions with a poet's eye. We can appreciate them as poetic devices rather than downgrading them as "substandard slang." Yes, there are poets all around us.

Poets convert thoughts into feelings and feelings into thoughts and then reveal them in language capable of evoking further feelings and thoughts in the listener or reader. This heightened language sweetens the most bitter business letter and enlivens the dullest debate. It also heightens our awareness of ourselves, our language surroundings, and our world. Poetic language should not be restricted to poetry; it contributes to the development of other forms of composition and communication and, surely, to that of communicators and their relationships.

Any aspect of language will lose its effectiveness if overused. Composition is not produced by mechanically adding elements together. It is accomplished by repeating and varying ingredients until one has fashioned the words to encapsulate the feeling. The attainment of artistic unity requires a skillful balancing of words and form. This balance in turn requires composers to turn on their perceptive powers and to turn toward the ideas that flow into composition, helping us to laugh, to weep, to dance with words.

SUGGESTED READING

Alexander, Arthur. *The Poet's Eye: An Introduction to Poetry for Young People.* Englewood Cliffs, N.J.: Prentice Hall, 1967.

Flesch, Rudolph. *The Art of Plain Talk.* New York: Harper and Brothers, 1946.

Gordon, Thomas. *P.E.T. in Action.* New York: Wyden Books, 1976.

Hayakawa, S. I. *Language in Thought and Action.* 2d ed. New York: Harcourt, Brace and World, 1949.

New York City Board of Education. "Developing Children's Power of Self-Expression Through Writing. Curriculum Bulletin no. 2, 1952–53 series. New York: Board of Education, 1953.

Queneau, Raymond. (Translated by Barbara Wright.) *The Infinite Fluidity of Language.* New York: New Directions, 1981.

7 From Language to Inventive Form

This chapter deals with language patterns fashioned by teachers and writers from the writer's own language. Called inventive language patterns, these self-initiated forms require one to rely on inner, self-imposed controls. They free writers to concentrate on their subjects, their feelings, and their natural language patterns rather than on forms designed by others.

Inventive expressions often appear spontaneous, and some of them are, but many are carefully designed. This is particularly true of the expressions of older writers. Relying on inner controls may be difficult for those used to depending on external controls initiated by some other person. For composers, freedom from formal restrictions affords myriad opportunities for a variety of language patterns to emerge, to be taken seriously, and to be appreciated in composition.

Composing without a predesigned form is, for many, similar to role playing and creative dramatics, expressive movements to music, and impressionistic painting — a way teachers can help people to see tangible results while enjoying the experience. The participants develop confidence in their ability and are likely to seek further experimentation.

Inventive patterns are shapes that the composer's language takes or is given to bring out the nuances inherent in the material. The language may be carefully fashioned, ordered, and reordered, but not according to a predesigned arrangement. The measure is variable rather than fixed. It is evaluated by the authors, the teacher, or the readers merely according to its appropriateness and effectiveness of expression.

Inventive patterns are not always new or formless. The oldest traditional literature, including much of the Jewish Bible, was composed in inventive patterns. Modern speakers and writers often use them without having studied them.

INVENTIVE PATTERNS FROM
LANGUAGE AND EXPERIENCES

Inventive patterns are often derived from spoken language, which is naturally rich in imagery and rhythm. Bubbling over with ideas, multicolored feelings, and memories, the language may fall into several kinds of patterns. Some of these associational patterns may be fashioned from our natural linking of one idea to another. This is the source of such forms as rhythmic dialogue, free-form responses to emotion, parallel expressions, litanies, prose poetry, narrative plot patterns, and patterns based on the logical order of ideas.

Rhythmic Dialogue

Language patterns may be heard in and fashioned from a student's impromptu conversation by any interested teacher. Three kindergarten lispers were sent to see the speech teacher. After introductions, they were asked to sing along with the teacher while he strummed "Skip to My Lou" (the only song he knew with sibilants) on his ukelele. The children's names were used in the song: "Mary had a red dress. Isn't it nice? Skip to my Lou, my darling." The children joined in, while an initial speech diagnosis was being made by the speech teacher. The children seemed to enjoy themselves, so he asked them what songs they liked to sing. He then asked them to tell him about songs. The children took turns and associated songs with past experiences as the teacher wrote down what they said.

First child:	A song is very nice.
	It makes you happy and gay.
Second child:	Some songs make you tired.
	Some songs are sad.
Third child:	[With a provocative wink] Some songs are bad.
All three:	Giggles.

When their responses were put down on paper, they found that they had composed a little rhythmic selection.

A song is very nice.
It makes you happy and gay.
Some songs make you tired.
Some songs are sad.
Some songs are bad.

The teacher read the dictation. One child remarked, "It sounds like a poem." They all agreed. They decided to say it over together line by line.

They repeated it in chorus as they returned to their kindergarten class-room.

Impromptu dialogue is often filled with rhythmic patterns. The simplest words or phrases have recognizable rhythms. When language is free-flowing, as it is in the playground, in the street, or in a relaxed classroom, the natural rhythms may even resemble jazz. Each syllable has a beat; some are short and some are long. Some phrases are spoken softly and some more loudly; some rapidly and others more slowly. Some words are tied together with final consonants followed by initial vowels. Other words are separated by stopped consonants or pauses to highlight the word immediately before or after.

Here is an example of impromptu language from a group of fourth-grade boys overheard in the playground. Each line was spoken by a different youngster. Each line has four syllables. The first, second, and fourth lines have the same rhythm. The third line uses an interesting variation. Together they demonstrate how inventive pattern may be found in impromptu dialogue.

> We have a bat.
> We have a ball.
> Let's choose up sides.
> Winner take all.

Language patterns fill the air and can be heard wherever there are people speaking freely. An interested teacher with a pad and pencil can catch a padful every day.

Free-form Responses to Emotion

INDIVIDUAL SOUNDS AND WORDS. Patterns may be fashioned from the words in the author's language storehouse. For the following writer, most words needed "a private line" on the page. This arrangement allowed the final consonant continuant sound (s) to be sustained and to heighten the imagery.

> Space
> Mysterious,
> Supernatural,
> Vastness,
> Midnight velvet
> Endless,
> Infinite, profound space.
> — *Robert, grade 6*

Two, three, or four words may be placed in sequence to compound their individual sound qualities. In Donald's selection below, the hunter is so quiet, so slow. The words "creeping" and "stealthily" must be said slowly. They alert us to the nature of the hunter. The hisses of the (s) sound in several words set the stage for the quiet but steady forward movement. The longer phrases add to the swiftness of the attack. The explosive (b) in "blinding" and (p) in "pounce" give force to the hunter's suddenness and power.

THE HUNTER

Creeping
   stealthily,
It
   silently stalks
An unsuspecting victim.

Scarcely showing
   its sleek physique
Slowly
   it closes the gap
Between itself and its prey.

Then with blinding speed it dashes wildly out
To pounce upon a grazing antelope.

Slashing with its paws and violently biting,
It conquers its meal.

                    —Donald, grade 6

PERSONAL FEELINGS. Patterns of language may arise from the personal feelings of the writer. Marty's choice of line arrangement is certainly appropriate to his feelings.

DEATH STRIKES

It is my kin
That does die,
I never win.
Now it is in heaven
She does lie.
Maybe it is better this way,
But not to me
Why can't I have my way to God,
Why can't he see?

I loved her so
Couldn't God have seen.

                    —Marty, grade 6

SENSE OF MOVEMENT.   Movement may be symbolized in language patterns and emphasized in a variety of line arrangements. Karen noticed how the flag in front of the school depended upon the breeze. The movement of the flag suggested her poetic composition and its arrangement on the page.

> The flag
> > flutters its pointed tips
> It
> > sags and
> > > BULGES TO THE END
> It
> > droops
> > > so lonely
> > > waiting for a breeze.
> SUDDENLY it swoops and straightens out
> With wing on wing it flies with ease.
> > > > *— Karen, grade 6*

ASSOCIATION OF THOUGHTS AND EXPERIENCES.   Patterns may emerge or be fashioned from the writer's natural association of one idea or experience with another. Sometimes groups of writers can cooperate in producing one of these word pictures or applied analogies. An intermediate-grade teacher asked her class one day, "What is an elementary school?" Her fifth and sixth graders wrote as a group:

WHAT IS AN ELEMENTARY SCHOOL?

A PLACE
> to get yelled at
> where you're given work to do
> where every now and then you go out to recess
> where if you're bad and fool around you get sent down
> > to the principal
> loaded with work, faulty radiators and hot classrooms

WHERE WE LEARN
> to read books
> the basic part of basic subjects
> to get along with other children
> about other places in the world

A TIME
> to store good thoughts
> to get rid of troubles

A JAIL for handwriting

A HEAVEN for science and math

A TORTURE CHAMBER

MISERABLE:
            BORING:
                        EXCITING:
                                    RUSH! RUSH! RUSH!
                                                YUK!

A mother, feeling a child's reaction to ridicule, arranged the words in an appropriate pattern (figure 7.1). Kathy Chapman links form with idea, connecting the child's feelings and words in an original and imaginative way. She applies the same technique to a social theme in her pattern poem "Hate Knows So Many Words" (figure 7.2).

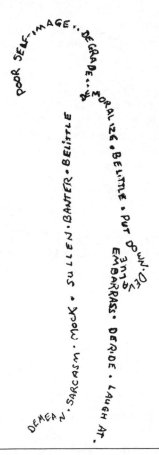

FIGURE 7.1.   Pattern poem: "Dejection"

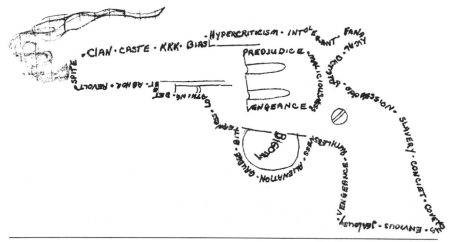

FIGURE 7.2.   Pattern poem: "Hate Knows So Many Words"

Parallel Expressions

Parallel expressions often suggest language patterns. Like catalogue verse, compositions consisting of parallel expressions have been used as far back as the Jewish Bible, notably in the psalms and prophetic literature. Parallel statements include comparisons, contrasts, and reiterations or restatements, whose echolike quality adds strength to a creative idea. Karen, a sixth grader, used parallel reiteration in arranging "Tomorrow."

TOMORROW

He was going to turn
Over a new leaf: Tomorrow
He was going to be
Unselfish: Tomorrow
He was going to be
Neater, politer, smarter,
Better to get along with;
Yes, all of these
He was to be: Tomorrow

Tomorrow he would
Straighten his room
Tomorrow he would
Answer his letters
Tomorrow he would
finish his work.

And repay debts;
Yes all of these
He was to do: Tomorrow

He was to do
This: Tomorrow
He would do
That: Tomorrow
Tomorrow he would do
Such and such;
He was to do so many things,
Isn't it a shame:
Tomorrow never came.

In another pattern, synonymous parallelism, two parts express the same idea. The second part is a restatement in different words. For example, "of everyone to whom an 'A' is given, much will be required; and those who do much schoolwork can expect a student's reward." In the antithetical or contrasting pattern, the second idea contrasts with the first: "The school was made for the child, not the child for the school." In progressive parallelism, the idea of the first part is developed in the second: "Those whom I like like me, and those who like me like my friends."

Litanies

Litanies may be composed privately or in groups to communicate inspiration or intense feelings. They, like parallel expressions, are biblical in background and use parallel arrangements of words. Once a topic is selected, a litany can be started in many ways. Anthony wrote a composition for Thanksgiving. As a seventh grader's prose composition, it left much to be desired. Rearranged as a litany by the teacher, it is more pleasing. The parallel arrangement heightens the writer's sentiments and the reader's appreciation.

A THANKSGIVING LITANY

Thanksgiving means that we are thankful
for the things we have like:

milk,
water,
food,
doctors,
parents —

and freedom:
for worship,

speech,
and for the things I have like:

schools,
clothes,
and food.

But most of all —
    my brothers and sisters
    my mother
    and father.

Composers may find the following list helpful in beginning their litanies:

We love our country . . .
We fear the bomb . . .
Help us work for peace . . .
I can hear Christmas . . .
I can taste Passover . . .
I can see Easter . . .
I can feel ____ [a season] . . .

Prose Poetry

A great deal of poetic writing first appears in prose form. Some may be considered prose poetry, a form that contains many of the qualities of poetry: strong imagery, intensity, encapsulated feelings, and rhythmic phrases. The distinction between poetry and prose poetry may be difficult or impossible to make. When poetic writing appears in paragraph rather than verse form, it may be called prose poetry.

Maureen could have written down the sentences in her composition in the form of verse. She chose instead to retain the prose paragraph form because it enhanced the reader's impression of the storm's intensity and at the same time underlined the ordinariness of the subject. Listen:

THE STORM

Waves lapped gently against the dock. The sun
partially hidden behind clouds cast an eerie
light upon the lake. Slowly, gradually, it
became darker. The wind howled fiercely and
roared with terrifying speed. All nature was
ready for the storm to break. Suddenly it
did. Rain poured down in angry torrents. The
sun was now completely hidden behind dark masses

of clouds. A flash of lightning lit up the
whole landscape. There came a crack of thunder
as though to shatter everything. The white-
capped breakers crashed into rocks and tore
at the beach. Then as suddenly as the storm
had come it was over. The sun shone once
more.

—Maureen, grade 7

Prose poetry may be left in paragraph form or rearranged in conventional poetic lines. In either case, the melodic flow of the lines will determine which form is most appropriate.

Narrative Plot Patterns

For centuries storytellers, as well as prose and poetry writers, have devised narrative plot patterns. Four of the following five simplified patterns were adapted from the Nebraska Development Curriculum Center series. These are: moving from security to insecurity, going from security to a confrontation with evil, escaping from an unfriendly environment to security, and opposing foolishness with wisdom. To these four, I have added a simple love plot.

In these plots, movement, security, and insecurity may be actual or psychological. Security may be represented by home, community, country, planet Earth, family, health, possessions, confidence, employment, protection, or self-worth. Insecurity may take the form of homelessness, rejection, poverty, friendlessness, lack of protection, fearfulness, or a sense of worthlessness. Definitions of movement, security, insecurity, evil, foolishness, wisdom, and love depend upon composers and listeners and their locations, times, and conditions.

FROM SECURITY TO INSECURITY. Moving from security to insecurity is similar to moving from the known to the unknown. These journeys are familiar to children, adolescents, adults and the aged—all who, spurred by curiosity or restlessness, have moved on and encountered isolation, loneliness, and hunger. They occur in all cultures, families, and walks of life. The journey is a universal story plot that we have experienced and will experience over and over again. We are interested in the stories of others who seek to know what's outside the door, across the street, over the hill, and beyond, and so the odyssey is a basic, universal plot pattern.

FROM SECURITY TO A CONFRONTATION WITH EVIL. Evil may be represented by complexity, conniving, selfishness, wickedness, and dishonesty, or by certain animals, insects, reptiles, birds, people, or groups of people, or by natural or artificial monsters and other creatures. (It should be kept in mind that the hero as well as the villian may be any of the above-mentioned creatures.) Evil may also take the form of the elements, disasters, epidemics, wars, hostile institutions, competition, selected authority figures, the establishment, or the rabble. Examples of this plot pattern are Genesis, "Little Red Riding Hood," "The Labors of Hercules," and "Jack and the Beanstalk."

FROM AN UNFRIENDLY ENVIRONMENT TO SECURITY.   The escape from an adverse environment and the creation or recreation of security underlie the plots of "Cinderella," "Snow White," "Hansel and Gretel," and "Peter Rabbit." Our forefathers also moved to a new land, to the suburbs, or to rural areas with others who sought security and valued freedom, natural beauty, openness, and a more responsive government. So many stories, biographies as well as fiction, have to do with dreams of an escape from a severe, unfriendly environment. Often the desire to create or recreate security is expressed in terms of the restoration of real or idealized traditions and beliefs. The Book of Exodus is a powerful expression of this desire. The old demand "Let my people go!" can become our story.

OPPOSING FOOLISHNESS WITH WISDOM.   Wisdom may take the form of intellect, thrift, education, experience, practicality, law, discretion, or far-sightedness. The foolishness it opposes may be ignorance, stupidity, gullibility, shallowness, or impracticality. Familiar examples of this plot type include "The Tortoise and the Hare," "Stone Soup," and, of course, "The Three Little Pigs."

SEEKING LOVE.   One typical simple love plot with a happy ending begins with A wanting B but B not interested; next, B wants A, but A now seems indifferent; finally, A and B desire each other. "True confession" magazines are filled with this plot pattern.

Another love motif is "love at first sight": Strangers' eyes meet, and suddenly they fall in love, as in the song "Some Enchanted Evening." These stories emphasize the beginnings of romance.

Star-crossed lovers are opposed by fate. *Romeo and Juliet* has a plot of this type.

After one has learned to recognize these plot patterns in stories or poems, one can look or listen for combinations of them. For example:

> An alligator was walking down the road one day and he passed a man
> and the man said, "Hi Mr." And the alligator replied, "I'm not a Mr. I'm

an alligator." Then they made friends and went down the road until they came to a tree and the man said, "What ya got for lunch, buddy?" and the alligator replied, "You" and he ate the man up. Then he took a sip of the man's beer.

—Andrew, grade 2

Without instruction, this second grader included several narrative patterns in his composition. The boy was sophisticated enough to create an antihero, the alligator, who moved from security to insecurity, outwitted the man and created his own feeling of security with the man's beer. When the writer reaches fourth grade, his hero may also be ready for love.

Patterns Based on the Logical Order of Ideas

Compositional patterns may also be arranged according to the logical order of ideas; that is, ideas are put into an expositional pattern that gives them form and logical direction.

The introduction to the following article described a kind of group behavior; this was the effect largely of the leader's behavior. The introduction was a way of illustrating the problem of an inadequate and superficial system of staff and program development. The balance of the article proposed solutions to this problem.

At 3:15 P.M., Mrs. Smith kissed the last bit of frosting from her thumb and forefinger, touched the back of her brand new haircomb three times, coughed quietly towards the rectangularly placed teachers, and assumed her duties as "Chairlady of the October Faculty-Discussion-Meeting."

"I'm sure you all join me in extending our thanks to the fourth grade teachers for acting as hostesses for today's meeting. I, for one, always look forward to October when the fourth grade teachers make those delightful cakes. Now, on with the meeting. Did you all receive a copy of today's agenda as you walked in? Some of you didn't? Miss Walker, would you hand out these extras to those people with hands raised? Thank you! Dr. Edwards (nods to her principal, seated on her left) has arranged an interesting meeting today, so let's begin with the P.T.A. report."

(This will be followed by the Red Cross report, the Science Fair report, the Publicity Committee report, the Social Committee, Civil Defense Committee, the Budget Committee, the N.E.A., the State Teachers Association new retirement recommendations, and then the Curriculum Improvement Committee.)

"We will conclude our meeting with a talk by our new French teacher about his program and how we can help improve the French program in our school.

"Now don't forget, we want to leave by 4:30, so everyone be as brief as possible."

. . . The cake eaters of today's meeting will be the cake bakers of next month's meeting; they will have gained weight, but they will not have gained one ounce of skill in group discussion methods, or leadership ability, or in group cohesiveness, or in problem solving, or in curriculum development, or in self-respect. Dr. Edwards has not done all he could do to help his teachers develop their leadership potential. He has sensed the uneasiness, the boredom, the stoic, clock-peeking disinvolvement. He has interpreted this to mean that teachers just don't like meetings, but unfortunately, he is responsible for having them. His course of action has been to vary the speakers, the hostesses, and the place mats in order to make this a simulated social experience. In a sense, by trying to make faculty meetings more palatable for teachers, he has tried to "placake" them. (I'm not sure if this is a Freudian slip or semantic pun.) The best way to motivate interest in problem solving is to start with the dissatisfactions felt by the group. If Dr. Edwards would only try this he might not need the trimmings.*

Common compositional patterns are cause to effect, topical sequence, space, time, elimination, effect to cause, comparison/contrast, general to particular, particular to general, problem/solution, and cumulative.

CAUSE TO EFFECT.   In the cause-to-effect pattern, one points to the cause and then to the expected result: "If you won't give me another cookie, I'll cry." "Peek-a-boo — I see you" (and you see me). "I'll cry and see who comes running." "If I do it, I'll get a spanking."

> The blue sky blackened.
> The trees seemed to hold their breath
> Expecting cold rain.
> *—Joan, grade 6*

TOPICAL SEQUENCE.   Topical sequence is the arrangement of ideas according to subject. "Let's talk about the gym program, the art program, the music program, and the French program." "I'll describe this vase — where it was found, how it was made, and what it's worth."

> The family clustered about,
> First, the girls
> All starch and giggles.
> Then the boys

---

*Robert Wolsch, "The Crystallized Faculty Meeting," *Today's Speech* (Speech Association of the Eastern States), April 1960.

March, march, shout.
The infant
Powdered and wiggly
Held by
The parents
Both a little stout.
                    — *Fred, grade 6*

SPACE.   A composition with spatial organization describes where things are, usually in relation to other things. "Election results are coming in from the New England, Middle Atlantic, Southern, Southwest, Northwest, and Great Lakes areas."

A gun was in his right hand,
A dagger in his left.
                    — *Jake, grade 5*

From the red-ribboned boxes below
To the silver star aglow
It stood proudly
At Christmas.
                    — *Diane, grade 6*

TIME.   Events or instructions may also be placed in a time sequence: 1, 2, 3; 1969, 1970, 1971; spring, summer; Monday, Tuesday. "I went to nursery school, kindergarten, and then elementary school; junior high school will be next."

Seed became flower,
As spring rain and summer sun
Were followed by fall.
                    — *Harold, grade 6*

ELIMINATION.   In a process-of-elimination sequence, all possible alternatives are discarded except one. "It isn't in my desk; it isn't in the closet; it isn't in my briefcase; it's not on my head; it must be at the lost and found." This type of reasoning is used by physicians, educators, and the writers of mysteries.

Who could it be?
The King, the Queen, the maid, the knaves?
The King was in his counting house
Counting out his money.
The Queen was in her chamber
Eating bread and honey.
The maid was in the parlor
Dusting things so shiny.

The Knave was all that's left,
And him so sly and whiny.
                    —*John, grade 7*

EFFECT TO CAUSE.   In the effect-to-cause order, a situation or feeling is analyzed by stating its cause. "I hate poetry because I had to memorize the 'Under the spreading chestnut tree' kind."

The lawn was lush green,
Fed, bathed and pampered;
A neighborhood queen.
                    —*Jeffrey, grade 7*

One can also use a flashback technique, beginning with the final situation and working back through a series of earlier causes.

COMPARISON/CONTRAST.   In the comparison/contrast format, things, events, or people may be related or distinguished: boys and girls, left and right, right and wrong, then and now, or advantages and disadvantages.

A toad is a fast runner
but a frog is faster.
The race
between frog and toad
was a disaster.
                    —*Jordan, grade 2*

GENERAL TO PARTICULAR.   A general-to-particular argument or discussion is a way of urging the acceptance of some specific proposition because its merits are derived from an accepted principle. "Everyone talks about acting fairly. Boys ought to be first sometimes."

AGE HAS ADVANTAGES

If bedtime hour
Depends upon
How old you are,
And Sam is only seven,
And goes to bed at nine o'clock,
Then we who've reached the age of nine
Should play until eleven.
                    —*Robert, grade 4*

PARTICULAR TO GENERAL.   Particular-to-general argumentation requires the use of several examples for one single conclusion. "My dad is always talking to my mom; my brother always hits me; my sister's always watching television; I'm tired of my family."

SISTER SUSIE SHOUTS A LOT

She shouted for her breakfast.
She shouted for her lunch.
She will shout for her supper,
Is my very next hunch.
—*Donald, grade 6*

PROBLEM/SOLUTION.   A simple statement of a problem may be followed by an obvious or surprising solution. "You wouldn't share your candy; I won't share mine."

The rats run in our house at night.
We want to run too.
—*Henry, grade 4*

CUMULATIVE.   Each new part of a cumulative composition adds a new idea and then repeats whatever came before in a chain of interlocking events, characters, or relationships. This is the technique used in children's memory games like "packing a suitcase," poems like "The House That Jack Built," and songs like "The Green Grass Grew All Around."

This is the book
   that I wrote.
This is one chapter
That's in the book
   that I wrote.
This is one part
That can be applied to prose, plays, or poetry
In the book
That I wrote.
—*Robert, age 54*

A communication program that emphasizes listening to, recognizing, inventing, and using narrative plot patterns and logical exposition provides a basic communication structure for people of all ages. On this foundation we can build higher levels of language insight and enjoyment.

RHYTHM AND THE DEVELOPMENT OF LANGUAGE PATTERNS

For a composition to be alive, it must have rhythm. Rhythm is the more or less regular repetition of some element. The universe is an infinite superimposition of rhythms: time, the tides, and the seasons, our waking and sleeping, our skating and skipping, the movement of and in our bodies. People, created in rhythms, die when their bodily rhythms are interrupted. Children develop rhythm first in utero and then through feeding, speaking, and listening to poems on their parent's knee. Nonmetered and metered patterns of language are developed from rhythm. Our breathing is rhythmic; our speech is rhythmic; our writing is rhythmic too.

Rhythms range from the hypnotic to the seemingly chaotic. They may be lulling, like beach waves, fireplace flames, and counted sheep. They may be scarcely noticeable; like the steady growth of one's children. Language may at first appear to be dysrhythmic, like the playing and writing of children. In short compositions, the variety of rhythms may not be as apparent as in longer ones. But the rhythms do vary from piece to piece, much like the rhythms of rope skipping, bicycle riding, and hot dog chewing. Each activity has a variety of distinct and individual rhythms; each poetic composition emerges from an appropriate rhythmic pattern.

The Unit of Measure

The writer or speaker must decide the rhythmic unit of measure and then proceed to use it in composing. In written discourse one usually thinks of the word or the sentence as the unit of measure. In fact, the rhythmic language unit may be a sound, an unaccented syllable, a word, a phrase, a line, a couplet, or a stanza.

THE SYLLABLE. In poetry the unit of measure is often the "foot" — the pattern of stressed and unstressed syllables. Counting all syllables, not merely the accented ones, is another way of measuring the rhythm of language. Haiku, for example, uses the syllable as the unit of measure.

THE PHRASE. The phrase is a basic unit of meaning in speech and oral reading. It is also a unit of measure suitable for invented composition. The phrase uses tones and pauses to convey meaning. How does one recognize a phrase? A phrase is a group of words surrounded by pauses. Pauses are used to take a breath or add a particular kind of emphasis to the phrase. Pauses give the listener time to arrange the lines according to the speaker's idiom.

Phrase hunting, a simple way to learn to recognize patterns in speech, writing, or reading aloud, is listening for the pauses, marking them, and then allowing a new line for every phrase. The line pattern developed from the phrases makes the meaning and the rhythmic quality of the composition more obvious. The line stands there and demands to be read. The literary pattern, therefore, follows and accentuates the writer's meaning and rhythm.

Concentrating on phrases instead of sentences and reorganizing paragraphs to resemble poetry has helped many hesitant people become better oral readers. It has enabled them to read with appropriate expression instead of being confused by sentences within paragraphs. The anticipated embarrassment of reading aloud before their friends is alleviated.

Adults may learn to sense the varieties of rhythms in people's compositions by listening to the rhythms of someone sleeping. Even the healthiest person's breathing is not metronomically even. Language too needs the occasional snort, sneeze, and sniffle to bring it closer to other forms of life. Using variety of rhythms avoids putting the reader to sleep.

Finding the rhythmic pulse of something previously considered lifeless is one of the joys of life for teachers as it is for physicians. The following selection required several oral readings by the teacher before the child's natural rhythmic pauses were noticed. Elizabeth's attempt to describe approaching spring looked like this:

> Spring is coming, Spring is coming
> How do you think I know the flowers are
> out the snow is not that's how I think I know.
> *— Elizabeth, grade 3*

The teacher added vertical slash marks to separate the phrases.

> Spring is coming/spring is coming/
> how do you think I know/the flowers are
> out/the snow is not/that's how I think I know/

The resulting line arrangement alerts the reader to the vitality of the third grader's poetic composition.

> Spring is coming
> Spring is coming
> How do you think I know?
> The flowers are out
> The snow is not
> That's how I think I know.

Oral expressions are often naturally rhythmic. Rearranging writing according to the rhythmic flow of speech offers many opportunities for original, self-initiated patterns. The speaker or writer may repeat a phrase over and over again to feel its taut rhythm. The phrase, with its accompanying image, is then allowed to run free, building a pattern around the rhythm of its own speaking. Repeating the first three lines enabled Elizabeth to build up momentum for another verse.

> Spring is coming
> Spring is coming
> How do you think I know . . .

Once the rhythmic pulse of this selection was felt, the teacher began to find new life in the writing of others. Even Abraham Lincoln's Gettysburg Address seems more artistic in a nonparagraphed form.

GETTYSBURG ADDRESS

Four score and seven years ago our fathers brought forth on this continent, a new nation, conceived in Liberty and dedicated to the proposition that all men are created equal. Now we are engaged in a great civil war, testing whether that nation, or any nation so conceived and so dedicated, can long endure. We are met on a great battle-field of that war. We have come to dedicate a portion of that field, as a final resting place for those who here gave their lives that this nation might live. It is altogether fitting and proper that we should do this. But, in a larger sense, we can not dedicate — we can not consecrate — we can not hallow — this ground. The brave men, living and dead, who struggled here, have consecrated it, far above our poor powers to add or detract. The world will little note, nor long remember what we say here, but it can never forget what they did here. It is for us the living, rather, to be dedicated here to the unfinished work which they who fought here have thus far nobly advanced. It is rather for us to be here dedicated to the great task remaining before us — that from these honored dead we take increased devotion to that cause for which they gave the last full measure of devotion — that we here highly resolve that these dead shall not have died in vain — that this nation, under God, shall have a new birth of freedom — and that government of the people, by the people, for the people, shall not perish from the earth.

THE GETTYSBURG ADDRESS

Four score and seven years ago
our fathers brought forth on this continent
a new nation
conceived in liberty
and dedicated to the proposition
that all men are created equal.

Now
we are engaged in a great civil war,
testing whether this nation
or any nation
so conceived
and so dedicated
can long endure.

We are met
on a great battle-field of that war.
We have come
to dedicate a portion of that field

as a final resting place
for those who here gave their lives
that this nation might live.

It is altogether fitting and proper
that we should do this.

But in a larger sense
we can not dedicate
we can not consecrate
we can not hallow
this ground.

The brave men
living and dead
who struggled here
have consecrated it
far above our poor powers
to add or detract.

The world
will little note
nor long remember
what we say here,
but it can never forget what they did
here.

It is for us the living
rather
to be dedicated here to the unfinished work
which they who fought here
have thus far
nobly advanced.

It is rather for us
to be here dedicated
to the great task remaining before us —

that from these
honored dead
we take increased devotion
to that cause
for which they gave the last full measure
of devotion —
that we here
highly resolve
that these dead
shall not have died in vain —

that this nation
under God
shall have a new birth of freedom —
and
that government
of the people
by the people
for the people
shall not perish from the earth.

Teachers and students who look and listen for invented patterns in the speaking and writing of others find themselves tapping out the rhythmic patterns, verbalizing the sound patterns, empathizing with the emotional patterns, visualizing the patterns of the imagery, and nodding in agreement with the often surprisingly reasonable order of oral and written language. People alert to inventive language patterns often find that they cannot listen to speaking or look at writing as they did before. They try to find a pattern for each piece rather than a piece for each pattern. The ability to develop an ear for their own patterns enables people to compose with naturalness, integrity, and gusto.

SUGGESTED READING

Ciardi, John. *How Does a Poem Mean?* Boston: Houghton Mifflin, 1960.

Gross, Ronald. *Pop Poems.* New York: Simon and Schuster, 1967.

Kimzey, Ardis. *To Defend a Form: The Romance of Administration and Teaching in a Poetry-in-the-Schools Program.* New York: Teachers and Writers Collaborative, 1975.

Martin, Bill, Jr., and Brogan, Peggy. *Sounds of the Storyteller.* New York: Holt, Rinehart and Winston, 1972.

Nebraska Curriculum Development Center. *A Curriculum for English.* Lincoln: University of Nebraska Press, 1966.

Spender, Stephen. *The Making of a Poem.* New York: W. W. Norton, Norton Library, 1962.

Williams, William Carlos. *The Autobiography of William Carlos Williams.* New York: New Directions, 1951.

8 Introducing Predesigned Poetic Forms

There are occasions, like weddings, Thanksgiving, Christmas, and Passover, when dinner tables are set in formal, prescribed ways. These are the occasions to use the damask tablecloth drawn evenly at each end, the matching napkins, and the best china; these are the times for everyone to sit in his or her prescribed place. At other times — around a campfire, for example — one may bring a box lunch or a can of beans and a canteen of water. Whatever the arrangement of the meal, it contributes to the mood of the occasion. Predesigned forms also say to the writer, "I am a particular kind of composition; get ready to work with me in a particular way." One may accept or ignore the command. Predesigned literary forms, like holidays, may serve superficiality, egocentrism, or gluttony as well as playful, didactic, or spiritual motives. This chapter will discuss predesigned poetic forms. The next chapter will deal with prose forms.

PREDESIGNED POETIC FORMS

Being in a writing program without poetic composition is like learning to march but not to dance. There are several reasons for including predesigned verse forms in the composition program. As writers mature, abstract thought and logic are added to the instructional program. In composition, predesigned forms provide a transitional stage between invented expression and more mature and rigorous exercises in poetic patterns with precise metrical and stanzaic units.

Some writers, perhaps the older, the brighter, or the more experimental, may grow weary of arranging inventive patterns. It is not unusual for prolific composers in the primary grades to put aside composition around the fourth grade. Predesigned forms present a new challenge worthy of renewed effort. Common rhymed forms suitable for beginning writers include limericks, clerihews, and some types of simple ballads, such as folk, blues, and nonsense. Other, unrhymed forms include the haiku, the senryu, the tonka, and the cinquain. All are discussed in this chapter. Having a variety of forms available, like having a variety of clothes, allows writers greater latitude in expressing themselves appropriately when moving from situation to situation.

Prescribed forms thus add another dimension to the development of precision in the use of language. These prototypes present additional ways of artfully controlling materials. Composing within the bounds of predesigned forms is a kind of self-discipline that some writers are both able and eager to handle. Predesigned forms even seem to help certain people begin composition, much as others find it easier to get on with the events of the day once a decision has been made about what they will wear.

Predesigned metered verse forms conform to standard patterns, but they may be long or short, complicated or simple. They are not mere artifices. They are shapes designed to carry strong thoughts in significant form. There are numerous kinds, from many countries and periods of history. Through use, these forms have become traditional and readily recognizable to those initiated into wide reading. Some authors find pleasure, others security, and some greater creativity through knowledge of some predesigned forms. These people may be uncertain or less effective in using original inventive patterns.

Depriving writers of the joys of composing in established forms is like depriving them of the predesigned forms of dances, games, and social usage. Some enjoy carrying on the tradition of using one or more established forms just as they enjoy carrying on the tradition of "trick or treat" at Halloween. Some enjoy the challenge of knocking on doors to see what they will get. Others enjoy the challenge of finding and filling the right form.

METER

As the rhythm of language becomes more and more regular, it approaches meter. Meters are measuring units that can be anticipated and counted like birthdays or grade levels. As children can grow without counting birthdays and can learn a great deal in nongraded schools, so they may begin their compositions without regular meter. Meter can always be added later, like innings and first downs in ball games.

Metrical compositions may be rhymed or unrhymed. They may use stress, syllables, or phrases as the unit of measure. Metered patterns may be initiated by young writers. Some seem to need the self-imposed restrictions of meter in order to express themselves openly. In these cases the meter may act as a mask. Composers are able to manage and focus their thoughts better because the meter helps them to establish boundaries for their content.

Meter is not necessary for writers, but like rhyme or salt and pepper, it may add zest to the product. Too regular a meter probably means that the writer has tried too hard to fit ideas and language into a pattern rather than let the pattern fit his or her purposes.

STANZAIC FORMS

Stanzas are verse units having a predetermined number of lines. They may also have a predetermined metrical pattern or a rhetorical device, such as a question and answer or a refrain.

Stanzas offer several advantages. They provide a kind of order that composers may wish to impose upon their compositions. Limits are set. One need not develop an original arrangement: the pattern used in the first stanza may be repeated in subsequent ones.

This section describes and provides examples of three elementary stanza forms: the couplet, the tercet, and the quatrain.

Couplets

A two-line unit with both lines in the same meter is called a couplet. The lines of a couplet cooperate to hold the section securely together, as in the following two selections.

> Animals big and animals small
> At the circus you see them all.
> — *Virginia, grade 2*

> We can't go out to play
> When it's a rainy day.
> — *Mary, grade 7,*
> *special class*

Couplets may be used independently, as in the above selections, or for some epigrammatic comment summarizing a longer passage; or they may be part of a larger selection, as below.

> THE CAT
>
> The black cat yawns and opens her jaws,
> Stretches her legs and shows her claws.
>
> Then she gets up and stands on all four
> Long stiff legs and yawns some more.

She shows her sharp teeth and stretches her lip,
Her small little tongue turns up at the tip.

Lifting herself on her delicate toes,
She arches her back as high as it goes.

She lets herself down with particular care,
She walks away with her tail high in the air.
                              — *Janice, grade 6*

Scavenger hunts and Easter egg hunts provide opportunities for writing couplets.

This is easy as can be
Its hidden behind the nice ____.

If someone sat, they'd sure yell "ouch"
This is underneath the ____.

Some are near and some are far
These are hidden in the ____.

This trail of ours has finally led
Right back to your own sweet ____.

Too many eggs can make you ill
These are on your window ____.

Bugs go here to hug and hug
Look beneath the LR ____.

Was it right to make a deposit
In the upstairs linen ____?

Some are near and some are far
Look inside the cookie ____.

Lucy, Lucy, Lucy Locket
Look inside your jacket ____.

A tired bunny just gets weaker
He left this for you inside your ____.
                              — *Lois*

Tercets

A three-line unit is called a tercet or triplet. Tercets may carry the rhyme in two lines or in all three. Some are complete units. In the first example only lines 1 and 2 rhyme.

Fans are proud
    to be allowed
To meet a movie star.
    —*Nancy, grade 4*

In the following selection, line 1 rhymes with line 3.

Doctor said, "Open wide."
He wants to see
What's down inside.
    —*Lisa, kindergarten*

Marvin rhymed all three lines.

I found a new dime
At just the right time
Avoiding a piggy bank crime.
    —*Marvin, grade 6*

Some selections include several triplet stanzas.

CHRISTMAS

Christmas is happiness
Christmas is joy
Christmas is getting many a toy

Christmas is cheerfulness
Christmas is fun
Christmas is presents for everyone

Christmas is stockings
Christmas is toys
Christmas is cards for girls and boys

Christmas is Jesus
Christmas is birth
Christmas is Frankincense, Gold, and Myrrh.
    —*Jane, grade 6*

Quatrains

Quatrains are four-line poems. Many children in elementary school compose short, one-stanza verses in this form.

There are nice days and bad days,
    all kinds of days.
There are days when people get spanked.
    There are days when God gets thanked.
        —*Bruce, grade 2*

A second quatrain stanza is usually added by older children in the intermediate school years.

NEWS OF SPRING

Boldly spring from the ground,
A crocus lifts its colored crown
Heralding news of a newborn spring
Leaving in its wake a happy ring.

Rows and rows of daffodils,
Marching straight and tall,
Breaking ranks to spread the news
That spring is here for all.
— Kathy, grade 6

RHYME SCHEMES

Rhyme schemes can add to the effect, the orderliness, and the unity of poetic compositions in stanza form. A rhyme scheme is the specific pattern or order in which rhymed lines occur. In the following selection, for example, the first two lines have one rhyme; the third and fourth lines have another. The first rhyme is designated the *a* rhyme and the second the *b*. The rhyme scheme in this quatrain is *aabb*.

CIRCUS

At the circus I saw a clown   (*a*)
He climbed ladders up and down   (*a*)
He laughed and made a funny face   (*b*)
And flipped and flopped all over the place. (*b*)
                          — Virginia, grade 2

The rhyme may be varied in other ways: *a b c b, a b b a*, or *a b a b*. Below are two examples of the first.

We tried and made some popcorn   (*a*)
It tasted very good,   (*b*)
In fact it was so delicious   (*c*)
That we ate more than we should.   (*b*)
                          — Karen, grade 4

The leaves are turning colors   (*a*)
The trees are black and bare   (*b*)
I know that autumn's coming   (*c*)
I can feel it in the air.   (*b*)
                          —Janet, grade 6

Each kind of quatrain may be enlarged with a couplet to make a six-line poem. Six or eight lines usually represent the limit for elementary school children.

The exact order of the stanza unit is decided by the composers. They decide the number of lines, the metrical pattern, and the rhyme arrangement. The stanza form is predesigned, but it is designed by the composers themselves.

SELECTED RHYMED FORMS

Several varieties of rhymed patterns are suitable for elementary school composers. They include the jingle, the limerick, the clerihew, and the ballad.

Jingles

Jingles are playful, easily remembered verse forms in which more emphasis is placed on sound than on sense. Some famous word jingles are: "Hickory, Dickory, Dock," "Eeny, Meeny, Miny, Mo," and "Reuben, Reuben, I've Been Thinking." Other kinds of jingles are nursery rhymes ("Little Miss Muffet"), war songs ("The King of France Went Up the Hill"), romantic lyrics ("Where Are You Going, My Pretty Maid"), popular songs ("Where, Oh Where Has My Little Dog Gone?"), lullabies ("Rockabye Baby"), street cries ("Peanuts, popcorn, crackerjacks," "Hey, get your cold drinks"), songs about historical personages ("Lucy Locket"), the words that accompany games ("Here We Go Round the Mulberry Bush"), and counting-out rhymes ("One, Two, Buckle My Shoe").

Teachers can use jingles to show that language can jingle and bounce, as the name suggests. These verse forms usually consist of a succession of sounds or a repeated phrase. Most people enjoy writing, listening to, or reading them. They have a place in the compositional diet, just as multicolored "sprinkles" add to the delights of certain desserts. Jingles are not to be equated with poetic composition and served as a total poetic diet. They might, instead, be saved for special times like birthdays, holidays, when someone needs cheering up, or when one wants to spoof or to play with language.

Limericks

Limericks have been popular for centuries, and are as unbending as an old castle. The limerick is a predesigned form well suited to humorous and nonsensical subjects. It has a highly metrical bounce, moves swiftly, and has a set rhyme scheme of *aabba*. The final line is often a repetition or variation of the first line, though some modern limericks include a witty final line, or "punch line," instead. The surprise ending is intensified by the fact that the last line rhymes with the first. The ideas often move from the possible in line one to the improbable in line five.

> There was an old teacher of math
> In such need of a dunk in the bath
> That when she described
> A perpendicular side
> We all held our noses and laughed.
> — *Robert, grade 7*

Some authors get caught up in the spirit of composing limericks. No sooner do they finish one than they are off working on another.

> Little Zachary Zump
> Sat on his camel's hump
> He slipped and fell
> Right down a well
> Did little Zachary Zump.

> Little Zachary Zump
> Sat on a tiny stump
> He started to drink
> Some red and green ink
> And fell over kerplunk.
> — *Billy, grade 3*

Limericks draw attention to real or imaginary situations and people. They often begin with a subject, a name, or a locality: "There was a young fellow named Ben," or "On the highway to Danbury." Teachers may wish to remind writers that limericks provide a literary way to poke fun or just play with language.

Clerihews

A clerihew is a humorous verse form, often a ridiculous biography or satire, consisting of two couplets of unequal length. The humor is developed in a deadpan manner. The silly or trivial is usually treated with pomposity.

> C. Columbus
> Sailed by compass
> He left his insignia
> Somewhat East of India.
> — *Robert, grade 7*

> C. Ovington Bloomer
> Started a football rumor
> Joe Namath can't throw
> And the Jet team is slow.
>   — *Kenny, grade 5*

Notice what is often included in the clerihew: a recognizable name, an accomplishment associated with this name, and a personal reaction to this accomplishment.

Clerihews are fun, too. Teachers who have used jingles and limericks may want to experiment with this relatively new verse form. Some youngsters may want to compose verses that bear their own name. Others can experiment with the names of famous historical personages or popular movie, sports, and television personalities.

Ballads

Ballads are usually story poems. Using the plain language of the common people, they describe dramatic situations with repetitive meters and refrains. Put to music, sung, or danced to, they are akin to folk songs, work songs, sea chanteys, cowboy songs, chants, spirituals, and blues. They may add great interest to the classroom.

Subjects for ballads are everywhere. They may focus on superstitions, ghosts, heroes, or villains. They can be sad, funny, realistic, or nonsensical. They may be spiritual and uplifting or mean and biting, but they are usually impersonal. Ballads are characterized by repetition, dialogue, action verbs, plain language, minimal description, and short stanzas. Some are made up of couplets or tercets, with a refrain inserted between the strong lines. When a quatrain is used, the second and fourth lines often rhyme (*a b c b*).

Some ballads are built up from a solo line followed by a single, unchanging response.

> Can I stay home from school today?
>   No, you can't my darling.
> Can I go out in the street to play?
>   No, you can't my darling.
> Can I skip my meat and eat my pie?
>   No, you can't my darling.
> Can I sock my brother in the eye?
>   No, you can't my darling.
> No, you can't. No you can't.
>   No, you can't my darling.
>   — *Allan, grade 5*

Robert drew on firsthand experiences for his ballad. He used an original idea, a follow-up idea, and a nonsense refrain.

> Johnny got spanked and his brother went, "Nyaa, nyaa."
> Bing-bang boppity no no.
> Then he got spanked and he cried, "Waa, waa."
> Bing-bang boppity, no no.
> Bing-bang boppity no no.
> Bing-bang boppity no.
>
> *— Robert, grade 6*

Robert then decided to use the same theme with another meter.

> Bing-bang the baby cried, "Waa waa."
> Bing-bang the baby cried, "Waa."
> Nyaa nyaa the brother teased, "Nyaa, nyaa."
> Nyaa Nyaa, Waa Waa.
> They both cried Waa.

BLUES. Blues are a special kind of ballad. They may be about failure, loneliness, school, parents, boredom, fear, living conditions, world conditions, or despair. Blues are personal. The first two lines are often repeated, followed by a fifth rhyming line to complete the thought. The following poem was written by a fourth grader after the teacher had discussed the blues with the class.

> I cried last night
>   When mom closed my door
> I cried last night
>   When mom closed my door
> Tonight I'll cry no more, no more.
> *— Franklin, grade 4*

NARRATIVE BALLADS. The next selection exemplifies the use of the quatrain in a lengthy narrative balladlike poem.

THE BATTLE FOR KING'S MOUNTAIN

> In the Southern Carolina hills there stands a mountain bold,
> On which the Tories and Rebels fought, is how the legend's told;
> The mountain boys and patriots, 900 stalwart men
> Advanced upon the Britishers, 1100 then.
>
> Clad in buckskin, armed with a rifle, the men for Liberty
> Defied King George and all his troops as their personal enemy.
> Then the signal, a wild war whoop, rang out upon the hill,
> And rebel riflemen charged in to get the finishing kill.

But then from the redcoat lines, there burst a withering fire
Which blazed down on the Patriots and forced them to retire,
Then with fixed bayonets, the British assaulted in vain,
But were shot down where they stood, so they fled, lest they
    be slain.

Regrouping with their leaders the Rebels invaded again,
And with their prize "sharpshooters," "picked off" the
    Englishmen
While under the barrage of a fire a solitary man
Stole past the Tory sentry to the powder wagons ran.

Then seizing a barrel of powder with his tomahawk he split,
And to the redcoat lifeline a glowing spark was lit.
The wagons with a deafening roar disappeared in smoke,
Whence the British troops surrendered and King George's morale
    broke.

In 1776 a Declaration signed,
Gave the citizens a nation, a nation in its prime
The Americans fought and struggled to make their country free,
And secured a land of promise from sea to shining sea.
                              —Bill, grade 6

WORK SONGS. Work songs are interesting topics for class discussion. Language has always accompanied work and play. We have endless poems for rope skipping, ball bouncing, and rowing. Some compose poems and work songs for snow shoveling, grass cutting, garbage can lugging, bed making, carpet sweeping, dish washing, window washing, sweeping, and rope climbing. Teachers can read work songs of various occupations and times and allow writers to compose songs related to their social studies units, chores, fears, boredom, victories, and work experiences.

    Harry, a fourth grader, made the following observation on sweeping.

SWEEPING

Push on the broom
Push on the broom
Watch all the dirt
Fly away zoom.

Helen and John also wrote songs for work and play.

DISH WASHING

Dishes, swishes
    Look what we just ate
Dishes, swishes
    Rinse away the plate

Now the plates
  are nice and clean
Cleanest plates
  I've ever seen.
        — *Helen, grade 4*

ROPE CLIMBING
Hand over hand
Hold on with your feet
When you get the knack of it
You will say it's neat!
        — *John, grade 7*

UNRHYMED POETIC FORMS

The delights of prescribed poetic forms are not dependent on rhyme or bouncy meter. Rhymed forms use repeated sounds and rhythm to bind their parts together. Unrhymed forms use connotation to draw the reader in. The reader then fills in the missing places mentally, as one would visually fill in an almost completed circle. Unrhymed prescriptions for poetic composition are as demanding and carefully measured as the prescriptions dispensed by the druggist.

This section contains descriptions of five predesigned unrhymed poetic forms: the haiku, the senryu, the tonka, and cinquain, and the diamante. The first three are Japanese forms; the fourth and fifth are American. Composers must pay attention to the imagery as well as to the number of syllables and the other requirements of each. Teachers have found that writers, especially beginning writers, enjoy these poetic forms.

The requirements of haiku and other nonmetrical forms are far from the preconceived notions of people who expect artistic writing to be limited to moon-June rhymed doggerel. With haiku and senryu, writers can concentrate on and catch a moment in time — no opinions, no moral messages, no rhyme, only an observation of one moment from nature's constantly moving merry-go-round.

The notable features of these unrhymed verse forms include their compression of language and imagery and the absence of judgment or opinion. They sharpen one's sensitivity to nature, words, syllables, and the relationship of each of these to all the others. Thus, practice in using these forms adds both strength and breadth to poetic composition.

Japanese poetic composition has been influenced by Buddhism. It tends to remind one of the ongoingness of the seasons, the importance of self-discipline, the uniqueness of all individuals, the infinite beauty of nature, and the oneness of all creatures and the universe. To know one moment and one thing is to better know all moments and things. These are some of the lessons of the East to be experienced through the haiku, senryu, and tonka.

Haiku

The haiku (pronounced hī′ ku) is an old Japanese form of composition. The people of Japan delight in it: haiku writing is a national pastime, a word game, and a test of creativity within the bounds of strict discipline. Over a hundred haiku magazines are commercially successful, and haiku are used as fillers in newspapers and magazines.

Haiku must meet four requirements:

1. They must contain seventeen syllables: the first line has five syllables; the second line seven; and the third line five.
2. They must be free of opinion.
3. They must include a hint of a specific time of day or season.
4. They must capture one precise moment.

A moment is not usually considered a very important amount of time. "May I have just a moment?" asks a door-to-door salesman, meaning an hour. However, the most important events of life take just one moment — birth, death, the first "I love you, daddy." Haiku capture these moments.

Teachers have found that many authors are able to use this strict form to describe moments of deep emotion.

> A frog in the pond
> Jumping at a small green fly
> Silence in the pond.
> *— Nancy, grade 5*

> Hovering over us
> The sky surrounds the world
> Invented by God.
> *— Billy, grade 3*

In a haiku, line endings do not break the cadence or distort the language. Nor do they break the natural rhythm of the line. Usually there is no end or internal rhyme in a haiku, though there can be so long as the image or symbol is not strained for the sake of the rhyme.

> Racing at twelve noon
> 'Twas a little bumblebee
> With a silver fly.
> *— Irene, grade 7*

Child lonely playing
In the cold and growling wind
Sees a lone leaf drift.
                —Ellen, grade 7

Winter had come now
Through the hazy candlelight
I saw the first flake.
                —Linda, grade 6

Every year the emperor of Japan chooses a topic and the people of the country enter the competition for the finest haiku about that topic. Just as all the entries in the emperor's contest do not meet all the rules and cannot be winners, not all the attempts by beginning composers are home runs. But who can say that these attempts are not valuable even though some of the rules are broken?

Senryu

The senryu (pronounced sen'ru) is another old Japanese poetic form. It may be used to precede or introduce the teaching of the haiku. It also provides a dignified category for compositions that may not meet the haiku's rather strict criteria. Some people are able to compose in a form that resembles the haiku, but their poems do not capture a single moment or give a hint of the season, or they use too many syllables or not enough. These poems may be called senryu.

I have a red heart
As red as red hearts can be
I have a real heart too.
                —Marilyn, grade 2

I forgot my coat.
Yesterday it was my hat.
In February?
                —Bruce, grade 2

Many senryu are humorous and are derived from incidents in daily life. Three children in one class wrote the following poems.

May I go outside
No! You may not go outside
May I please go out.
                —Audrey, grade 2

I like my baby
She is in her bed today

I like my dog, too.
— *Theresa, grade 2*

I am not playing
Because you do not play fair
So, I am going.
— *Sharon, grade 2*

Tonka

The tonka is a Japanese poetic form that is more than a thousand years old. It has the same structure as the haiku, with the addition of two seven-syllable lines to take one beyond the haiku's single moment. It therefore contains thirty-one syllables.

Footprints in the snow
Leading to the icy brook
Who has put them there?
They were not there yesterday;
Should we run home for father?
— *June, grade 4*

The icy wind blows
Over the sleepy meadows
And in the town's streets.
Only one small bird still flies
Hoping to reach his warm nest.
— *June, grade 4*

For some writers the haiku moment is not enough — they need something more to summarize or complete the thought or tie it in with something else. The tonka may satisfy their needs. A series of tonka related around a central theme or period of time may be composed. Where a haiku captures one moment, a tonka may show a progression of ideas or events. Writers may continue a theme from day to day, class to class, and year to year using the tonka form. This way of continuing an idea is well within the spirit of the tonka.

Cinquain

A cinquain is a poem of five lines, usually unrhymed. It consists of a two-syllable topic line followed by lines of four, six, eight, and, finally, two syllables. The cinquain can be introduced in the intermediate grades to complement the haiku, tonka, and senryu. Writers are often intrigued with the line arrangement. Teachers may suggest cinquain verse to composers who have an appropriate idea and seek a form.

Silence
Means it's quiet.
Impossible for me.
Silence, is golden, means I'm broke.
QUIET!!!!!
            — *Leonard, grade 6*

I need
Lots of money —
Lots and lots of money.
What to do with lots of money?
Spend it.
            — *Leonard, grade 6*

Morning
Sunshine's warm rays
Warm the earth's atmosphere
Then on to turn the fields of wheat.
Golden.
            — *Nancy, grade 5*

Firetruck's
Siren blowing
Went zooming down the street
"Where's the fire?" shouted someone.
"False 'larm."
            — *Elena, grade 5*

Hatred
Breeds more hatred
Hatred rots, rots people
Hatred rots lots of good people
Stop it!
            — *Patricia, grade 6*

Girls camp.
Beautiful girls
Across quarter-mile lake
I like two girls better than one.
Like me?
            — *Leonard, grade 6*

Brother!
Little brother
Rotten little brother
When I catch my brother — poor kid.
Brothers!
            — *Leonard, grade 6*

Diamante

The diamante is a seven-line verse in the shape of a diamond. It usually begins with a noun subject and ends with a word that is that noun's opposite: for example, love-hate, peace-war, friend-enemy, prison-cathedral.

A teacher may start by requesting an interesting noun, or one may appear during a social studies or science lesson; interesting parts of speech may be saved in folders for later use in poems.

The skeleton of a diamante is arranged as follows:

noun
2 adjectives
3 participles (-ed, -ing)
4 words (noun related to subject)
3 participles (-ed, -ing)
2 adjectives
noun

The following selection was handed to a social studies teacher.

peace
sweet, calm
smiling, laughing, loved
Dream   of   the   world
frowning, crying, hated
bitter, violent
war
— Henry, grade 8

Just as the appearance of a building sets the tone for what goes on inside, or a cake may offer clues to an occasion, the pattern of a piece may also signal its content. In successful writing and speaking, structure and substance can never be separated without altering the meaning.

Predesigned forms are initiated by someone other than the writer, but, like forms initiated by the writers themselves, they provide a framework for encapsulated feelings, precise language, and a unified arrangement of the parts. What is different about predesigned forms is that the molds have already been made and are available. Practice with them may give authors new ways to convey their particular feelings, experiences, and ideas.

People learn foresight and consistency from handling a rhyme scheme. Learning to use the unrhymed forms is like learning to use one's allowance at the candy store. The seventeen-syllable haiku is a lesson in word thrift; fourteen more syllables may buy a tonka. It takes twenty-two syllables to make a cinquain. Seven syllables for this line, only five for another. Economy of words is a basic requirement for speakers and writers of all kinds.

SUGGESTED READING

Anderson, Harold G. *Haiku in England*. Rutland, Vt.: Charles E. Tuttle, 1967.

Hartman, J. M. *Writing Poetry: A Beginner's Guide*. Los Angeles: National Poetry Association, 1961.

Hopkins, Lee Bennett. *Pass the Poetry Please*. New York: Citation Press, 1972.

Perrine, Lawrence. *Sound and Sense: An Introduction to Poetry*. New York: Harcourt, Brace and World, 1956.

Preminger, Alex, ed. *Encyclopedia of Poetry and Poetics*. Princeton: Princeton University Press, 1965.

Samples, Robert. *The Metaphoric Mind: A Celebration of Creative Consciousness*. Reading, Mass.: Addison-Wesley, 1976.

Whitman, Ruth, and Feinberg, Harriet, eds. *Poemmaking: Poets in Classrooms*. Lawrence, Mass.: Massachusetts Council of Teachers of English, 1975.

9 Introducing Predesigned Prose Forms

As noted in the last chapter, predesigned poetic forms help some people to communicate. Speakers and writers have confided to us their need for the restraints of a predesigned prose format to guide their flow of communication. Bypassing decisions about form allows them to spend their creativity directly on content.

This chapter about predesigned prose forms is not intended to be all-inclusive. Narrative forms traditionally assigned in composition classes — comparison, contrast, description, analogy — are discussed throughout this book and are therefore not treated separately in this chapter. Instead, we have included forms that meet the communicative needs of beginning writers in a generally ascending order of difficulty. The purpose was to get writing started — to make it enjoyable and part of everyday life. Writing is like driving a car: it's easier to turn the wheel and change direction once you're rolling along.

The predesigned prose forms discussed here are journals, captions, signs, notes and letters, autograph albums, recipes, epigrams and mottoes, catalogue "verse," flowcharts, brochures, scripts, interviews, stories, reviews, and reports.

JOURNALS

Journals are writers' scrapbooks — they help writers remember things that got to them and that they wish to savor. They are places to record impressions, private, informal collections of intellectual or sensory excitements, celebrations of the ordinary. They can also be used to practice enlarging on these fleeting impressions and storing them away for future use. They need not be carried everywhere: pages can be pasted or stapled in and later taken out and put to work in a manuscript.

Photographers keep proof sheets. One $8\frac{1}{2} \times 11$ inch contact print may contain all thirty-six pictures from a roll of film. That one contact sheet can be examined, marked, and referred to again and again. Decisions can be made before one invests time, effort, and money in enlarging each of the thirty-six pictures. Some are not worth another thought; some can be used in part; this one would look better if we added clouds or cropped the garbage can; this one should be shot again on a brighter day; this one must be printed on a paper that adds contrast; this one should be redone with a model wearing a red hat; this one can be part of a series or a montage. A writer's journal can be made to work the same way. Writers should look over their journals about once a week and bracket ideas that they want to come back to. Then they can expand these, add what they forgot, delete the unimportant elements, rearrange, and write more clearly.

Remember that journals can include all types of writings, and even drawings (figure 9.1). They exist to record important memories and inspirations. Journals are meant only for the author, but he or she should write clearly enough that the notes will be legible at a later date.

A young man, Peter Selgin, says of his journal:

> I can't imagine being a writer and not keeping a journal. I was introduced to journal keeping by an eighth-grade English teacher who became my best friend. The journal is my place for revealing everything. The pages have no lines, no boundaries. I can doodle or write energetically. I can swear; I can yell and scream. I can scrawl huge, angry letters or tight, tiny, insecure words. If my mood tells me to blacken a page with charcoal, I'll do it. If it says, "Tear this page out," I'll tear it out. If it says put in a leaf or a poem, I'll do it. I call them journals, but they could be called "mood books." In their pages I've learned to think less and create more. I've become better at experiencing life and writing.

CAPTIONS

Writing is as much fun as putting mustaches on pictures (figure 9.2).

Adding captions to cartoons, sound/slide shows, and silent movies is a pleasant way to practice dialogue and introduce sequence and exposition. Giving new captions to used commercial cards puts them back in circulation. Pictures cut from magazines can evoke conversations and class discussions from which captions can be extracted and written down.

SIGNS

Signs are usually public, short, sweet, and right to the point. This second grader's note (figure 9.3) was short and right to the point, but bitter.

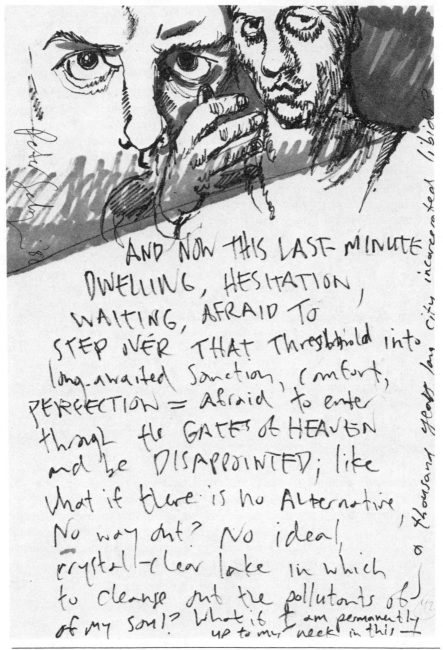

FIGURE 9.1.   Page from a journal

1. The mystery birthday boy

2. Mr. Jones (the principal)

3. [Add your own.]

FIGURE 9.2.   Captions

With maturity the form may change; the idea remains constant. Rub-on letters in Old English type were used in the message reproduced in figure 9.4.

NOTES, LETTERS, AND CONTRACTS

Notes, generally private, informal, and less demanding than letters, provide opportunities for communicating clearly and forcefully. In time, formal letters are sure to follow.

FIGURE 9.3.   Sign   FIGURE 9.4.   Sign

To Momy
I love you
and I by you a gift
Love
Lisa
                    —*Lisa,*
                kindergarten

It takes courage
to talk and to read
and when it was the first day
you went to work.
                    —*Lisa, grade 1*

Mom,
After this
I won't bug ya
but please make
my bologna sandwich
Love,
Lisa
            —*Lisa, grade 2*

Dear Mom,
I had some of the macoroni and cheese
and I hated it!
Love
Lisa

Can I
have another donut
to cheer me up
Love
Lisa

how come
everybody teases me
Yours truly
Lisa
                    —*Lisa, grade 3*

WHAT I WANT FOR MY BIRTHDAY

1. Some Money
2. Some clothes
3. A *real* birthstone ring
4. Rock Candy 1.25 LB
5. Giant BEAR
6. Puppy Calender

FIGURE 9.5. **Note with visual aids**

> 7. My room done over
> 8. Pant suit
> 9. Go-Go Boots
> 10. Two More Pairs OF Jeans
> 11. A couple of dresses
> — *Lisa, grade 4*

Some notes include visuals (figure 9.5).

Parents and friends are always eager to receive notes, and others, years later, may find such material fascinating.

> Dear Mother:
> . . . Well I am still here yet but might go out to night for all I know. I am pretty certain it will be soon anyway. . . .
> Cantonment Insurance Office
> Camp Upton, NY
> May 16, 1918

> Dear Mother:
> Well we are up where the shells are dropping a little ways from us. Once in a while we hear some going over our heads and nearly every night aeroplanes drop bombs near our place where we are all camped

out, but we get used to it and I sleep through it about all the time. . . . We
expect to go in the line very soon which most of us will be glad when we
get a shot at *Fritzie*. We play ball nearly every after noon and the British
soldiers like to see us play. Last night our regiment gave us a concert and
the boys nearly went wild when they started playing ragtime. . . . By the
way did you get the two handkerchiefs I sent you for souvenirs, well here
is another for Mayme. . . .

France
June 1, 1918*

The writer never returned. Can you imagine how many times those lines
were read?

Notes and letters can help extend school or club activities. Invitations
can be sent to authors and various experts to speak or give workshops; directions can be written and sent. When a speaker's question-and-answer
period is too short, writing down and sending him or her questions stretches
the time budget. Follow-up thank you notes are always appreciated, and
they may spark additional letters.

Letters to Santa, relatives, friends, other classes, the principal, the superintendent of schools, the mayor, and celebrities provide useful experiences in composition.

> Dear Bobby Murcer,
>> I have seen you play and I think you are my favorit Yankee.
>> So please send me an autographed picture of yourself.
>>> Yours truly,
>>> —*Andy, grade 2*

Notes can also be intimate and therapeutic when exchanged by friends
in classrooms, by lovers, and, later, by spouses, parents, or children for
marriage and family enrichment. One can write to a parent, spouse, child,
or friend something one might neglect saying to them, and the blank page
of paper will not interrupt, contradict, or sidetrack the writer. The notes
can be read silently, privately, and without interruptions to generate face-
to-face interaction followed by further note writing. "I love you" is often
easier to write than to say.

Writing and passing notes to friends goes on in most classes. It can be encouraged. Parents and teachers have individual and private mailboxes, and
so can classrooms. Everyone should have the freedom and opportunity to
send and receive written messages. Teachers may differ on when youngsters should read them. Anytime? Special mail-call times? Mail time evokes

---

*As appeared in *Clio*, Western Connecticut State College (Fall 1978): 38.

excitement in the armed services or at camp; it can be an exciting part of any school day too. Providing private mailboxes is a natural method of encouraging written communication.

Letter writing is an old art form that should be revived. In addition to the methods described above, letter writing can be encouraged by:

> Publishing a class or school Aunt Blabby column (advice to the lovelorn)
>
> Compiling lists of friends and neighbors in hospitals, the armed services, and nursing homes
>
> Writing to: people in jail, people in mental hospitals, relatives of victims of accidents and disasters, old friends, coworkers, previous teachers, a doctor, a coach, a counselor, relatives, celebrities, politicians, pen pals (in other schools, other states, other countries)
>
> Sending group or individual letters to the editor (of the school or local newspaper) on any subject

There are no limits on the relationships that can be developed through the mail. Tape pals, who use and exchange tape cassettes, are an interesting new variation.

Notes and letters come in many forms and perform many functions. Contracts are a fact of life in our culture. Interest rates vary.

> I Jordy Wolsch
> owe Dad
> A favor.
> > —*Jordy,*
> > grade 5
>
> > Contract
> IOU   June 15th, 1968
> > to Dad
> Borrowed .12¢
> Intrest $.01 (4 milk)
> Owed — 13¢
> > —*Bill, grade 5*

RECIPES

Writing down and sharing recipes can also start the writing juices flowing.

LISA SPEISHIL INGRIDENTS

take a hot Dog
bun slop two
pieses of balony
And then slop tuns of musterd
on the balony
and take a little
fork and a cherry and
poke it on the bun.
                    —Lisa, grade 2

Youngsters usually enjoy rhyming awful recipes, like "Great Big Gobs of Greasy Grimy Gopher Guts." Real recipes can be exchanged by older writers. Like telling jokes, sharing recipes gives good practice in getting all the information in and getting it in the right order.

EPIGRAMS AND MOTTOES

Epigrammatical sayings are small but reasoned voices. They are concise and often picturesque. People sometimes spontaneously express themselves in pithy and practical ways. For example, a kindergarten teacher called on Lisa just as another child asked Lisa for some help. Lisa replied, "I can't go both ways; I can't be two of me." William, a second grader, angered by a series of reprimands, challenged, "Don't push me; I'm not a button."

Epigrams are difficult to compose consciously. A fourth-grade class collected the epigrams written down in class. They called them:

SMALL VOICES FROM A FOURTH GRADE

We often say it's wicked to have the things we want the most.
We often think, I'll get around to it later, but he's sloppy.
We often think, I'm sure, but he's stubborn.
We often think, I'm young, but he's a baby.

Note that these epigrams do not have the spark of those that erupt spontaneously out of deep feelings. Sometimes mottoes and slogans add impetus and direction to prose composition. We are familiar with mottoes like "Be Prepared," and "Always Ready, Always Faithful." Other well-known sayings have come from books, the theater, and the words of famous people.

It never rains but it pours.
All that glistens is not gold.
To err is human; to forgive divine.

We enjoy savoring them and try to imitate them.

The more you put in the bank, the more you'll get.   *—James, grade 2*

Little things amount to big things.   *—Elena, grade 3*

Don't count the chips till everything is tried.   *—Doug, grade 4*

Don't laugh, 'cause everything is possible.   *—Nancy, grade 5*

Sometimes epigrams arise from experience, like this maxim by Henry, a sixth grader: "Don't sweep until the sawing's done." Sometimes they appear in the form of new definitions or discoveries:

Dresses are those things girls wear to school and
church when their jeans are being washed.   *—Henry, grade 5*

The wind sighs its troubles to the trees.   *—Beta, grade 6*

The earliest epigrammatical compositions were probably the epitaphs found on Egyptian tombs. The Greeks also took great pride in the epigrams carved on their buildings and statues. Everyone may take pride in composing and collecting reasoned, short poetic sayings. Unfortunately, spray-can graffiti appear to be our present mode, but we can hope that this stage will soon pass.

Autograph albums may provide composers with an incentive to invent epigrams. Besides soliciting epigrams from friends, collectors can think of a particular person—a friend, an enemy, a famous person—and imagine asking him or her to write something in their autograph books. Anything is acceptable. Results are often surprising: "From your secret admirer."

CATALOGUE VERSE

Catalogue "verse" is not verse at all; maybe we should have another name for it, like "cata-lists." Like slide shows and some television commercials, it gives us a quick succession of flashes that collectively create an impression of the marvelous complexity of the subject. Catalogue verse is a listing of things that have something in common. It is an ancient device used around the world. It has been used in story, prayer, modern song, and the newspaper column. Catalogue verse can be of any length. The imagery, the vocabulary, the sound, and the rhythms all add to the picture created. It is used to inform, teach, convey the flavor or power of something, express pleasure or enjoyment.

The following composition records a second grader's dictated stream of language associations. When read aloud, it conveys his excitement in talking about his great passion—cars. It is an example of the beginning of catalogue verse composition.

hmmm
tires
stick shifts
racing
trophies
hmmm
hub caps
hmm
Fords
winning
pit stops
flashing red lights
ambulances
hospitals
first aid
money
green flags
fixing cars
Indianapolis
Daytona
East Islip
car dealers
Mustangs
Bob Slade's going to
    kill me if my car
  wins
production lines
cuts
smashed cars
racing helmets
goggles
racing gloves

shoulder harnesses
safety belts
roll bars
night
steering wheels
Lotuses
safety belts
time
seconds
numbers
hmmm
grandstands
hot dogs
enjoyment
winners
POWERFUL ENGINE
hmmm
slicks
chrome engine
hmmm
hmmm
tow trucks
enemies
smashups
spinouts
checkered flags
race tracks
dirt
cement
doctors
nurses
good sports

sports
bad sportsmanship
fire
fire trucks
dragsters
hot rods
cars
nuts
brass nuts
weather
people
bandages
beginning of
    transportation
stunts
tricks
tires
engines
models
I'm running
    out of gas
antennae
radios
transmissions
grills
bumpers
lights
red lights
learning
hmmm
hmmm
    —*Jonathan, grade 2*

Catalogue verse can also be written in paragraph form, with items separated by commas or dots: hmmm . . . tires . . . stick shifts . . . racing . . . trophies . . .

FLOWCHARTS

Flowcharts are arrow diagrams that illustrate plans for reaching an objective. They may consist of direct, simple paths or networks of interrelationships. They require thinking and writing.

Flowcharts call for concise language, a careful consideration of alternatives, and decisions on the sequence of steps in the particular event or process to be communicated. Usually the first stage includes a listing of ingredients — as in a recipe. The second requires checking to see whether every ingredient has been included. Third, the steps are put in order and checked off. Finally, the time needed to achieve the objective is estimated.

Not everyone agrees on the symbols used in flowcharts. Those shown in figure 9.6 are common. Some people, however, prefer to devise their own symbols, like smiling or unhappy faces, stars, and bull's-eyes.

Events may flow in a series, be parallel, flow in several directions at once, or merge (figure 9.7). They may also be timed (figure 9.8).

Once the basic symbols are known, flowcharts may be used for simple directions: to show the way from home to school, from school to the firehouse, from the classroom to the boys' room or the principal's office, or to illustrate how to make a peanut butter and jelly sandwich. They can also be used to demonstrate the solution of math problems, report the events in a story or play, or prepare for an examination or project. Professionals, military and political analysts, and business managers compose flowcharts, which are an important element in the Program Plan Evaluation and Review Technique (PERT). School and personal planning could be done this way too. For example, Kathy's flowcharts, shared with the class by means of an overhead projector, helped explain her busy schedule. Figure 9.9 shows how she went about buying a car.

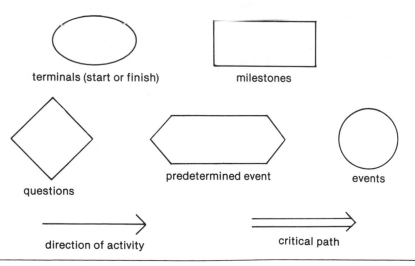

FIGURE 9.6.   Flowchart symbols

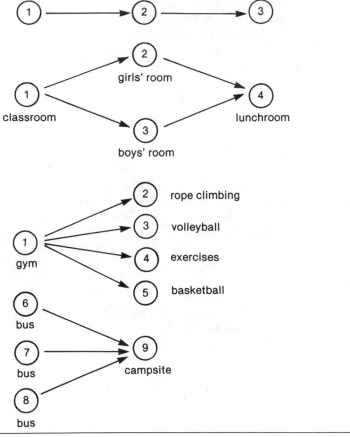

FIGURE 9.7.   The flow of events

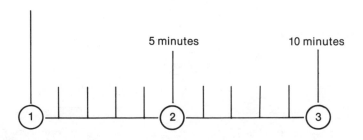

FIGURE 9.8.   The timing of events

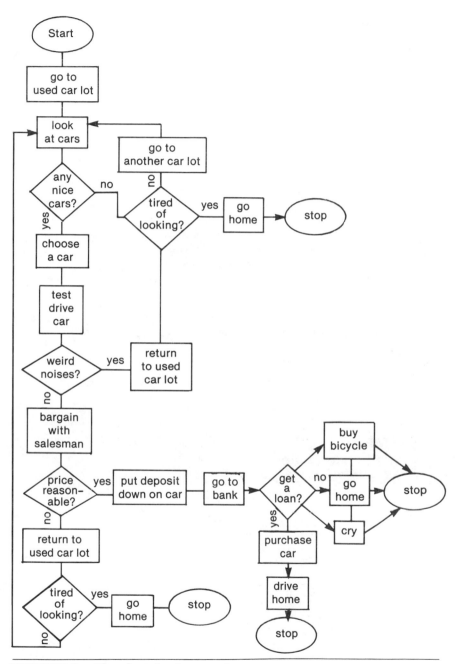

FIGURE 9.9. Flowchart: buying a used car

BROCHURES AND CARDS

Brochures arrive in our mailboxes every day. They attempt to inform, advise, or persuade us (figures 9.10–9.12).

A sheet of paper folded in half or in thirds yields four or six pages for a brochure. Appropriate visuals and lettering help get the message across. Brochures can be duplicated and distributed as part of a larger project: advertising campaigns, dances, football games, school plays, and social welfare programs. A brochure-producing project was organized by Suzanne Wilson and her friends. Suzanne's mother describes its success.

> The TV is gathering dust in our home after school. My daughter and her four friends have initiated a creative workshop after school that encourages writing and oral reading. They made brochures of their thoughts on a rainy day. The used their school photos to "Meet the Author." A child is sick in the neighborhood and the kids taped their original writing for him to listen to. They invited the child to tape his thoughts. They gave their brochures to the pediatrics ward in the Northern Westchester Hospital.

Paper can also be folded to make cards. Lisa, a second grader, created a birthday card that was better than any storebought kind (figure 9.13).

Announcing!
The MASTER OF SCIENCE DEGREE IN EDUCATION
with a concentration in
COMMUNICATION ARTS

For additional information contact:
Coordinator: Robert Wolsch, Ed.D.,
professor of Communications
and Education
or
Dean of Graduate Studies
Western Connecticut State College
181 White St.,
Danbury, Ct 06810

FIGURE 9.10.   A brochure intended to inform

FIGURE 9.11. A brochure intended to convince

FIGURE 9.12.   A brochure intended to persuade

FIGURE 9.13.   Card

SCRIPTS

Scripts use both dialogue and stage directions to represent a mood and a point of view to an audience. The following dialogue comes from a script based on the Book of Genesis. It was used for a Sunday school winter solstice celebration.

Reader 1:	In the beginning
	God created the heavens
	and the earth.
	And God said:
Congregation:	"Let there be light."
Reader 2:	And there was light.
Congregation:	And God saw the light.
Reader 3:	And it was good.
Congregation:	And God divided the light from the darkness
	and God called the light Day
	and the darkness was called Night.
Reader 1:	And there was evening
	and there was morning,
	one day.
Congregation:	And God made the two great lights
	The greater light to rule the day
Reader 2:	And the lesser light to rule the night.
Congregation:	The stars were also set in the heavens
	to give light upon the earth
	and to divide the light from the darkness.
Reader 3:	And God saw that it was good.
Congregation:	So God's first creation was light.
Reader 1:	Some think of God as light
	or the source of light
	and the Bibles as lights
	to light another kind of darkness.
	And there are other great lights.
Congregation:	The stars
	round planet stars
	sun stars
	five-pointed stars
	six-pointed stars.
Reader 2:	Stars that light the heavens
	Stars that lead travelers today
	as magically and brightly
	from mantels and mangers.
Congregation:	Since humans began to reach above themselves.
Reader 1:	The pagans lit their fires
	for warmth
	and to keep away wild animals

	to keep away their enemies
	to keep away the night.
Congregation:	They said,
	"Let there be light,"
	and there was light.
Reader 1:	They also said,
	"Let there be beauty
	and warmth,
	comfort
	and good cheer."
	And they gathered greens from the countryside
	and brought them in
	to their caves and their houses.
Congregation:	And they lit their lights
	and told their stories
	sang their songs
	and endured the darkness.

Scripts can be as simple as the preceding example or much more complicated, with directions for music, photography, actors or readers, sound
effects, and graphics. Script writing requires preproduction planning, logical organization, legibility, and literacy. Experience in writing and reading scripts can be applied to the writing of announcements, commercials,
interviews, stories, reviews, and reports, and to the production of materials
for various media — radio, video, films, pageants, slide shows, film strips,
puppetry, choral speaking, reader's theater, and combinations of these.

Scripts can be used to raise school spirit and combat apathy. Classes can
practice and tape them. Good programs are always in demand.

INTERVIEWS

Interviews usually use someone else's language. The writer need not invent anything but the questions, and sometimes the fewer of them the better.

The jazz trumpeter Clark Terry was interviewed in Danbury by college
students and children.*

Q: How do you produce a shake?
A: You either vary the "chops" — the embouchure — or you move the
    trumpet closer and back.
Q: How do you vary the tone?

---

*Frank Merkling, "Clark Terry: Sounds of the Head and Heart," (Danbury, Ct.) *News-
Times*, 11 March 1980.

A: You keep the vowel sounds in your head: daydle, deedle, dittle, do-
     dle, doodle.
Q: How do you play the blues?
A: You got to bend the tone.
Q: When did you start playing the trumpet?
A: About your age [eleven] on an old instrument.
Q: What are those things the drummer uses?
A: Those are brushes. In a slow ballad you swish them over the head of
     the drum like bacon is frying.

Interviewing, like such other forms of communication as public speaking, oral reading, discussion, and listening, is a way of teaching people. To
obtain specific information one asks closed-ended questions: for example,
In what year did Columbus discover America? Open-ended questions
evoke broader concepts: What conditions led to Columbus's voyages and
the discovery of America?

Ways of listening vary according to the listener's intent. Active listening
is a way to get to more than surface information. The feelings, concerns,
perceptions, and thought processes of the speaker are important to the active listener. Active listening requires concentrated attention; the listener
must work with the speaker.

We have learned the importance of interviews from students in our
speaking, writing, and storytelling classes. Tony came to Bob's office on the
first day of school late in September. "Remember that assignment you gave
in Speech Fundamentals class last year?"

"Sure."

"It was the best thing I ever did. I want you to know I'm glad you made
me do it."

"Let's sit down while you tell me about it."

"I interviewed my Grandma, right?"

"Right."

"I also used open-ended questions and active listening. I've been writing
to her ever since. I never did before; well, maybe I signed a birthday or
Christmas card my mother sent her. I never knew my grandmother. We'd
visit on a holiday. She'd open the door, greet us, maybe pat my head, tell
me how I'd grown, kiss my cheek, tell me she had a big bowl of something
for me to eat.

"I'd get lost watching T.V. 'till dinner time'; we'd eat, do the dishes, and
go home. On the way out the door I'd say 'thank you' for the delicious dinner and the present she may have given me. That's all till next year.

"Last winter holiday, I told her I had to do an interview for a college
class. I wanted to know about her as a little girl and as a young woman,
why and how she came to this country, and some experiences she had here

as an immigrant. We spent two hours together. The next month, I went back alone — just to see her. She's quite a gal. I'm very proud of her now. I write to her, and I visited her again this summer. The interview helped me love my own Grandma. Thanks."

Another student in our graduate class on "Reading and Telling Stories" interviewed her grandmother for ethnic stories that were not written down — the kind that had been told in the family, but only to children.

"I always thought of my Grandma as an old lady who talked a lot and never listened. I brought my tape recorder and focused her attention on stories from the old country. I used two ninety-minute cassettes. I put them together for your class project on ethnic stories, remember?"

"I'll never forget it."

"Well, she died this summer. I've had about thirty requests from relatives for copies of that tape."

The third student was in another graduate class, "From Speaking to Writing." Not fortunate enough to live near a grandparent, she interviewed an elderly neighbor who related his "forty years as a fur fluffer." It seems that Danbury was at one time the hat center of the world. Using probing questions, she learned that it was not unusual there to see people with odd movements, like the Mad Hatter in *Alice in Wonderland*, because the mercury used in treating the fur also poisoned workers. There were jobs to do in those days that only the old hatters remember. Our interviewers are collecting them.

Other old-time residents of the area remember their experiences during the Danbury flood. One student's interview included an account of the New York City fire trucks that traveled all the way to Connecticut to help pump out the town.

Two of our students interviewed relatives who survived Nazi concentration camps. Other students interviewed immigrant relatives who had been Nazi party members, Luftwaffe pilots, or members of the S.S. Some interviewed old sailors who had served aboard four-masted schooners, policemen, clergy, parents, children, and friends.

Being interviewed is often a flattering experience. It can also be a humbling, a loving, and a learning experience, and the same is true of interviewing someone else. Interviewing the writer Isaac Bashevis Singer must have been all of this for L. S. Dembo and Cyrena N. Pondrom, who published the following exchange with Singer in their collection of interviews, *The Contemporary Writer*.

> Q: When you use the words "good" and "bad," you're really using them on the basis of revelation, are you not?

A: No, on the basis of human needs. I mean, you are a good man if you don't make people suffer. This is the only measure; there is no other measure. The Ten Commandments and all the commandments in the world are built on this. *

Interviews of teachers by students and of students by teachers add another dimension to their relationships. Every interview is an opportunity to enhance a person's place in the world, but it is especially true that the dignity of ordinary people is enhanced by offering them an opportunity to talk about themselves, their roles, their trials, and their contributions. Through this mode of communication, we can come to know each other better and identify with family members, friends, or heroes.

BIOGRAPHY AND AUTOBIOGRAPHY

Biography and autobiography (and their subgenres obituary and epitaph) are ways of introducing people. Just as it is easier to introduce someone else than to introduce oneself, it is also less embarrassing to write about another person. Collaboration can be helpful in filling in details for brochures and resumes or relating parts of one's life story. Producing a book jacket for one's own composition or a classmate's is a good exercise in this kind of writing. The following biography was accompanied by a xerox of the author's school picture.

MEET THE AUTHOR

Suzanne Wilson was born in Mt. Kisco, N.Y. in 1969 on the first day of spring. During her childhood she played with her baby brother and her pet kitten, Tiny.

She is the best dodge ball player in fifth grade at Increase Miller Elementary School in Goldens Bridge, New York. Recess and lunch are her favorite "subjects."

Being a member of the basketball team is important to her.

She is a member of Girl Scout Troup # 1013 and likes to go camping in the fall and spring.

Why wait? Composers can devise fitting tombstones and obituaries for friends, relatives, pets, enemies, themselves. They can consider celebrities of today or earlier eras. The project may be serious or just for fun. They might begin with any of the following phrases:

---

* *The Contemporary Writer: Interviews with Sixteen Writers and Poets* (Madison: University of Wisconsin Press, 1972), p. 97.

Life lover . . .
Too soon . . .
We miss you . . .
We will always hear her laughter . . .
So kind . . .
At last . . .

Autobiographical writing does not have to depend upon classrooms and teachers. Retired and resettled in Florida, Bud Mackta recollects his old home town in response to his nephew's interest.

When I was a child, growing up in Knoxville, Tennessee, our town was no longer a frontier town. There were two traffic lights, and the main street was paved. There was a livery stable and trolley cars, and a pail of draught beer could be had for ten cents. There were a few automobiles in town, including one battery-driven car, and that was just about it. Dusty roads and streets were the rule of the day, and during the rainy season these roads became sloppy quagmires. Cotton mills from back East were beginning to move South to avail themselves of cheap labor, not to mention nearness to the source of supply. The news soon reached the hill and mountain folk, and they were deserting their rocky hill farms and coming to town seeking jobs in the cotton mills. They came by the hundreds, flooding our community with jolt wagons pulled by beautiful spans of Missouri mules, coops of chickens, cows, household belongings, and passels of blond, blue-eyed, emaciated "young'uns."

The average pay for a mill worker was about $6.00 per week, but several members of the same family worked, including children ten years of age and sometimes younger.

We lived near the mills, surrounded by disease and mountain people we did not understand; we were different. My mother was referred to as the "furrin lady." The nearest neighbor that shared our foreign culture and heritage lived about three miles away.

Labor organizers began to filter in, and soon there were strikes and lay-offs at the cotton mills. That meant trouble for the commissary. These people still had to live. They had no reserve funds, and the unions were of little help. My mother "carried" the mill workers during these bad periods, and more than once her business was all but bankrupt. These hill people had a certain code by which they lived: "once on strike, on strike they stayed." Why not, as long as they continued to get supplies from the general store. When the strikes were over and the people were back at work, they loyally paid off their accounts, sometimes as little as twenty-five or fifty cents per week, while maintaining their current accounts.

STORIES

Storytelling draws on other skills, like dialogue and biography. The following excerpt from a story composed by a seventh-grade youngster reflects his experiences with people in school and with dialogue in literature.

ELROY

Elroy felt a fist hit him in the chest. He turned around half wheezing and saw Tommy Martin laughing.

"Who did that?", said Elroy.

"Not me", said Tommy, red in the face.

"The heck you didn't!", said Elroy.

"Detention!", was what he heard.

"Elroy, you're not supposed to talk in class", said Mr. Fairchild, Elroy's 7th grade teacher. "I'll expect you tomorrow at 2:15."

"Buzz!" The bell rang, ending 5th period. Elroy ran to the stairs only to have Tommy trip him. Books, papers, tests, and pencils were everywhere.

"I'll get you!", said Elroy now crying, "I'll get you!"

Elroy picked up as many books as he could as the kids kicked his books down the stairs. What a day! He was so sick of this day that he threw up in 7th period all over his desk. . . .

That night, when Elroy went to bed, he thought about Tommy Martin. "I'll kill him!", vowed Elroy, and he went to sleep.

— Dan, grade 7

The development of story composition is analogous to learning to photograph with a variety of lenses — telephoto, average, and wide-angle.

Telephoto lenses limit the subject matter. The composer moves from one subject to another: "Elroy asks, . . . " "Tommy tells, . . . " "Mr. Fairchild hears, . . . " "the kids run . . . ." Some compositions have no structure linking people, ideas, or events, but only separate pictures. Others concentrate on one character or theme: "Elroy felt, . . . " "Elroy said, . . . " "Elroy cried, . . . " "Elroy went. . . . " Each picture can be appreciated as a separate entity. None is dependent upon any other. Any can be left out.

Average lenses can show some relationships between one character and another: "Elroy ran because Mr. Fairchild was angry." Others lead from one character or event to another: "Elroy turned to Tommy because Tommy said, . . . because Mr. Fairchild said, . . . " or "because the bell rang and Tommy tripped." Stories like these can resemble soap operas, where things just happen and happen without returning to the plot or the initiating problem or event; they seem never to end.

Wide-angle lenses capture the larger picture. They show the connection of the characters to the central plot or problem and the resolution of that problem. The storyteller who can zoom to the most appropriate schema and language for his or her material and audience is well equipped and bound to be successful.

Another way to look at stories is described by Carol Westby and A. N. Applebee. They proposed that six levels of narrative structure can be seen in children's stories as their powers of composition develop. These levels may be defined and applied to Elroy's story as follows:

> Level 0: *Heaps*. The story consists of ideas or events with no linking structure or central core: "Elroy says, . . . " "Tommy tells, . . . " "Mr. Fairchild hears, . . . " "The kids run, . . . "
>
> Level 1: *Sequential*. The story has a central core, character, or theme. Events are narrated in the past tense and with a formal beginning: "One day Elroy felt, . . . " "Elroy said, . . . " "Elroy heard, . . . " "Elroy cried, ..." Each frame can be appreciated as a separate entity; none is dependent on any other; any can be left out.
>
> Level 2: *Primitive*. In primitive narratives connectives ("and," "because") are used as starters. "And Elroy felt, . . . " "Because Elroy was mad . . ."
>
> Level 3: *Unfocused Chain*. The story has no central core, but the narration proceeds from one event to another. "Elroy turned to Tommy because Tommy said, . . . " "Because the bell rang and Tommy tripped . . ."
>
> Level 4: *Focused Chain*. On this level events do not seem to be caused by attributes of characters; they just happen. Elroy and a succession of other characters, somewhat like Old Man River, just keep rolling along. The story has no ending.
>
> Level 5: *Narrative*. Reiteration is used to connect characters to a central plot or problem. Eventually there is a resolution of the problem that is related to the initiating event.

Setting

The setting comprises the time, place, customs, and social attitudes that constitute the background of a story and influence the decisions made by the characters. For example, Tommy's father owns the mill in which Elroy's whole family works and controls the major source of income in the region.

Beginning

The plot begins with the introduction of a human or an animal who has one or more problems to solve and with some sort of action. The story usually ends when this character's largest problem is solved, and this solution is related to the initiating event.

Point of View

The point of view refers to the author's way of presenting the actions of the plot and his or her attitude toward those actions and toward the characters. Events may be described from the perspective of any character or an omniscient narrator outside the story. Elroy's mother's narration would be different from Elroy's or Tommy's. Sometimes an author shifts from first- to third-person narration to mark a change in point of view.

Plot Patterns

Knowing a variety of compositional patterns (including patterns based on the logical order of ideas and events and the basic plot patterns described in chapter 7) gives Dan and other authors great latitude in deciding which ways their stories can go.

Plot patterns are developed through the series of separate but related situations that a story's characters have to confront. Combinations of incidents and problems make up the story. One of the five basic plot patterns could be used in a story about Elroy:

1. from security to insecurity: Elroy's journey to isolation or some sort of trial
2. from security to a confrontation with evil: Elroy's encounter with a monstrous situation or thing—perhaps Tommy or a police dog
3. from an unfriendly environment to security: Elroy's rescue from a harsh situation, such as a gang of boys picking on him, and the creation of security, perhaps through a new group of friends
4. opposing foolishness with wisdom: a conflict between Elroy's wisdom and Tommy's ignorance
5. a love plot: a love story involving Elroy and Tommy's sister

Antagonist

Plots usually have three aspects — the main character, an issue or controversy, and some other person, place, or thing. In Dan's story, for example,

Elroy is the main character; the issue could be his loneliness or his involvement with drugs; and the other person could be his enemy, Tommy, his teacher, Mr. Fairchild, or a police dog. The author's choice of the person or thing to fill the role of antagonist will influence the plot and its solution.

Character Motivation

Character motivation, or characterization, refers to the means of creating, describing, and representing a character — Elroy, for example. Authors can use his voice and diction, his actions, or what people say about him to help depict Elroy's personality. Elroy may be motivated mainly or partly by his needs for protection, social status, possessions, sensory pleasures, or membership in something larger than himself — a cause (for example, the movement to get Congress to adopt a simplified English spelling).

Theme

A work's theme is the main idea or meaning of the material — for example, the idea that bad guys eventually lose. The theme is the answer to the question why is the author telling this and not some other story? A clear theme helps keep every detail on target.

Language

The language of a story comes from the voice and vocabulary of the characters and the narrator, the rhythm of their speech, and their articulation. Any of these features may be used to establish the mood, the place, the date, and the attitude of the author toward each character and situation.

Kinds of Stories

Several kinds of stories may be used to begin storytelling and writing: adventure stories, animal stories, biography, folk stories, historical fiction, and science fiction. Let's look at Elroy as he would appear in various kinds of stories.

Adventure stories usually include an unusual undertaking with an uncertain outcome, possibly hazardous, involving luck and courage. In an adventure plot, Elroy might be doing undercover work for the local police, attempting to find out who is selling drugs at his junior high school.

Animal stories are of two kinds. One kind — folk tales and fables — humanizes animals; they think, talk, and act like humans. Stories of the second kind treat animals as animals. Fido, Elroy's dog, might have marvelous insights and counsel Elroy on how to get even with Tommy.

Biography is, of course, the story of a person's life. A biography could tell how Elroy grew up to be heavy-weight champion of the world.

Folk tales — fairy tales, myths, fables, and heroic legends — form part of the tradition of a people. People usually remain contentedly in their village and their class. Some, with the aid of miraculous forces, are wisked into the unknown. In such a story, Elroy's magic godfather might turn him into a fourth-degree black-belt Judo champion, enabling him to quickly dispose of Tommy.

Historical fiction uses the people, customs, and language of a previous time and place to entertain. It might, for example, describe the experiences of Elroy, the first black boy to attend Broadview Junior High School in 1942.

Science fiction draws heavily on knowledge of the physical or social sciences. Some authors build their plots around a change in one aspect of life; in their stories everyone is deaf, blind, or web-footed or lives under water. Others describe the life of the future or another planet. A science fiction author might give Elroy dragon breath — the ability to spit real fire which he would only use under extreme circumstances, to defend himself or help people.

Logical Order

The organization of a story is agreed to by both storyteller and listener or reader. "Sequence" or logical order helps the author to organize his or her ideas so that they make sense. A partial list appears in chapter 7.

Cause-to-effect reasoning directs the reader or listener's attention to an event, focusing it on the effect or effects of a certain action. Topical organization focuses on the parts that together make up an event. A chronological narrative informs the audience: "Such and such happened at 12:00. At 1:00 something else occurred, and by 3:00 it was all over." A time sequence often combines nicely with a space sequence: "I left the house at 12 o'clock and arrived at the courthouse at 3:00." Effect-to-cause sequence is the basis for a story that says, "This is the way it is. This is how it got that way." Mystery stories apply the process of elimination: "It can't be this, and it can't be this, and it can't be this. It must be this." A problem/solution story explores a problem and offers a solution: Prince Charming could not find his princess; his solution was to try the glass slipper on all the maidens in the Kingdom until he found the one it fit.

Endings

Something has to happen at the end of a story. The most satisfactory ending is a resolution of the problem by either the author or the audience. The resolution may be expected or unexpected. Some stories require surprise endings.

Listing on a grid or checklist the story elements discussed above can help the author organize his or her ideas and decide how to proceed. Adding and combining these ingredients to cook up stories thickens the soup and provides a vast variety of flavors.

Other authors just write their ideas down, and the elements seem to fall into place. There's no one way to compose.

The "round-up and review sheet" (table 9.1) may be used as a check list by writers, a review sheet by storytellers, and an assignment sheet by teachers.

REVIEWS

Book reviews require original thinking, and not the story line copied from a book jacket often found in book reports. Four questions provide the skeleton to be fleshed out by the writer.

1. What do you believe was the author's purpose or theme?
2. How was that purpose accomplished (or why was it not accomplished?)
3. Were literary techniques used well or badly?
4. For whom is this to be recommended and why?

A teacher asked the class these questions about the story "Cinderella." He expected to hear, and did hear, that goodness will prevail, that the book was about the relationships of stepsisters, stepparents, child labor — even the effects of uninvolved or absent fathers. Who would have predicted that a freckle-faced pig-tailed fifth grader would write, "The author's purpose in writing 'Cinderella' was to prepare a manual on how to get a man." The rest of the three-page review contained glorious details supporting her opinion.

Plays, assemblies, television shows, movies, books, and stories and reports written by friends may also be reviewed. Everyone could review the same work, and each review would be a unique and interesting learning experience.

Following are some excerpts from reviews by two popular Danbury re-

TABLE 9.1.   Writer's Round-up and Review Sheet — Long Form

1. Setting
   A. Time _____
   B. Place _____
   C. Customs _____
   D. Other _____

2. Beginning
   A. Action _____
   B. Reaction _____
   C. Problem _____

3. Point of View
   A. First person _____
   B. Third person _____
   C. Variation _____
   D. Other _____

4. Plot Patterns
   A. Insecurity _____
   B. Confrontation with evil _____
   C. Rescue _____
   D. Foolishness vs. wisdom _____
   E. Love _____
   F. Other _____

5. Antagonist
   A. Person _____
   B. Place _____
   C. Thing _____

6. Character Motivation
   A. Protection _____
   B. Social status _____
   C. Possessions _____
   D. Sensory pleasures _____
   E. Involvement in cause _____

7. Theme _____

8. Language
   A. Voice _____
   B. Vocabulary _____
   C. Diction _____
   D. Rhythm _____
   E. Other _____

(continued on next page)

TABLE 9.1.   continued

9. Kind of Story

   A. Adventure _____
   B. Animal _____
   C. Biography _____
   D. Folk _____
   E. Historical _____
   F. Science fiction _____
   G. Other _____

10. Logical Order

   A. Cause to effect _____
   B. Topical _____
   C. Time _____
   D. Space _____
   E. Effect to cause _____
   F. Elimination _____
   G. General to particular _____
   H. Particular to general _____
   I. Comparison/contrast _____
   J. Problem/solution _____
   K. Cumulative _____

11. Ending

   A. Action _____
   B. Reaction _____
   C. Resolution of initial problem _____

viewers, Millie and Morton Siegel, illustrating their responses to our four questions.

Question 1: What was the composer's purpose?

A BOOK

The author has been criticized for writing only about the upper middle class WASP. But this is the life style he knows and understands — the cocktail drinking, chain smoking suburbanite, searching for happiness, satisfaction and self-esteem.

Cheever says in his preface that his stories hold memories "of the women and men I have loved and the rooms and corridors and beaches where the stories were written."

A FILM

This week's presentation of Robert Anderson's "I Never Sang for My Father" is a change of pace from slapstick farces and sex comedies. This serious drama is a sensitive and moving portrayal of an uneasy father-son relationship.

A MUSICAL

A true nostalgia treat is waiting for theatre goers in the Western Connecticut State College production of "Take Me Along."

A PLAY

Robert Bolt's "A Man for All Seasons" is a masterful example of how to make history palatable for contemporary theatre goers. . . . Concern for human rights under law, in the face of powerful ambitions, makes for empathy not levity.

A CONCERT

The opening concert of the Newtown Arts Festival, featuring the New England Conservatory Ragtime Ensemble, conducted by Gunther Schuller, was an excellent example of the belief that instruction can be interesting when properly presented.

Even the most devoted fans of ragtime, and other forms of early 20th century American music, would have discovered exciting enlightenment.

Question 2: Was the composer's purpose accomplished?

A PLAY

It is doubtful the play will make it to Broadway with the imperfections which were revealed last night.

MUSICALS

The entertainment values of this Bob Merrill musical are many, and the Department of Speech Communication and Theatre Arts has put together a presentation filled with delights.

The show is filled with many rewarding and excellent elements but the total impression is that it is somewhat lacking in the elusive qualities that spell "hit" for New York City.

Question 3: Were literary techniques used well or badly?

A PLAY

Much of the premise is plausible, but some of the plot convolutions are far-fetched and a few of the lines of dialogue are utterly unrealistic. . . . The solution is improbable, but possible, and not hinted at previously. What hurts most, however, is the 1930's mystery-movie vintage dialogue that the writers have given some of the characters to speak.

STORIES

It is no surprise that the publication of "The Stories of John Cheever," a collection of 61 of his memorable works, has been greeted by readers and by the publishing world as a major literary event. . . . He writes with sensitivity about love in the suburbs, with nostalgia for rented summer houses and with insight into people adrift in their private lives.

His characters are idiosyncratic but believable. You feel their joy, their despair, their anticipation.

They are not happy stories. Cheever is more fascinated by heroic losers than winners.

He writes of them, and of life, with affection and occasionally the joy of celebration. He revels in sensual pleasures: "the wet leather smell of the loud waters and the keen woods offer a smashing pair."

Question 4: For whom is this work to be recommended?

PLAYS

Audiences, especially younger ones not familiar with the play, will find plenty of amusement in this offering.

[*Sleuth*] is solid entertainment which can be recommended to anyone not familiar with the story.

It is pleasing to be able to report that the youngsters who witness this production [of *As You Like It*] are equally enthralled. The play has always been a good introduction to Shakespeare for the young, and this presentation is fast moving, funny, and filled with memorable moments.

"A Man for All Seasons" offers solid, adult theatre.

STORIES

The collection is the best of Cheever. Those who enjoy his tales will enjoy re-reading their favorites and discovering unfamiliar gems.

NEWS STORIES

News stories require a headline, a lead, and a body. The headline consists of a line or two of large type that attracts attention to the story and makes people want to read it. The lead paragraph or paragraphs tell the essential facts. The body of a news story gives details of what happened, who was involved, and where, when, and why the event occurred (the five Ws). It gives a more complete picture than the headline or the lead paragraph of the story.

Other elements of a news story include the dateline, identifying the city in which the report originated, and the wire service identification, crediting a story to the Associated Press (AP), the United Press International (UPI), or some other service.

Journalists describe their way of reporting a news event as an inverted triangle or pyramid. The most important questions — who, what, where, when, why — are answered in the first part. Details are given in succeeding paragraphs, in order of their importance. News stories are usually cut from the bottom when space is needed for advertisements, pictures, or other items. Every reporter understands this system and knows that if the news story is cut, it will be cut from the bottom or point of the triangle.

Arnold Brackman, my colleague, assigns first-year journalism students to rewrite a children's story as a news event, in inverted pyramid style.

HUMPTY DUMPTY

ENCHANTED KINGDOM (AP) — Famous egg Humpty Dumpty died of injuries yesterday after falling from the east side wall, a Kingdom spokesman announced today.

Dumpty apparently lost his balance and tumbled to the ground, scattering eggshell fragments over several square feet. After being rushed to the Royal kitchen in a cookie truck, Dumpty expired on the operating table while a team of surgeons, and several horses, attempted to "put Humpty Dumpty back together again," a kitchen spokesman said. According to Kingdom officials, there is not much known about Dumpty's background. "He was just there," an official said, "always hanging around."

"He was a real hard-boiled type," another official said. "He was definitely no softie."

Dumpty's remains will be cremated over-easy or poached, depending upon His Majesty's choice. Mourners may call between the hours of eight and nine o'clock in the breakfast nook.

— John Fusto

SNOW WHITE

NEVER-NEVER LAND, Conn. (UPI) — A young woman, later identified as Miss Snow White, was found this morning in a comalike state in a glass box in the Enchanted Forest by Prince Charming, a regional dignitary. Mr. Charming performed life-saving techniques which revived Miss White.

Police arrived at the scene and Miss White told them she ate an apple given to her by an elderly woman passerby when she felt faint and apparently lost consciousness.

Miss White resides in a miner's cabin where she works as a housekeeper for its seven occupants. One of the men, Mr. Bashful, declined to comment.

Police have impounded the remnants of the apple and seek information regarding the identity of the fruit vendor.

Mr. Charming and Miss White, introduced at the scene, have announced their engagement. One of her employers, Mr. Grumpy, said he was displeased but Mr. Happy expressed his joy.

Miss White is the daughter of Mr. Charles King and the late Mrs. Queenie King. The second Mrs. King was unavailable for comment.

— Debra Johnson

GINGERBREAD MAN

DANBURY, Conn. (UPI) — The alleged gingerbread man was finally consumed today by a fox in the Housatonic River after a three-hour search, police said.

Mrs. Evan M. Sigmon of 44 Red Oak Lane said at 2:00 P.M. she was removing the approximately 12 by 6 inch cookie, a surprise she baked for her husband, from her oven when it suddenly jumped up and ran across the kitchen laughing.

Mrs. Sigmon said she cried, "Stop, we want to eat you!" The gingerbread man laughed and replied, "I am the gingerbread man, I am, and I can run, I can, I can."

Mr. Sigmon, gardening in the yard, saw the cookie leave the house. He said he and his wife, both 60, chased it about a quarter-mile but had to stop.

Police reported Dottie L. Nichols, 42, 12 Sycamore Lane, said she saw the gingerbread man at 3:00 P.M. with her horse. She said they appeared to be talking to one another.

Police said another witness, Samuel T. White, 42, 35 Oscoleta Road, heard a similar dialogue between the cookie and a cow at 4:00 P.M.

Taylor said he saw the cookie and fox go into the river together at 5:00 P.M. The fox reportedly escaped across the river.

— Laura F. Linden

NURSERY RHYME

NEWTON, Conn. (UPI) — Pandemonium broke out today at Middlegate School on Cold Spring Road when police arrested a lamb. The lamb had apparently decided to attend classes with his mistress, reported Miss Gertrude Hotchkiss, fourth-grade teacher.

Whitey apparently followed his owner, Mary S. Jones, 10, daughter of John and Evelyn Jones, Huntingtown Road, when she walked to school.

"I did not know he was behind me," said Mary. "I thought I heard something, but I was afraid to look. Those woods are scary."

School principal Hans Schmidt said, "I did not really want to call the police, but we have this Lamb Rule. He is not a bad lamb, as lambs go."

"The children were having a great time," according to the janitor, Joe Brown. "It is going to take me a week to clean up this mess," he said.

John Jones said, "We have had a lot of trouble with that lamb. He just follows Mary everywhere. I try to keep him locked in the barn; I have even found him in the house."

Mrs. Jones agreed that it was a real problem. "I have to vacuum a lot," she said.

— Susan Dugan

REPORTS

Reports, like speeches, can provide interesting and accurate information in a logical form. A report should contain the following elements:

1. Introduction: tell the reader what is coming.
   A. Get the reader's attention.
   B. Consider the reader's concerns.
   C. Describe the subject and sources.
   D. Describe what will appear in the body of the report.
2. Body: tell the reader the facts.
   A. Present the facts in a logical order.
   B. Include appropriate visuals.
   C. Give credit to sources.
3. Conclusion: tell the reader what you have told him or her.

William, aged eleven, was determined to do a report about snakes. Armed with camera and tape recorder, he set off a set off for a museum specializing in vipers. He photographed several exhibits, read the fact sheets on the display cases, and tape recorded his own observations and opinions. At home, William listened to his taped notes, developed his film, read further, and finally felt that he was ready to write his report. He selected his categories, arranged a table of contents, added an introduction, a conclusion, a bibliography, and a cover. He then provided his class with "almost everything you would want to know about the subject." Excerpts from William's report follow. First, the title page:

SNAKES

ALL KINDS

BY WILLIAM

Then the outline:

SNAKES

I. Kinds of snakes (lists and reports)
   A. Non-poisonous
      1. Garter snake
      2. Milk snake

        3. DeKay's snake
        4. Corn snake
        5. Bull snake
        6. Smooth green snake
        7. Hog-nosed snake
        8. Indigo snake
        9. King snake
       10. Queen snake
       11. Reticulate Python
       12. Anaconda
       13. Boa constrictor
    B. Poisonous
        1. Diamondback
        2. Sidewinder
        3. Copperhead
        4. Water moccasin
        5. Coral snake
        6. King cobra
        7. Spitting cobra
        8. Sea snakes
 II. Warning devices
    A. On rattlesnake
    B. On coral snake
    C. On Indian cobra
III. How snakes catch and eat their victims
    A. Stalking
    B. Injecting venom
    C. Swallowing
 IV. Medical knowledge about snakes
    A. Relieving snakebites
    B. How to prevent snakebites
  V. Conclusion

The introduction:

This report isn't about cars, bears, or George Washington. It's about snakes. Why did I write it? Because I like them. Some people like frogs, or horses — I like snakes. The pictures in here were taken at the Staten Island zoo, where the largest collection of snakes in the world are found.

The conclusion:

CONCLUSION

The length of this report was shortened because of delaying factors. Otherwise, it has almost everything you would want to know about the subject.

> I must add that there are people who are afraid of snakes. For one main reason; they see movies of giant, monstrous snakes who make unprovoked attacks upon a helpless girl. Not so. The biggest snake is a python, which is afraid of human beings and is afraid to look at them. Also, snakes with fangs 6 inches long with venom (of course very lethal venom) that will kill you in a second still is not true. If you are afraid of snakes, don't walk in fields, ponds, marches, or even in Central Park. Snakes are everywhere!

The prescribed forms described in these last two chapters are only appetizers for the beginning writer. Composing within the bounds of prescribed forms is a kind of self-discipline that authors need if they are to control and represent emotions in language artfully. With guidance, beginning writers can experience the challenge offered by predesigned forms and know the craftsman's joy in a well-fashioned product.

SUGGESTED READING

Applebee, A. N. *The Child's Concept of Story*. Chicago: University of Chicago Press, 1978.

Brady, John. *The Craft of Interviewing*. Cincinnati: Writers' Digest Books, 1979.

Bruce, B. "What Makes a Good Story?" *Language Arts* 55 (1978):461–66.

Cheyney, Arnold B. *Let's Write Short Stories: A Book for Boys and Girls*. Miami: E. A. Seamann, 1973.

Day, Robert, ed., and Weaver, Gail Cohen, assoc. ed. *Creative Writing in the Classroom: An Annotated Bibliography of Selected Resources (K–12)*. Urbana, Ill.: National Council of Teachers of English, 1978.

Edmonds, Robert. *Script Writing for the Audio-visual Media*. New York: Teachers College Press, 1978.

Freedle, R., and Hale, G. "Acquisition of New Comprehension Schemata for Expository Prose by Transfer of a Narrative Schema." In *New Directions in Discourse Processing*, edited by R. O. Freedle. Vol. 2. Norwood, N.J.: Ablex, 1979.

Maloney, Martin, and Rubenstein, Paul Max. *Writing for the Media*. Englewood Cliffs, N.J.: Prentice-Hall, 1980.

Nebraska Curriculum Development Center. *A Curriculum for English*. Lincoln: University of Nebraska Press, 1966.

Rockness, Miriam. *Keep These Things, Ponder Them in Your Heart: Reflections of a Mother*. New York: Doubleday, 1979.

Rumelhart, D. E. "Notes on a Schema for Stories." In *Representation and Understanding: Studies in Cognitive Science*, edited by D. G. Brown and A. Collins. New York: Academic Press, 1975.

Stein, N. L., and Glenn, C. G. "An Analysis of Story Comprehension in Elementary School Children." In *New Directions in Discourse Processing*, edited by R. O. Freedle. Vol. 2. Norwood, N.J.: Ablex, 1979.

United States Postal Service. *All About Letters.* Urbana, Ill.: National Council of Teachers of English, 1979.

Wigginton, Eliot. *Moments: The Foxfire Experience.* New York: Teachers and Writers Collaborative, 1980.

Wood, Pamela. *You and Aunt Arie: A Guide to Cultural Journalism.* New York: Teachers and Writers Collaborative, 1979.

10 Criticism That Dignifies Composition

> Composers only tell the truth
> as they alone may view it.
> And all they really ask of you
> is that you don't undo it.

How can one learn to remain open to criticism and continue to explore the sometimes dark and awesome doorways to composition? We focus now on ways to receive and dignify compositions and composers. The tactics may vary with the individual teacher, but the strategy remains the same: give helpful, encouraging, confidence-ensuring criticism.

This chapter concerns criticism as a way of reaching out to help others. It is addressed to the teacher-pupil-peer relationship between the first draft of a composition and its final revision. It assumes that there will be a thoughtful examination of the product followed by an appraisal that may be favorable, unfavorable, or mixed. Criticism must stress the positive and successful aspects of a composition; it must never deteriorate into fault finding, censure, or carping. Such behavior by an authority figure may intimidate writers. They will anticipate rejection and avoid it in various ways, including writing only what they can spell or what they think the teacher wants. Too many will sit blocked, staring, with pencil poised, at the blank page or at a phrase. This anticipatory-avoidance struggle is a kind of stuttering for writers. Criticism in this chapter means a way of encouraging a search for value and beauty that adds dignity to creative work.

A DIGNIFIED RECEPTION FOR COMPOSITIONS

After creating something in clay, one has to take the chance that it may explode in the kiln. If we avoid the risk, we are left with a piece of clay. Like the potter, the writer takes risks in order to create products of greater

217

and more enduring value. When people become aware that they can compose with words, they have passed through the first stage — the evocative or vision stage — of composition. Learning precision in the revision of language is the second stage. Finding ways to share those visions — now compositions — with others is the third. Thus, criticism is the last milestone of Stage Two. The composer makes sure that his or her work is ready to be widely shared. As Harold Taylor writes:

> The purpose of engaging the student in the act of writing is the same as the purpose of engaging him in true reading — to reveal to himself what it is he really thinks, what he honestly feels. He is not being taught to write poems, plays, stories, or essays so that he can publish them and be recognized in order to become a writer. . . . In writing, the student engages himself in the discipline of expression; he is learning to know the discipline of an artist by becoming one. The task of writing is undertaken to enable him to become aware of the reality of art, to learn to recognize the truth that is in it, to enter more easily into this form of knowledge for the rest of his life.*

Attitudes that foster dignity are taught through the criticism of teachers and friends. Self-respect and self-development undergird the educational process. Without these, a person cannot fulfill his or her potential. All of society suffers from this extravagant waste.

Approaching the teaching of composition with insight and concern is natural to some teachers. "Who has something for me to see?" asks the teacher, noticing a few writers move away from their papers. "Come up here! Let me see what you've composed." The first three stand at the teacher's desk with their papers. The teacher takes the first one, reads it carefully, and comments on its important and interesting subject or precise use of language or appropriate arrangement on the page. "Your composition is fine. Don't disturb it," the teacher cautions. The next one is told, "An exciting idea! Do you want to work on this viewpoint some more or start another composition?" The third student is sent back to work on his line arrangement.

Another author hands in her paper. The teacher reads on. The line of authors grows, waiting for criticism. When several are finished, the teacher speaks to one privately: "May I share yours with the class?" As he reads an apt phrase, the classmates are encouraged to express their appreciation or offer suggestions. The composer returns to her seat ready to revise this composition or compose another. Meanwhile, the class listens and learns how to recognize and point out what is successful in their own and their friends' papers.

Art and the Intellect: Moral Values and the Experience of Art (New York: National Committee on Art Education, The Museum of Modern Art, 1960), p. 17.

Some people get caught up in the excitement of composition and may compose several selections at one sitting. Others work toward the improvement of one.

Respecting Privacy

Composers care about their work when others show interest and appreciation, but composing is a very private act. Asking authors to share their compositions is, in fact, asking them to expose their real selves. This means that teachers and other helpers must make a commitment to special care for such people. Helpers must prove that they share the author's concerns. If they do, they will begin to see behind composers' public masks. They will realize that composers develop protective devices for their private faces: they hide them, dirty them, wrinkle them, or blank them out. Encouraged by a trusted teacher, they may also expose them. A teacher who asks a pupil to show his or her private face has assumed an obligation to treat the flaws and scars there with the secrecy of the confessional and the sensitivity of the therapist.

A person who is persuaded to offer his or her private thoughts and then finds rejection by word, look, or red pencil may mistakenly perceive those private thoughts as unacceptable. Even worse, some perceive rejection of their work as rejection of themselves.

Teachers who believe that every person is a potentially creative individual handle personal expressions carefully. Primitive as it may be, a person's composition is the best he or she is able to do at that moment. Once teachers encourage their students to be honest, they owe them confidence, respect, and acceptance. To withhold these is to renounce their own word and the composer's faith.

Encouraging Pride and Growth

The main role of the teacher is to encourage pride and growth. These cannot be generated unless the teacher receives the student's offering with respect. No matter how simple or crude the work, the author can feel somehow appreciated when assured by the teacher or a small peer group or both that his or her composition is respected.

There are many ways to communicate positive attitudes about written work. Three common threads linking the reports of successful teachers are prizing inventiveness, using small peer groups, and timing critical judgment carefully. First, teachers must set an example and be inventive in the ways that they promote and reward inventiveness if they wish to draw out the creative. Many, teaching by example, write along with the group. Second, they must avoid acting as literary judges and thereby cutting off too many new buds. They must help writers to help one another by responding positively to what seems successful and asking questions about what needs to be made clearer.

PRIZING INVENTIVENESS.   Styles of teaching vary, but effective teachers are able to show that they prize inventiveness. "Just right," a teacher is heard to say. "Did you have that word handy or did you use the thesaurus?" Another time: "Class, we need a word. Who can suggest one for Andy?" Occasionally: "Ladies and gentlemen, close your eyes. Listen to Helen's selection. What pictures does she paint with her words?" Sometimes: "What an unusual idea," or "I never would have thought of that, Henry." The teacher attempts to treat each work as unique and respond appropriately to it.

USING PEER GROUPS.   A teacher gives individual guidance within the group setting. The teacher may help one at a time, but the others may listen and gather clues and cues for their future work. Sometimes authors may be encouraged to read their work to the class or a small group and obtain help, which the author can accept or reject. This is one way writers may improve their work and retain a sense of pride in and identification with their creations.

TIMING.   Point out only the positive aspects of beginning composition. Early negative opinions often choke off creative growth. Successful teachers of composition understand that when beginners are doing the baking, one may bite into an occasional walnut shell. They do not throw out all the cookies or the new baker.

There is a better way. Many adults have wished that they had waited a while before mailing an emotional personal or business letter. Time may help one notice fuzzy thinking and unreasonable feelings. Composition is so often personal and intimate. The teacher sometimes merely accepts a composition with thanks and keeps it until the heat of self-conscious exposure has passed, which might take a week or more. Some prefer to wait a day or two and then look for particular things: an unusual point of view or an original form.

There are other times, known best by the perceptive teacher, when it will be helpful for the others to hear at once something that is obviously good. But routinely waiting a week or so before offering criticism of the composition has an advantage for the teacher related to the planning of class time. All compositions do not have to be read or criticized immediately after they are produced. If a teacher or group helped three writers each day, each member of a class of thirty could have personal assistance every two weeks.

Encouraging Trust

Writers who have received true praise readily share their papers about their times of pleasure, loneliness, or pain. Those who have been hurt or have known failure may need an impersonal writing box in which to place their work. Many teachers recommend using a drawer of the teacher's desk for this purpose. Some teachers may find "anonymous" writing in their coat pocket, in their mail box, or in their car in the teachers' parking lot.

Teachers can help writers offer their compositional gifts as they would help them present other personal gifts: by tidying them up; suggesting or supplying a suitable box or container; helping them with appropriate wrapping; and proposing methods of delivery. If this can be done for a person going to a birthday party, shouldn't as much be done for someone going to write? Teachers can help writers put their words in order and inspire them to present their carefully carved ideas to others in a spirit of friendship, affection, and esteem.

Writers bring to their writing their background, their confusion, their language. The teacher can help them develop a sense of pride in each aspect of their writing. This is the time when the teacher assumes a new role — the role of editor.

TEACHERS AND FRIENDS AS EDITORS

After the right amount of time has elapsed since composition, the teacher may act as editor. The teacher-editor helps the author select, arrange, revise, and otherwise make the composition into a trim product. Is this honest? Won't the product then be the teacher's?

Professional speakers, reporters, novelists, poets, and writers of all kinds and abilities have editorial assistance before publication. Aren't the introductions of books bursting with thanks to colleagues near and far, to spouses, professors, and secretaries who also helped in typing the manuscript? James Thurber obviously had great respect for his editor:

> Having a manuscript under Ross's scrutiny was like putting your car in the hands of a skilled mechanic, not an automotive engineer with a bachelor of science degree, but a guy who knows what makes a motor go, and sputter, and wheeze, and sometimes come to a dead stop; a man with an ear for the faintest body squeak as well as the loudest engine rattle.

Even though a beginner's work is not for wide publication, neither is it just for grading or practice. It is for learning how to express important experiences and feelings in language that can be communicated to an audience. And by acting as editors, teachers can help beginners to do this.

Like fireflies, beginning speakers and writers may flit from idea to idea, not linking ideas or people or events to one another or to a central idea or problem. Some of a composition's characters or happenings could be left out with no loss to the sender or receiver. Other compositions seem to ramble on and on without apparent motivation on the part of the characters and without a plausible ending in sight. It takes a special friend to help someone who has created these fireflies or broken records to see the material more objectively and improve it.

Teacher-editors do not tamper with creativity. They may never change a word, but they may ask questions and offer suggestions to make the writer's thought clearer. They may also involve the student's peers — a few friends who care enough to respond helpfully.

Suggestions may be made for a word change here, a new phrase or line arrangement there. The composer maintains the right to make the final decision and must not be intentionally or unintentionally coerced. The writers must leave the experience as they entered it — as the only composers.

Citing Errors

Many well-meaning teachers not only discourage composers but deprive them of opportunities to think and learn by their manner of correcting papers. Leland Jacobs taught, first, to put questions and encouraging responses on the right side of the student's paper; second, never to mark a composition with red or blue pen or pencil, which mutilates the paper; and third, not to deprive the student of a thinking opportunity by indicating and naming the specific mechanical problems in his or her composition: spelling, word order, verb-subject agreement, and so on.

When the teacher uses underlining and a light penciled check to the left of the sentence to signal a mechanical problem, the student is required to think about the reason for the teacher's concern. If the student is unable to figure it out alone, friends are to be asked for help. Thoughtful discussion ensues, and learning by discovery is possible. Only after repeated attempts by the author and friends fail is the teacher to be asked.

Then, if the composer agrees with the teacher, revisions may be included in the next draft. The student maintains control of his or her composition and dignity. The teacher has not "corrected" the paper but helped the author to focus and learn.

Increasing Sensitivity to Literary Structure

The teacher or friends can increase a speaker or writer's sensitivity to literary experience by asking questions, adding comments, and criticizing positively.

ASKING QUESTIONS.   In suggesting ways to expand or narrow a topic, the teacher, friend, or peer group may ask specific or open-ended questions. For example, to a composer imagining himself or herself an astronaut in space: What sort of things do you feel when you are there? About an unexpected event: How do you feel about this? On anything: What does this remind you of? Why? Were there any other people there? Was this in the city or in the country? What was the name of the street? What else do you remember about it?

ADDING COMMENTS.   Like open-ended questions, appreciative comments will help writers to think in a variety of ways. For example, on new puppies: "Yes, birth is exciting; there are many exciting things happening." On death: "Yes, it is sad to think about that. There are many sad things to think about." This teaching technique requires both a confirmation of the student's ideas and the suggestion that there are more avenues to explore.

CRITICIZING POSITIVELY.   What can one write or say about a friend's paper that will be truthful, helpful, and encouraging? Some teachers try to make a few positive comments followed by a summary statement at the end of the selection. The sensitive teacher knows how and when to add more direct suggestions for improving writing. In written comments, the teacher can direct attention to three aspects of composition: the felt experience, the form, and the use of language.

Teachers may find the following words helpful in giving the beginning composer positive criticism on the use of language:

> adventurous, bold, carefree, hearty, vigorous, energetic, exciting
> artistic, colorful, original, creative, imaginative, new, dreamy, inventive, wistful
> conscientious, painstaking, clear, complete, firm, solid
> funny, gay, lively, pleasurable, happy, cheerful, playful, blithe, festive, whimsical, jovial
> honest, frank, sincere, truthful, meaningful, sound, ethical
> interesting, engrossing, fascinating, intriguing, absorbing
> rhythmical, flowing, soothing, restful, lilting

> sensitive, tender, warm, gentle, polite, perceptive, sympathetic,
> kind, keen, friendly, trustful, thoughtful, appropriate, cool

Why a list of words? Only to remind us that there are more appropriate things to say than "pass," "fail," "good," and "bad." Suppose one writes "creative" on one paper and "imaginative" on another. Why two words that are so close in meaning? The words are like the writers — similar but different; composers deserve specialization and personal treatment in the teacher's remarks.

It is a joy for students to read on their papers evidence that their teacher cares about them as persons and cares about what they have to say and how they say it. As the students' confidence develops and they become more secure, they can take a firmer grip on their expression. They may then seek help with their line arrangements, word choices, and other techniques. Logic, metaphor, whimsy, wonder, and inventive language are left alone. The teacher helps composers look more sympathetically at what they are trying to do. The teacher realizes that the writers have done the best they can do at that particular time.

At first, the teacher may want to read the material aloud to the composers. Then the writers read it again to see if their interpretation is similar to the teacher's. As long as the teacher and classmates remain on the side of the writer, they can be helpful. They are able to look at the work with an outside view, which, if presented sensitively, can help the author to polish the composition.

Improving the Language

One way of improving the language of any writer or speaker is to point out skillful ways of putting words together. This is more effective than pointing out an error or lack of craftsmanship. The following are some guidelines that teachers and friends may point to when appropriate.

1. The opening line, like a sergeant, orders the direction a composition will go.
2. Poems, paragraphs, and lines in poems and paragraphs should be balanced, like canoes. The strongest words or phrases should usually paddle in the front and the rear; having them in the middle often diminishes their effectiveness. Nouns and verbs are the steaks and chops of language; adjectives and adverbs are the herbs, gravies, and spices. A strong noun or verb adds muscle power; using many spices may be an attempt to cover a bad choice of meats, poor cooking, or immature taste.
3. Using vague, noncommittal language is like marking time: march!

4. The feeling of a word must match the meaning, so that "running" feels like running, and "crawling" feels like crawling.
5. Using unnecessary words is like wearing too much jewelry.
6. Writing and speaking styles, like modes of dress, may add clarity or cause consternation.
7. Repetition, like uniforms or his and her outfits, may be used to underline similarities, but it should not degenerate into monotony or sameness, and it should allow for differences.
8. The necessary transitions should be effective as bridges enabling the reader to move from one place to another.
9. The terms of another art form may be used to improve language. Suggesting a bit of bright red on a gray canvas might help some children more than hearing that they need variety or contrast.
10. A speaker or writer with a meager offering might be asked, "How would you say what happened before or after this?" or "What are the words you'd use to tell where this was?"

Criticism based on these guidelines will be more useful than a mere indication of poor word choice or triteness. Genuine inquiry and advice help people enjoy a feeling of status as composers.

Improving the Form

The following is a seventh grader's description of the sky.

> I looked up and what do you think I saw? A beautiful clouds going through the air. It was so white and puffy it look like a soft blanket in the sky. The clouds had a ring of gold around it so.
> The wind was sing a beautiful sound it was like a very beautiful lullaby.
>
> *—William, grade 7*

The teacher read the composition aloud to the author. William noticed the need for subject-verb agreement and consistency in tense. The youngster suggested some places where changes should be made, and these were underlined by the teacher. After each natural pause, the teacher marked a new line with a slash mark. Checks before a sentence indicated the corrections needed. The selection then appeared as follows:

> ✓I looked up/and what do you think I saw? A beautiful clouds/going
> ✓ ✓through the air./It was so white and puffy/it look like a soft
> ✓blanket in the sky./The clouds/had a ring of gold around it/so./
> ✓ ✓ The wind/was sing a beautiful sound/it was like a very
> beautiful lullaby./

After reading the teacher's arrangement, both silently and aloud, the writer made the decisions regarding the final form of his selection. Here is the result of the teacher's helping a writer to reconsider and dignify his composition.

I SAW A BEAUTIFUL LULLABY

I looked up
    and what do you think I saw?
A beautiful cloud
    going through the air

It was so white and puffy
It looked like a soft blanket in the sky

The cloud
    had a ring of gold around it

so —

The wind
    was singing a beautiful sound

It was like a very beautiful lullaby.

This is an example of the adventure of phrase making. It exemplifies one of the four choices open to the teacher. He or she may accept the work, reject it, help the writer modify it, or prescribe a new form for it, like the tonka. This time the teacher chose to modify the line arrangement. Suddenly the writer is an artist. What a difference a phrase makes!

Improving the Mechanics

The mechanics matter. Neatness, spelling, punctuation, and handwriting have a place, but that place is last. Moving them out of that position is putting the caboose in front of the engine.

NEATNESS. Expecting clean, white composition paper to be returned clean and white after a writer's first encounter with an idea is like expecting Marines in dress uniforms to hit a beach, engage the enemy, secure a victory, and return to the flagship ready for a white-glove inspection. White dress uniforms and white composition papers properly come well after the encounter. Real authors know that.

SPELLING. Spelling, like typefaces or the graphic style of the artist or calligrapher, can add to the message. The word "Antiques" or "Shoppe" over the door sets the stage differently from "Anteeks" or "Shop." The appropriate spelling is the one that will attract the least attention, usually the most common. New, odd, or phonetic spelling will do in early drafts but may interrupt the reader's concentration. Spelling, like pronunciation or any other mechanical aspect of speaking and writing, can aid or deter communication. The sender-writer must consider the audience-reader, make a decision, and take the consequences.

I look forward to the benefits of simplified spelling as I look forward to simplified income tax forms. The burden of making these changes should not be placed on beginning writers and taxpayers. Instead, they will require the work of professionals and politicians, who will not deliver these reforms before your next papers or taxes are due. So, for now, spelling must have a place in the curriculum.

Spelling's place in language study depends upon whether and how much one cares about it. Drills, tests, rules, long lists, treatment of spelling as a separate subject — these are the "spelling demons," not difficult words. Some poor spellers have hearing or vision problems. Other poor spellers just don't care.

Spelling depends upon meaningful word study. It helps if the writer cares whether the reader is able to read his or her important piece.

PUNCTUATION. Punctuation, like spelling, is a part of the larger study of language. Punctuation is used not to provide a basis for grading, but to help a writer make his or her meaning clear, as a composer uses time and emphasis in a musical selection. If the rules are confusing, composers should set them aside, read their work *out loud*, and then put punctuation only where it will help them communicate to the reader the pauses and emphasis that their voices would convey in conservation.

Proofreaders' marks (figure 10.1) may help editors and writers communicate more easily.

FOOTNOTE FORMS. The business of counting indented spaces and lines from the bottom of the page and placing commas here and periods there makes many footnote forms a complicated mystery that requires footnote specialists, just as tax forms require income tax specialists.

Teachers understandably do not expect children to use complicated footnote references. Too many youngsters, however, never learn that copying out of encyclopedias and magazines without giving credit is inappropriate. They soon learn to plagiarize without guilt.

On the other hand, too many conscientious footnoters interrupt their reader's concentration and natural left-to-right reading by forcing them to look at the footnote on the bottom of the page and then return to the text.

&	Ampersand (and)	⊓	Move up
✓	Apostrophe	no ¶	No paragraph
✳	Asterisk	¶	Paragraph
✕	Bad type or broken letter: reset	( )	Parentheses
rom	Change to roman type	⊥	Push down type
⌒	Close up	?	Query author to verify copy circled
⊙	Colon	?	Question mark
⋀	Comma	;	Semicolon
eq.#	Equalize spacing in a line	bf	Set in boldface type
spellout	Figures should be spelled out	≡ caps	Set in caps
!	Exclamation point	ital.	Set in italic type
⋀	Insert copy	lc	Set in lower case
#	Insert space	≡ sc	Set in small caps
/=/	Hyphen	‖	Straighten type
/2	Inferior characters	2	Superior characters
L/S	Letter space	ℐ	Take out
stet..	"Let it stand." Used in margin when copy has been inadvertently crossed out.	tr	Transpose (letters, words, or lines)
⎵	Move down	9	Turn over (letter, line, etc.)
⊏	Move to left	fi	Use ligatures, as fi, fl, ffi, ffl
⊐	Move to right	wf	Wrong font (type belongs to another face)

FIGURE 10.1.   Proofreaders' marks

The footnote also interferes with communication on the writer's side by causing concern about line spaces, punctuation, and other details.

There is a simple way to cite sources that is appropriate even for children. Include the work's title or the author's name within a sentence and add the page number (in parentheses) after it — or put all this information in parentheses. The rest of the information (publisher, date of publication, journal, volume number) is placed in an alphabetical bibliography at the end of the paper:

> Jones said, "Blah, blah, blah . . . " (p. 19).
> Or "Blah, blah, blah . . . " (Jones, p. 19).
> Or "As Jones's *Guide to Blah* says . . . (p. 19)."

If Jones wrote two books listed in the bibliography, the style is:

> Jones said, "Blah . . . " (1976, p. 24).

If Jones wrote two articles that year:

> Jones said, "Blah . . . " (June 1976, p. 28).

This simple reference format requires no footnote numbers, no writing or typing at the bottom of the page, no counting spaces. It is easy enough for children to use, and it is similar to the accepted mode of citation for publications of the American Psychological Association and the American Medical Association and the scientific format of the Modern Language Association.

HANDWRITING. Handwriting, not to be confused with writing or composing with words, fascinates and arouses emotion. It is also a complex expressive gesture that requires communication from the brain to the point farthest from the brain to initiate an automatic movement. Handwriting reveals one's response to internal and external stimulation. Like voice and diction, handwriting, though changing, is unique and identifiable throughout a person's life. It is second only to speech as a means of communication.

Speech pathologists include handwriting analysis in the battery of tests used in some aspects of clinical work. Studying the handwriting behavior of people who have, or are suspected of having, language processing problems is often helpful to the physician or therapist. We can examine handwriting for evidence of problems that also influence reading, composition, speaking, gestures, and listening. In handwriting, as in speech, we can note tensions, delays, lack of clarity, variations in speed, accuracy, repetitions, self-corrections, distortions, blocking, cluttering, omissions, intrusions, irregularities in rhythm, and degrees of muscle strength. It is important diagnostically to know whether someone has a motor control or a sensory problem — that is, whether he or she has the ability to copy a text but is doing so without comprehension. Changes in handwriting, as the result of an injury, for example, are noted in the appraisal of a patient's condition and prognosis and in planning treatment. Handwriting should not be subjected to a superficial analysis based on traditional educational practice.

Individual variations in handwriting, gestures, speech, voice, language, reading, hearing, listening, and vision are based not only on will and practice, but also on individual neurological and muscular patterns. Speech depends upon the brain and nervous system, and the large and fine muscles. Handwriting is the written counterpart of speech.

Scribbling, common to children from ages two to five, is the graphic equivalent of oral babbling. Though only random at first, babbling and scribbling later take on rather stable patterns unique to each person and distinguishable from the babbling and scribbling of others. When established, the pattern remains a sign of individuality and self-expression. We recognize cheerful sounds and anxious sounds, and we recognize expanded and upward lines as cheerful, constricted patterns as anxious, and downward slopes as sad. These oral and written patterns, learned well before school, may remain in each of us throughout life.

Bearing the message from writer to reader, handwriting, spelling, letter forms and the arrangement of words on the page, like voice, diction, and physical gestures, tell much about the sender. The mechanics of speech and writing convey information on three levels: (1) the intended, conscious message; (2) nonverbal, emotional messages conveyed through the voice, gestures, smiles, and frowns: and (3) unconscious, subtle, and recurrent messages, often suggested by slips of the tongue or the pen, that reveal problems that block or filter communication. This third level is often evident only to professionals — speech pathologists, psychologists, and graphologists.

Clearly, handwriting is not a simple skill that can always be improved by more practice, homework, or willpower. Pressure to improve handwriting may have a positive effect, or it may merely evoke anxiety and tension.

Handwriting problems need to be studied and treated as carefully as any other aspect of communication breakdown or difficulty. Handwriting problems have not yet attracted the same attention as reading and speech problems. It was not long ago that stutterers and lispers, the hard of hearing, and people with voice problems, foreign accents, and ethnic dialects were ridiculed. We are becoming aware of our use of sexist language. We realize that communication is a complex process involving intellect, emotions, brains, nerves, muscles, social ties with parents, peers, and others — a personal commitment. Handwriting is not easily or uniformly learned by everyone. Neither are spelling and punctuation. Problems in these areas deserve the same understanding and counseling as any other learning problem.

Yes, the mechanics matter. The mechanics of communication are intended to speed the message to the listener or the reader. In speech, anything that detracts from the message is considered a problem. A speaker who repeats, "Ya know, ya know," moves around too much or too rapidly, wipes a nose, tugs on a girdle, wears distracting clothing or makeup, has a marked lisp, substitutes (w) for (r) or (l), uses unexpected pronunciation or unusual word order, or has an irritating voice quality, volume, or rhythmic pattern may cause the listener to attend to the unusual mechanical feature rather than the message. How many times did she scratch her head or tug on her ear? Such mannerisms are a problem because they interfere with the audience's ability to listen to the message. They are a kind of static.

Writers have the same concerns. The audience — the readers of the final copy — must not be distracted from the message by mechanical problems. Untidiness, poor spelling or handwriting, usage errors, excess words, complicated footnotes — anything that turns the reader's attention from the writer's message may be considered a problem to be alleviated.

Rewriting

To deny beginning composers the first aid of rewriting is a questionable tactic. Scissors are the writer's scalpel; plastic tape or staples are the suture; cutting and reordering is the method of most writers and editors who want to improve written work. Composers should, therefore, write on only one side of the paper. To be effective, writing must follow the thoughts of the writer, but the final copy need not always mirror the order in which these thoughts occurred.

Dylan Thomas, according to his wife, "put so much faith in the Word that he would write and rewrite a line fifty or a hundred times; . . . took so much pride in his craft that . . . he said, 'I use everything and anything to make my poems work and move in the directions I want them to: old tricks, new tricks, puns, portmanteau words, paradox, allusion, paranomasis, paragram, catachresis, slang, assonantal rhymes, vowel rhymes, sprung rhythm.' "*

A recent eighth-grade "convert" to composition reports that his early literary experiences included forced memorization, irrelevant subject matter,

---

*Stanley Kunitz, "The Tumult of Dylan" (review of Constantine Fitzgibbon, *The Life of Dylan Thomas*), *New York Times Book Review*, 31 October 1965.

unstimulated writing on demand, writing only for the teacher, and rigid schedules. In addition, he pointed to the lack of opportunity for rewriting and the premature criticism of mechanics that took the place of attention to the purpose of composition, the language, and the arrangement:

> What soured me against poetry was that in third grade we had a poet of the month, and we had to memorize a poem each week — poems of the "Under the spreading chestnut tree" type. . . .
>
> An important part of getting the class to write this year was assuring them . . . that their poems would not be graded on spelling and grammar.
>
> *—John, grade 8*

After criticism and before rewriting, it is advisable for the authors to read their compositions aloud again. Do they sound better?

As was noted above, reworking should begin after some time has elapsed. Attempts at reworking that are too early often find their way to the wastebasket. Then they must be retrieved by alert teachers and quietly filed away. Later, insights gained from hearing the work of others may help the composer to appreciate this compositional fragment.

In fostering rewriting, the teacher should try to nourish the feeling that the writer may accept, reject, or modify criticism (including the teacher's). A time cushion between the writing and the criticism is helpful to both teacher and writer. Making one appointment for writing, another for criticism, and a third for rewriting provides a natural progression and a dignified atmosphere. There are more opportunities for perception, and teachers are able to organize their schedules more realistically. These are important considerations for the real world of the classroom.

STOPPING.   When do writers stop revising? When the teacher tells them? When time is up? When they run out of paper? When the pencil breaks? When another boy or girl hits them with a paper airplane concealing a secret message? Or do they stop when they have heard enough opinions and come to respect their own composition? The teacher helps authors make this decision, which should be based on accumulated evidence and intuition.

The following short form of the story review sheet (table 10.1) is an impersonal instrument that can be adapted for prose, poetry, or plays. We call it the "round-up and review sheet" — short form (the long form is printed in the preceding chapter as table 9.1). Storytellers and writers can use it alone or with the teacher's help as a checklist before a performance or the preparation of final copy, just as a pilot marks a check sheet before take-off. Narrowing one's concentration to check a word, a phrase, or a sentence sharpens one's focus. An itemized list of missing or problem

TABLE 10.1. Writer's Roundup and Review Sheet — Short Form

SELECTION _____

AUTHOR _____

FORMAT _____

ELEMENTS

 1. Setting _____

 2. Beginning _____

 3. Point of View _____

 4. Plot Pattern _____

 5. Antagonist _____

 6. Character motivation _____

 7. Theme _____

 8. Language _____

 9. Kind of story _____

10. Logical order _____

11. Ending _____

COMMENTS: _____
_____
_____
_____

REPLY: _____
_____
_____
_____

areas in the writing is sometimes easier to accept on the round-up and review sheet than it would be orally or on the composition itself.

Some writers fill in the form before they write; some check off items as they write; and others use it afterwards. Some teachers hand out a copy as a pre- or post-writing assignment and use it during their personal counseling time with the writer. A few use it for grading.

When the writers have decided that they are finished, they should be encouraged to prepare a final copy of their composition. When that is done, the teacher should accept the composition without reservations.

MAKING A FINAL COPY. Final copies depend on the author's intent. If something is to remain a personal composition, the writer may not wish to do anything except file it in its original form. Sometimes, however, writers may wish to put their very best penmanship, punctuation, and spelling on the cleanest, whitest, or most beautifully colored paper available. Sometimes a typewriter or a word processor may be available to them, or even an interested typist. The final form depends upon the intended audience and the composer's estimate of the worth of the piece.

Preparing a final copy may facilitate both the reader's and the writer's appreciation of the composition. Private, first-draft manuscripts are strictly for the writer and the members of his or her classroom family. They may be indecipherable to anyone else. For public purposes, such as displays outside the classroom or school magazine publication, a wider audience must be considered. The composition is then put into the best manuscript form possible, handwritten or typed.

OTHER CONSIDERATIONS IN DIGNIFYING COMPOSITIONS

The Teacher's Considerations

In composition, teachers are, in effect, asking people to expose their most personal experiences, both real and imaginary. The piece of paper handed to the teacher is a representation of the author. The handing in may represent trust or fear, depending upon the composer's past experiences. A teacher must ask himself or herself, "Will what I do help the pupils trust me again? Will they be able to learn from me over a period of time? Will they gain trust in themselves? Will what I do help them to see themselves positively? Will it help them look upon their work objectively? Will they learn how to interact positively with more people because of this?" If teachers can answer yes to all of these questions, they have prepared the ground for deeper author involvement in the evaluation process.

The Writer's Considerations

Self-criticism begins with the first germ of an idea. Initially this criticism is probably on the unconscious level. Later on, speakers and writers consciously work at uncovering and encouraging their own artistic efforts. From the model set by the teacher and peer group, composers may learn that what interests them can be expressed in a way that is interesting to others; they may learn that their helpers are honest in appreciation of them and their ideas and interested in working with them to improve their compositions. They may also learn that they can try numerous ways of putting their ideas and feelings together with words; they can become more sensitive to their own feelings and more appreciative of the feelings of others — their audience.

Pupils think, talk, and write about many things that would not pass the censors. For teachers to intimate that they will accept only certain kinds of expression makes their relationship with writers precarious. Bathroom graffiti, glandular poetry, and "nyeh-nyehs" often make up a large share of the underground composition program. When these come to the attention of the teacher, usually through the custodial or playground staff, they might be handled like all private compositions and kept private.

Maintaining a Sense of Dignity

Criticism depends upon the strengths of the learner and the insight and empathy of the critic. Helpful, respectful criticism between teacher and student or student and student demands particular understanding and concern for the composer. The example set by the teacher is often followed by classmates in dealing with each other.

For communicators to feel satisfaction with their own language product, they must know consciously or unconsciously how to evaluate it. When their work reveals some facet of their personal existence, the revelation is a moment of satisfaction for them. It may be born out of trust in themselves, in their teacher, or in their peers.

The successful expression of genuine feelings in appropriate language and form is a step along the road to maturity. When people are able to separate their expression of feelings from actual experience, they are growing. The ability to see and represent things from a new angle marks an important level of development. It is for this reason that learning pride and confidence in oneself as a composer is the first stage in this program of communication arts.

Generating Another Product

What is the teacher's role after a composition is completed? What possible experiences will encourage the composer and the teacher to try again? Success breeds success. This point in the communication cycle is a time for the author to reflect on his or her achievement and the satisfaction it brings. Interest in further composition is often kindled by the satisfaction and pride of seeing one's final copy.

The most important thing that teachers can do to encourage further composition is develop the habit of respectful criticism. They must make a point of looking for the feeling, idea, language, or form in compositions.

Composers can learn to do the same for each other and for themselves through the example set by the teacher or their friends.

Authors look to friends for inspiration, illumination, appreciation, explanation, and instruction. They do not look for pontification and humiliation. They look to teachers who read aloud or otherwise demonstrate an interest in their writings, rather than to teachers who "correct" their papers. It is important to dignify work by accepting it, no matter how poor, if it is all the composer can produce now. A sense of freedom is equally important. As Leland Jacobs points out, "The reader must feel receptive to the author's ordering of life through the imaginative elements in the writing."*

As the composers' confidence develops and they become more secure, they will compose again and again. They may then want help in learning techniques and skills to facilitate their writing. Their private feelings and their expressions of these feelings must, however, be left alone.

Teachers stimulate people to write something that others can read and understand by giving imaginative assignments, receiving them graciously, and helping composers to value the work of their classmates. These are the teachers who keep files of students' writings and can point to improvements in their ability to handle well-developed ideas with ease and clarity. Students are spurred toward further self-appraisal when their work is appraised constructively.

Artists do not always know the value of what they have produced. Teachers can help them comprehend their accomplishments by asking the following questions, even of beginners:

> What is it about this that I like?
> Did it say what I wanted it to say?
> Do I want to share these ideas with others?
> Have others listened?

Self-criticism and self-appraisal are appropriate for middle graders.

> Did I get my ideas across to my listeners or readers?
> Can I read this without interruption?
> Is it in the best form for my listeners or readers to appreciate what I have to say?
> What can I do to make it better?

As communicators mature, their ability to question the specific language, unity, simplicity, beauty, or form of their own compositions will evolve. In ways the maturing authors can understand, teachers can pose other questions.

---

*Leland Jacobs, "More Than Words," *Childhood Education* 37 (1960): 160–62.

> Is the idea too common, prosaic, or trite?
> Is the work too long and diffuse?
> Does it start well but fizzle toward the middle or end?
> Is it too flowery or moralistic?
> Is it lacking in imagery?
> Is it too repetitious in rhythm, rhyme, or meter?
> Are all the elements appropriate to the subject?
> Can all the scene be experienced by the reader or the listener?

We trust teachers who prove that they know we are not mere containers of information, attitudes, and emotions stored for use in college or beyond. Many teachers realize that students already have all the qualities necessary for worthwhile productions. But people require evidence of their worth. If teachers expect pupils to aspire to greater things, a realistic appraisal must be made of their present achievements. We have to believe that what we have done today is useful in order to plan for what we may do and become tomorrow.

Evaluation is a serious and complex process. Expecting people to change without telling them why they should is asking them to act like leaves blown in the wind. In order to change the communication habits of others, we must try to understand our own. In order to change things in ourselves, we must try to understand our own limitations.

> Which of our own aspirations for others
> cannot be fulfilled?
> We may need to renounce our own errors.
> We may need to remove commitments
> that no longer nourish others
> but, unintentionally, hurt them.
> We may need to give our energies and our will
> to deeds that will fulfill
> us *and* our students
> and help improve communication.

With this introduction we can proceed to the use of an evaluation sheet — a device to help detect and display the value and effectiveness of an attempt at communication.

Some teachers and peer groups use a communication grading sheet (table 10.2) to summarize their comments and judgments before the final draft is composed. Perhaps this form can be used to re-evaluate the five compositions in chapter 1. Have you or your classmates changed your judgments? If so, why?

Symbols (plus or minus, check marks), letters (A to E), and numbers (0 to 5, 0 to 20, or 1 to 100) can be used to assign values to different features of a composition. Some teachers prefer to use a brief verbal description

TABLE 10.2. Communication Grading Sheet

	E 0–9	D 10–12	C 13–15	B 16–17	B + 18–19	A 20
Feeling/ Ideas						
Language						
Form/ Organization						
Effect on audience						
Mechanics						
				Grade =	Total =	

("static," "less effective," "fair," "effective," "helpful," "memorable") in order to get away from the grading process. The communication grid can be used for evaluation in several ways.

1. With letters, numbers, or other symbols in the column heads, the teacher can use xs or a bar graph to display the various strengths and weaknesses of a composition.
2. Teachers can flesh out letter or number grades with brief verbal comments. For example, a teacher can print "trite" at the intersection of "Language" and "C" or "imaginative" at the intersection of "Form" and "A" to explain why these grades were given.
3. The form can be used to grade and compare several compositions or several versions of the same composition. In this case the columns would be headed "Story #1," "Story #2," and so on (or "Draft #1," "Draft #2"), and the teacher would use letters, numbers, symbols, or words in the body of the table.

Note the following items on the evaluation sheet and the evaluations associated with different levels of achievement.

FEELING/IDEAS

Effective: The composition is generated out of commitment, interest, knowledge, honesty. The composer has communicated concisely and clearly. Varied and related types of supporting material (facts in a report, setting and character motivation in a story) add to the believability.

Fair: The speaker/writer may not be believable. Plot or arguments seem vague and not well supported.

Less Effective: The composition is difficult to follow, unsupported, or not believable.

LANGUAGE

Effective: The composer shows interest in using language imaginatively, clearly, and appropriately.

Fair: The language used seemed tired, slanted, commonplace; it was intended to impress rather than communicate.

Less Effective: The language was inappropriate, careless, unclear, or unskillful.

FORM/ORGANIZATION

Effective: Material is in an appropriate and logical format with a dash of creative flavoring.

Fair: The work is conventional, with less important parts stressed over the central ones.

Less Effective: No clear direction is evident; the work appears impromptu.

EFFECT ON AUDIENCE

Effective: The work is original, believable, revealing, memorable.

Fair: The composition is without helpful or colorful specifics.

Less Effective: The composer has achieved less than expected for the occasion.

MECHANICS

Effective: The work is usually correct, with appropriate variations and clear concern for the audience.

Fair: The work is often correct, with some errors that may obscure the composer's meaning.

Less Effective: The work is difficult to follow, and mechanical errors detract from the message.

Finally, hearing and seeing the products of one's peers or composing materials for other people can help renew the composition cycle. Some teachers have turned their classes into newspapers and publishing houses, encouraging small groups to help one another and at the same time allowing their students to write for a real audience rather than a teacher. Offering this kind of help seems more realistic than having one teacher "correct" a whole stack of compositions, a procedure that furthers dependence on teachers rather than independence.

The kind of constructive, peer-oriented criticism recommended here should keep in mind the Oriental concern for helping people save face. It is one aspect of the rhythmic cycle of creativity that includes the stimulation, then tension, commitment, work, and finally the release of fulfillment and celebration. These experiences encourage composers to share their work with a wider audience.

SUGGESTED READING

Ashton-Warner, Sylvia. *Teacher.* New York: Simon and Schuster, 1963; Bantam, 1964.

Elbow, Peter. *Writing Without Teachers.* New York: Oxford University Press, 1973.

Emory, Donald. *Variant Spellings in Modern American Dictionaries.* Urbana, Ill.: National Council of Teachers of English, 1973.

Hawkins, Thomas. *Group Inquiry Techniques for Teaching Writing.* Urbana, Ill.: National Council of Teachers of English, 1976.

Holbrook, David. *The Exploring World: Creative Disciplines in the Education of Teachers of English.* Cambridge: Cambridge University Press, 1967.

Holt, John. *How Children Fail.* New York: Delta Books, Dell, 1964.

Jacobs, Leland. "More Than Words." *Childhood Education* 37, (1960): 160–62.

Lanbuth, David. *The Golden Book on Writing.* New York. Viking, 1964.

Roman, Klara G. *Encyclopedia of the Written Word.* New York: Frederick Ungar, 1968.

Shaughnessy, Mina. *Errors and Expectations: A Guide for the Teacher of Basic Writing.* New York: Oxford University Press, 1979.

Simon, Sidney, and Bellanca, James A. *Degrading the Grading Myths.* Washington, D.C.: Association for Supervision and Curriculum Development, 1976.

Smith, Vernon H. "An Investigation of Teacher Judgement in Evaluation of Written Composition." Ed. D. Dissertation, University of Colorado, 1966.

Stanford, Gene. *How to Handle the Paper Load.* Urbana, Ill.: National Council of Teachers of English, 1979.

Stibbs, Andrew. *Assessing Children's Language.* Ward Lock Educational Publications, 1979, distributed by Hayden Book Company, Rochelle Park, N.J.

Strunk, William, Jr., and White, E. B. *The Elements of Style.* New York: Macmillan, 1972.

Sullivan, Sheila. "Beginning Poetry and Its Survival." *Teachers College Record* 67 (1966): 508–14.

Taylor, Harold. *Art and the Intellect: Moral Values and the Experience of Art.* New York: National Committee on Art Education, Museum of Modern Art, 1960.

Stage Three
SHARING VISIONS
BY READING

Compositions are products to prize and to share. Stage Three deals with ways friends, parents, and teachers can help composers reach out to others through the performance, display, and publication of their compositions. Consequently, this stage of our language sensitivity program emphasizes reading.

11 Sharing as Reaching Out

A composition is the author's own to share, if he or she so desires, with teacher, family, and friends. It helps composers to share the laughter that comes from inventive play with language. Composition provides a way to share secret human experiences, visions of struggles, insights, and fears. Sharing compositions affords classes, peer groups, and families opportunities to call a truce in their pushing and grabbing world to join together and admire something created with words that stirs them.

There are many ways to share compositions. Such devices as repetition, chants, and rhythmic phrases have been used since ancient times and are still used in tribal cultures. In the Middle Ages the ballads of wandering minstrels carried art along with news and gossip from place to place, from the conquered to the conquerers, and from generation to generation. Coinciding with the development of mass communication in the last century was the development of universal education. Learning has become an active-expressive process rather than a passive-receptive one. The learner is now expected to speak up and assume a vigorous role in the educational process. Students too are responsible for transmitting ideas. Sharing their compositions is one way for them to do this.

Sharing a composition with one helper is a relatively private experience. The helper's encouragement contributes to the composers' self-esteem and motivates them both to compose some more and to share their efforts with their peers. Recognition by an appreciative person — friend, writer's club member, teacher, parent, grandparent, or even a child — is important to beginning writers. Appreciation of their efforts by their peers may be even more important.

Peer approval ratifies the teacher's encouragement and confirms the author's ability and effort. Sharing helps composers perceive how their writing brings joy to others. They may begin their sharing with the teacher and then go on to their classmates, peers outside the classroom — a writer's club, for example — and an ever-widening audience.

Leland Jacobs tells of the kindergarten word-painter he observed standing before an easel upon which was a freshly painted, rainbow-colored bull's eye. "Tell me about it," asked the visiting professor.

"It's a letter to my grandma."

"Read it to me."

Starting with the smallest, the boy pointed to each circle and read his letter aloud, with longer sentences corresponding to the larger circles:

> Hello grandma.
> How are you today?
> I'm fine, and so's Momma and Daddy.
> Are you coming to visit us for Christmas this year?
> I hope you come, but this time I want lots and lots of presents.

A composition — a play, a story, or a poem — is a work of art and should be treated as a work of art. It is a kind of art to be shared rather than confined, to be looked at, listened to, and felt by the reader and listener, as well as the composer. It is a product that the teacher and the composer's peers have a role in enhancing. They can help it stand alone.

A composition can be performed like any other performing art. It can be displayed like a picture. It can be published. Composition is a multimedia art with endless possibilities.

SHARING COMPOSITIONS BY PERFORMANCE

At one time all books were intended to be read aloud. Then only children's books were. Today interest in reading aloud is growing again. Varieties of language, voices, accents, and ways of conveying meaning have invaded our lives through radio, television, film, and recordings. The intensity may have diminished our ability to hear, but what we have left is fine-tuned.

Poems, plays, and stories can be read aloud by the teacher, the author, or groups of people (figure 11.1). One selection or several may be read. A number of readings may evolve into a program. Musical accompaniment, scenery, action, and special effects may be added to contribute to the mood and intensify the artistic impact.

Teachers who read aloud effectively add dignity to their pupils' compositions. What could thrill a composer more than to have the teacher read his or her work to the class? Students' work may be included in the class's reading-aloud hour. Hearing their work read along with the works of famous authors gives writers status. Some teachers make a tape recording of the reading, to be used later in class or by individual class members or to be

FIGURE 11.1.   The Wolsch family rehearses a performance of children's compositions (drawn by Chris Durante, 1980)

taken home. Tapes may be shared with other classes in the school or district
or even exchanged with another school district. Some may be appropriate
for faculty meetings and in-service courses for teachers.

Teachers can learn to read aloud effectively with preparation and practice. Marking off meaningful phrases with slashes or setting them on separate lines is useful. It may also help to mark the text for pauses, emphasized
words and phrases, volume, and rate, as musicians and professional readers
do. Teachers should find the practice just challenging enough to make
them sympathize with their pupils' struggles. Perhaps then people will
learn to read aloud to communicate rather than to be tested for speed and
comprehension and rewarded by moving to the next reading level. Perhaps
then reading will be fun as well as fundamental and will become an important part of students' lives. Perhaps then teachers will treat reading as one
part of the encoding-decoding process, one aspect of the cycle of listening,
speaking, writing, reading, and thinking. Perhaps then reading will be
mainstreamed into the curriculum rather than treated as an end in itself
and a cure-all for personal and societal problems.

Marking Directions for Reading Aloud

Look at the "Pledge of Allegiance" written in three ways: first, the paragraph as usually droned; second, the paragraph with appropriate pauses indicated; and, finally, the paragraph reset with each phrase on a separate line for easier reading.

> I pledge allegiance/to the flag/of the United States of America/and to the republic/for which it stands//one nation/under God/indivisible/ with liberty/and justice/for all.//

Notice how much easier it is to understand the pledge when pauses are appropriate to meaningful phrases.

> I pledge allegiance/to the flag of the United States of America/and to the republic for which it stands//one nation, under God/indivisible/ with liberty and justice for all.//

> I pledge allegiance
> to the flag of the United States of America
> and to the republic for which it stands
> One nation, under God,
> indivisible
> with liberty and justice for all.

First note that when people recite the "Pledge of Allegiance" they usually pause eleven times. Why? No one seems to know. Some say because of punctuation; others say because it is easier to remember that way. The result? Lack of understanding and failure to communicate the meaning. No wonder so many are confused. All the meaning has been squeezed out. Reciting the pledge becomes a mere exercise in intoning words in a rhythm that adds nothing.

Now try the other two ways. People of all ages, previously labeled "problem readers" by teachers or by themselves, have little or no difficulty reading aloud the version with one phrase to a line. Hundreds of young people have told us that this format helped them sound interesting to their friends, whereas "the usual way of reading aloud makes me sound dumb." They agreed that the conventional paragraph format was like having too much on your plate: you lose your appetite. We know a youngster who can eat ten hamburgers, but he couldn't eat them if they were all heaped on his plate at once or lined up in front of him.

Phrase-a-line forms are easier to read than paragraphs because, according to vision-training optometrists, eyes can handle the smaller phrases in one sweep from left to right. It is easier to write in this manner too, and hearers find it easier to understand a text read phrase by phrase. This format has been used by speech teachers, radio announcers, and choral-speaking conductors.

Marking directions for reading aloud helps the reader interpret the composition as the writer intended it to be interpreted. In a musical score, the composer or arranger can help the interpreter of the selection with specific directions. There are similar considerations in oral reading. Performing music and reading aloud require variations in volume, rate, emphasis, inflection, and quality, and the timing of pauses. The following list includes directions that can be marked on the oral reader's script. This practice will help them avoid last-minute indecision, blundering, and anxiety. These directions need not all be used for every reading, but they may help readers to recall and share key aspects of their interpretation of a composition.

VOLUME

pianissimo — very soft (pp)
mezzo piano — moderately soft (mp)
piano — soft, subdued (p)
mezzo forte — moderately loud (mf)
forte — loud, with force (f)
fortissimo — very loud (ff)
crescendo — gradually louder (cresc.)
diminuendo — gradually softer (dim.)

RATE

acceleranda — gradually faster (accel.)
adagio — leisurely, slowly
allegro — fast, lively, brisk
andante — rather slow and even

EMPHASIS, INTONATION, AND QUALITY

change — two thick bars **‖** indicate a change in emphasis or rate
emphasis — sounds, words, or phrases to be emphasized can be underlined one, two, or three times
falsetto — high voice
fröhlich — cheerful
inflection — rising $\nearrow$ and falling $\searrow$ inflection marked before the word affected
legato — smooth and connected; indicated with a curved line
monotone — no variation
pause — between sounds, words, or phrases, a pause may be indicated by vertical bars. A single bar | means a short pause; two bars || mean a long pause; and three bars ||| mean a very long pause (may be used instead of or in addition to commas and periods)

parenthetically — read as an aside

repeat — two dots before a double bar :|| signify that the part before
the double bars is to be repeated; dots on both sides :||: signify
that the parts before and after the double bar are to be repeated

ritardando — retard, become gradually slower (rit)

sotto voce — in an undertone

staccato — abrupt, disconnected, discontinuous

stress — marked just béfore 'accented 'syllable

sustain — sounds held longer than usual; sign is a dot or dots under the
sound to be sustained.

tie — words can also be tied or said together

tutti — all performers to take part

After decisions are made about the phrasing that best communicates the
meaning, one may wish to consider how words or groups of words should
be sounded. Not every word should be spoken separately. We speak, and
should read, in lumps or groups of words, depending upon the rhythm and
meaning we wish to convey. Our language is rhythmic and tonal, filled
with music — jazz, pizazz, and razamatazz. Just listen to the way we speak
and then read the same way.

First, words are tied together when a word ending in a consonant sound
is followed by a word beginning with a vowel sound ("pledge allegiance,"
"flag of") or when one word ends with the same sound that begins the next
("yes sir"). These words *should* be spoken together, just as double consonants within a word should be pronounced as if there were only one consonant. You would not ask someone to pass the but-ter, would you? (Try it tomorrow at breakfast.) That dash between the two consonants is to show the
typist where to break a word at the end of a line. Too many teachers have
misunderstood that dictionary mark and told children to speak the word as
if there were two consonants. Nonsense! By the same token, readers should
not strictly separate one word from the next unless staccato delivery contributes to the beauty or sense of a passage.

Next, try for real sounds in oral reading. To read our language aloud as it
is spelled is to add to communication problems. To pronounce "toes,"
"rose," "blows," and "of" as they are spelled is to speak in a foreign accent.
These words are in fact pronounced in the United States as follows:

     z   z   z v

    toes, rose, blows, of

Here is one reader's guide for the "Pledge of Allegiance." Note that he
has numbered the lines.

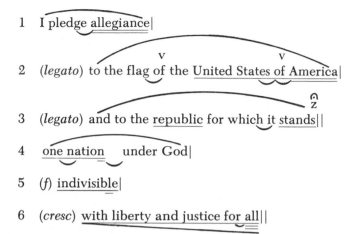

1   I pledge allegiance|

2   (*legato*) to the flag of the United States of America|

3   (*legato*) and to the republic for which it stands||

4   one nation   under God|

5   (*f*) indivisible|

6   (*cresc*) with liberty and justice for all||

Read it aloud the way it has been marked. Isn't this what a musician does when practicing and performing? Why not afford the same anxiety-reducing, communication-expanding opportunity to oral readers? Try it and then notice whether listening has improved. Will writing follow an improved oral reading? You will know only if you try.

Choral speaking wherein people read their original works as a group has been found to be a successful way of promoting the sharing of compositions. Choral speaking can be simple to stage and fun to do. Several types of arrangement are possible. The entire selection may be read in unison. Or each person in a group may have a line to say, with the last line said in unison. In the two-part type, the readers are divided into two groups according to sex or height or voice quality. Question-and-answer poems lend themselves well to two-part readings: the deeper voices ask, "Pussy cat, pussy cat, where have you been?" and the higher voices answer. Simplicity is the watchword for choral speaking. Strong rhythm, clear images, and action should be sought in choosing the selections.

Original compositions may also be used as the prologues or epilogues for other types of performance. A program of individual readings may center on a single theme, such as a holiday, a season, a special event, or a problem. Composers may record their work, as if for a radio show, and use the school's public address system to bring their work to selected classes. These recordings may become an integral part of the district's audiovisual library. They may also be listened to by individuals wearing earphones in a corner of the classroom or in the library.

Compositions may be used to set the mood for a musical selection, just as music may be used to introduce or accompany reading. It was noted above that music can be helpful to writers. Listening to Debussy's *La Mer* inspired Marjorie to write "The Sea" (see chapter 1). Some people write as they listen to music. Music can also help readers. Professional readers often use musical backgrounds for dramatic effect, and yet amateur readers like youngsters in school are expected to perform acappella.

With the right music, we lift the heaviest anchors or send the military off to war. And the music that has evoked a composition can later be shared along with that composition if it is the right music for the audience too. How does one find the right music? One should ask questions, become knowledgeable, and have it available. Ask music teachers, musicians, filmmakers, actors, disc jockeys, radio engineers, skating and gymnastic coaches, dancers, music librarians, and those who sell music, records, tapes, and commercial sound tracks. Music can be taped from the radio or television.

Below is a beginning list of recordings to have available. It is meant to be supplemented as favorites emerge. The collection can be cross-referenced. Categories may include Americana, animals, anthems, children, cities, comedy, cultures, drama, dreams, fairy tales, holidays, love, make-believe, military, parades, nature (storms, pastoral, water, etc.), space, special occasions, sports, supernatural, suspense.

AMERICANA

Copland	"Shaker Tune"
	A Lincoln Portrait
Dvořák	Symphony no. 9
Gershwin	*An American in Paris*
Ives	Last movement, Symphony no. 2
Joplin	"Maple Leaf Rag"
	"The Entertainer"
Schuman	*New England Triptych*

ANIMALS AND CIRCUS

Copland	*Circus Music*
Donaldson	*Under the Big Top*
Saint-Saens	*Carnival of the Animals*
Stravinsky	"Circus Polka"
	Petrouchka

DANCES

Borodin	Polovetsian Dances
Brahms	Hungarian Dance no. 5
Copland	"Hoe-Down"

Khachaturian	Russian Dance (*Gayané* Suite no. 2)
	Armenian Dance
	Mazurka And Galop (*Masquerade* Suite)
Lecocq	Can Can ("Mlle. Angot," from "La Fille de Mme. Angot")
Mozart	Country Dances
Rossini-Respighi	Tarantella, Waltz
Smetana	"Dance of the Comedians"
Vaughan Williams	*Folk Dances from Somerset*
Waldteufel	"Skater's Waltz"
	"Espana Walzes"
Weber	*Invitation to the Dance*

FANTASY

Busoni	*Indian Fantasy* Op. 44
Debussy	*Prelude to the Afternoon of a Faun*
Prokofiev	*Cinderella*
Schumann	*Carnival*
Strauss	*Till Eulenspiegel's Merry Pranks* Op. 28

LEGENDS AND SUSPENSE

Berlioz	*Symphonie fantastique*
Dukas	*Sorcerer's Apprentice*
Liszt	"Mephisto Waltz"
Moussorgsky	*A Night on Bald Mountain*
Saint-Saens	*Danse macabre*
Stravinsky	*Firebird* Suite

MACHINES

Anderson	"Fiddle Faddle"
Honegger	*Pacific 231* (train)
Mossolov	*Symphony of Machines*
	Steel Foundry
Schuller	*A Twittering Machine*

MARCHES

Berlioz	Hungarian March
Prokofiev	March
Rogers	"The March of the Siamese Children" (from *The King and I*)
Schubert	March Militaire

NATIONALISM

Bizet	*L'Arlésienne* Suites no. 1 and 2
Falla	*El Amor Brujo*
Finney	Scottish Dances Op. 32
Gershwin	*Rhapsody in Blue*
Glière	"Russian Sailor's Dance"
Granger	"Londonderry Air"
Grieg	*Peer Gynt* Suite
Honegger	*King David*
Ives	*Decoration Day*
Mendelssohn	*The Hebrides* Overture
Moussorgsky	*Dawn on the Moskva River*
Offenbach	*Gaieté Parisienne*
Ravel	*Rhapsodie Espagnole*
Rimsky-Korsakov	*Capriccio Espagnol*
	Russian Overture
Sibelius	*Finlandia*
Tchaikovsky	*Capriccio Italian*

NATURE AND MAKE-BELIEVE

Beethoven	*Moonlight sonata*
Debussy	*Clair de Lune*
	Nocturnes
	Images Pour Orchestre
Donaldson	*Season Fantasies*
Grieg	"March of the Dwarfs"
Respighi	*Fountains of Rome*
	Pines of Rome
Rimsky-Korsakov	"Flight of the Bumble Bee"
Schubert	Moment Musical in C Major Op. 94 no. 1
Schumann	*Forest Scenes* Op. 82
Tchaikovsky	*Papillons*
	Nutcracker Suite
Torjussen	*Prelude to the Rising Sun*
Vaughan Williams	*A Pastoral Symphony*
Vivaldi	*The Four Seasons*

PICTURES AND PATTERNS

Brahms	*Academic Festival* Overture Op. 80
Liszt	Hungarian Rhapsodies no. 2 and no. 6
Mozart	*Eine Kleine Nachtmusik*

Moussorgsky	*Pictures at an Exhibition*
Rossini-Respighi	Pizzicato (*Fantastic Toy Shop*)
Schumann	*Kinderszenen* Op. 15
	The Wild Horseman

SPRING

Britten	*Spring* Symphony Op. 44
Schumann	*Spring* Symphony
Stravinsky	*The Rite of Spring*

STORM

Wagner	"Ride of the Valkyries"

WAR AND FIRE

Beethoven	Third Symphony (*Eroica*)
Tchaikovsky	*1812* Overture
Wagner	"Magic Fire Music" from *Die Walküre*

WATER AND THE SEA

Debussy	*En Bateau (In a Boat)*
	La Mer (The Sea)
	Clouds
Donaldson	*Harbor Vignettes*
Handel	*Water Music* Suite
Wagner	Overture to *The Flying Dutchman*

Listening to and categorizing music and sound effects is a way of familiarizing oneself with the possibilities for applying music to the communication arts. Discussions follow; writing and reading aloud emerges; and the communication cycle moves on.

Small Group Performance

Small group performances of compositions lend dignity to the work of the individual. Attention can be paid to the diverse ways authors have worked well with language. Small group performances in a class, at home, or with friends allow one to read aloud a strong line or an apt word from the work of a person who otherwise has few opportunities to shine within the group. Such performances also afford opportunities for composers to help one another with suggestions for improvements. The selections may even stir others to follow the composer's pattern or cover the same theme in a different form.

Assembly Performance

Teachers should be on the alert for compositions that are suitable for assemblies. Assembly performances do not have to be dramatic auditorium productions. They may be readings in the classroom, the cafeteria, the library, the schoolyard, the town park, a nursing home, or a hospital — anyplace where some teachers and composers can share their compositions with other groups. Like strolling players, they can perform their work in a variety of places.

Pleasantly surprising was the response of the fourth, fifth, and sixth grades in one elementary school to the announcement of the formation of a writer's club. Those interested met once a week during the second half of their lunch period (normally used for outside play) in the school auditorium, where they wrote, criticized helpfully, and used pantomime, dance, and music to interpret their written compositions. Choral speaking in the spirit of a Greek chorus added to the dignity of several of the selections.

Nancy wrote a short selection for the club meeting one week. The teacher read it aloud to the club members.

> The last snowflake fell
> The new fallen snow sparkled
> as the night crept on.
>   — *Nancy, grade 5*

"Turn on the blue lights, and read it again," a club member suggested. The teacher read aloud under the blue light.

"Can we act it out?" asked a small voice. The teacher read aloud under the blue light while boys and girls turned, leaped, spun, fell, stretched out their arms, and tip-toed off the stage.

"Can we say it too?" asked a fifth-grade boy. The teacher kept quiet this time as the children turned, leaped, spun, fell, and stretched out their arms while they spoke the lines in chorus. Their voices became a single whisper as they tip-toed off the blue-lit stage.

"Can I add some music?" asked another fifth-grade boy. "It's a practice exercise that I've been doing on the piano. This reminds me of it."

"Go ahead." The youngster played.

"Too fast." He played again.

"Start fast and end slowly." He played again.

"Yes, yes, that's just right."

The bell rang. The children ran to their classrooms. Everyone was back the next week to put it all together, and perhaps hear another composition by a friend.

A third-grade teacher combined several arts for a meaningful assembly program that climaxed in a performance in the auditorium before the entire school. After covering a social studies unit on Manhattan that included a bus trip to the big city, a discussion of city problems, and playing city-type games, a teacher read to her class Henry James's simile "the skyscrapers are like gigantic pins in a cushion." Each child wrote a one-line description of New York City. Later they elaborated on their original first lines. Demi's poem looked like this:

MANHATTAN

An island of beauty,
An island of adventure,
An island of skyscrapers,
An Empire island,
A Dutch island,
A big island,
An old island,
A good island,
An island of people,
An island of fun,
An island of joy,
An island of pets,
An island of illions of things!!
                        — Demi, grade 3

Audiovisual aids added sensory pleasures to the compositions. Each child illustrated his or her writing with simple line drawings that, together with the composition, were transferred to plastic overlays. Five pictures and poems were selected to be projected behind and through a large sheet suspended above the stage like a movie screen. During the performance the class, standing just below the projected pictures, spoke the original selections in chorus as each picture was projected.

Printed programs, including the compositions, were prepared in class. A copy of the program and an invitation to the assembly were mailed home, accompanied by a letter from the teacher that used several extracts to describe the project. Her letter follows:

Dear Parents,

In connection with our study of Manhattan, I put this quotation on the board "The skyscrapers are like gigantic pins in a cushion" — Henry James. After reading and discussing a few more quotations, I asked the children to try to think of some descriptive sentences themselves. I thought you would enjoy some.

A skyscraper looks like ninety thumbtacks at night — *Kenneth*
Manhattan looks like a big lily floating in the water — *Louis*
The buildings look like shining silver — *Jim*
The bridges lighted look like beads — *Susan*
Manhattan looks like a make-believe city — *Richard*
The buildings look like giants on a ball — *Susan*
I think the small buildings are children and the big ones are
     parents — *Nancy*
One building reminds me of a bottle of beer — *Donna*
The skyscrapers look like enormous pencils — *Wendy*
The skyscrapers look like floating stars — *Walter*
If you never saw a skyscraper before and you saw one now, your hat
     would blow off — *Billy*
Manhattan looks like an island of beauty — *Demi*

This is an outstanding example of teacher-pupil involvement. In order
to produce this program, several factors had to be considered. What can be
done to enhance the sharing of the writer's feeling? Is movement appropriate? What kind? Should people move or should we use projected images?
Will sound be helpful? Will voices help? Constant voices? Occasional
voices? Voices in chorus? What kind of music? Instrumental? Drums? Records? A soloist? Perhaps the school orchestra? Do we need help from the
music teacher? The speech teacher? The dramatic teacher? How about the
language arts consultant? (In the end this teacher and her class thought it
out and worked to get help from all of these specialists in order to enhance
their compositions.)

Performances for larger groups have a different purpose from classroom
performances. There the individual is not the focal point. The composition
itself and what it can add to the occasion for others is the central consideration.

A poetry, play, or story festival is a natural assembly program. It may involve an individual class, a school, or a whole district. It may include original compositions, read or recited by individuals or groups. An assembly
helps people share common concerns, "spread the word," entertain, and in-
struct indirectly but often forcefully.

There are obviously many ways to share compositions through performance in the classroom or around the school, and there are specific advantages in such performances for composers and audience alike. We want
here to stress the feeling of involvement that develops between the students
and the teacher. Working together, they attempt to share original work in
the way that best elicits an appreciative response from the audience.

SHARING COMPOSITIONS BY DISPLAY

Displays of compositions require exploration for places and ways to show them to best advantage. Displays may uncover new talents and add new spirit to a school, community center, or hospital. Some people may first be attracted to composition by helping with the planning, preparation, and posting of the displays. Others may have their interest in composition sharpened through reading displays of their own works or those of others.

Room Display

Classmates come to know one another as a kind of family. A person's compositional strengths and weaknesses are more likely to be known in his or her classroom than they are in the library or the classroom down the hall. Displaying a selection in a classroom is different from displaying it in the lunchroom or the main hallway of a school or hospital. Room display, like room performance, is a semiprivate affair. In the classroom, living room, art room, or hospital ward, a person's composition is displayed because it is the best work he or she has done. Having a composition displayed is an expression of both pride and hope — pride in the composer's accomplishment (no matter how small) and hope for further composition.

Room displays should enhance the author's work. A corner of the room may be devoted to an artistic display of items like a vase of fresh flowers, a beautiful picture, a piece of sculpture, a well-designed model or mobile, a fascinating example of pop art. Why not compositions? Bulletin boards and cork stripping may be used to display compositions along the walls. Folding screens, wire ropes, mobiles, window panes, and shades can also be used. Whatever the device, room displays of original compositions require more than a haphazard arrangement. All art should be displayed with dignity.

School Displays

There are many places throughout the school to display compositions. Hallway bulletin boards, special stands, and showcases may all be used. The center hall of the school, the library and the hall just outside it, the principal's office, the superintendent's office, and the faculty room bulletin board may occasionally be appropriate for original compositions. Lunchrooms, often forgotten, provide excellent display space. The bulletin boards near or in the cafeteria also offer possibilities.

Students are often heard to exclaim, "Hey, Charley, look at this! That's a neat way to say it." Or "I didn't know Harry could write like that. He's sure a better writer than a runner!" Some supervisors have used the space near the teachers' or nurses' mail boxes to display a pupil's picture or mobile or story for the appreciation of other pupils and the teachers.

School-wide displays are more impersonal than room displays. Their purpose is usually to inform others of the accomplishments of a class and to encourage all who need to be shown that original compositions are particularly desirable reading.

Compositions chosen for school-wide display should exemplify new ideas or interesting craftsmanship. Writing and other creative arts are acquired tastes; excellence and originality must be pointed out in order to help people recognize them. Outside-the-classroom displays provide opportunities to exhibit and promote those acquired tastes.

Public Displays

Displays outside the school — in the local library, hospital, or shop windows — are aimed at relative strangers. Strangers will not search for subtle ideas, nor will they usually have much time to examine a display. This must be kept in mind in arranging the display. Casual observers must be enticed. The display should appeal to their interests and their aesthetic sense. The compositions should have a mounting that provides space and contrast so that they will stand out and insist on being read. Finding appropriate colored backgrounds and titles for displays is crucial. Care must also be taken to ensure that compositions are at the right height for young passers-by who stop to read.

A clear cursive or printed text on clean white paper may be appropriate. Colored felt pens or typed copy, however, may add clarity and dignity, and the legibility of large primer type becomes more important as the distance from reader to display increases.

Writing has always been displayed. Early writing was akin to drawing — a fusion of picture and thought. Pictographs later became ideographs, as in Chinese and Japanese writing. Then came phonetic symbols and, later, alphabets. Writing has been influenced by economic needs, the tools and materials available, and cultural pressures.

There has always been a conflict between the demand for speed and the demand for legibility. Most systems of writing — in all parts of the world — eventually developed two styles: the careful, formal, artistic, often beautiful writing used in important official documents and displays, and the rapid, informal writing used in daily business. Informal, cursive handwriting is to formal, artistic calligraphy what dialect is to literary diction. There is a need for variety. One language is no better or worse than another; each has a usefulness in certain places and at certain times. So too with writing styles. There is a place for artistic calligraphy. The Caroline round hand of the tenth century, the early and later Gothic of the eleventh and fifteenth centuries, the nineteenth-century Spencerian hand, the italic, cursive, manuscript, and Palmer writing of the early twentieth century — each has a history. Studying them is a way of studying history. Penmanship is a fascinating study for art, history, or language classes. If we had, literally at our fingertips, the ability to write in a variety of styles, perhaps more people would enjoy writing and reading.

The compositions for display can also be typed in a pica, elite, or modern executive style, or a large primer type. Typewriter companies have proven that varieties of type styles can make the printed word more exciting. The ability to go from Old English to Italic to Future with the flick of an element is surely one way to make the form fit the function and the display fit the situation.

Teachers should be constantly on the alert for new ways to display compositions. They should also vary the kinds of material displayed. Original class and school mottoes, banners, and songs may be posted and may contribute to school spirit. Writings can be organized and displayed in groups — big ones or little ones, fat or skinny, long or short, soothing or shattering, fast or slow, happy or sad, in invented or predesigned form.

Teachers and composers should ask, "What can we do to enhance this piece?" Does it need a frame, like a picture? What color? What texture? Does it need special lighting? Should it be placed on a wall or a bulletin board, or made into a transparency and shown with an overhead projector? Should it be stationary? (This would be appropriate for a composition or a program about a wall, building, or mountain.) Would swinging it on a string be more fitting for a poem about a butterfly or an airplane? Try sharing writing on posters, photographic slides, book covers, T-shirts, book plates, and bumper stickers. Or add it to photograph albums. Or try transferring compositions to mobiles, plates for mounting, or wall plaques with help from the art teacher. Any other ideas?

One fourth-grade child found a way to put a thought on a rock that the children passed on the way to and from school. The child cleaned a large rock, wrote something on it with a felt pen, and covered the rock with shellac. He had left a token and given the place a name with his offering: "The opera house of frogs."

Displays can be planned and arranged by the teacher, by the composers, or cooperatively. Teacher-organized displays are the most expedient because of the pressures of time and the expense of materials. Displays planned and arranged by composers, however, have additional value. The participants in the preparation of classroom displays have opportunities to learn how to make writing visible and to recognize the accomplishments of their classmates. Cooperative efforts of teacher and pupils also offer many benefits.

SHARING COMPOSITIONS BY PUBLICATION

Publication of original works, in booklets, broadsides, the school or community literary magazine, or the local newspaper is fairly common. This kind of sharing enables authors to contribute helpful materials to the communication program.

Classroom Productions

Writers enjoy reading their own works and those of their peers. It is not uncommon for teachers and counselors to take each person's best compositions of the year, bind them, and place them in the reading corner. Devoting a whole page in the class booklet to each selection enhances its importance. Little compositions, like little people, are just as important as big compositions and big people.

In order to exhibit compositions to best advantage, certain questions must be answered. What can be done to enhance the sharing of the author's feelings? Should a work be handed out as a single selection or as part of a collection? Should a collection have one theme or several? What can be produced in the school or community center? Can we get help from the art teacher, the librarian, or the school print shop? What kind of spelling will be appropriate: old, modern, or simplified? What kind of writing instruments should we use? Will a pencil do? Soft or hard? Will a ball-point pen be acceptable? What color? How about a felt-tip pen? Pens with flat tips? What kind of lettering will be appropriate for this selection: manuscript, cursive, italic, Old English?

Those hungry but wonderful duplicating machines may be fed colored paper or colored masters. Composers may choose their favorite colors or colors appropriate to their themes — winter white or blue, spring green, and so on. Paint and fingernail-polish manufacturers take great care in developing and naming their many colors. Study them. Authors and editors also need time to choose colors. Using just the right color assures authors that their writing is something special.

Some authors or helpers may bind the books with cardboard covers. Others may paint and letter the covers and paste original drawings or wallpaper on the end pages inside the covers. In schools where people regularly compose their own books, they need the help of a book production group. Some work alone; others cooperate. People may type, illustrate, run the duplicating machine, or collate and staple. Each contributor may be recognized for his or her specific assistance on the title page or on a page of acknowledgments. What could be more encouraging than the librarian's arrival to ceremoniously type two library cards with the new author's name? One card will be placed in the pocket of the library copy of the book and the other will go in the official authors' index along with Mark Twain and Shakespeare.

More than one writing club has an author's party each week in the library; several homemade copies of a third grader's new book are available for the author to autograph for friends as they drink juice and munch cookies. Schools with exciting programs fill their libraries with books written by the children. Retirement villages, community centers, camps, and colleges can too. Handmade books often are among the most actively circulated books in the library; authors are so eager to read their friend' works that the books may wear out in a few months.

School Productions

Many institutions — schools, hospitals, community centers — have some form of newspaper or literary magazine. Such publications can be valuable. However, teachers should not be arbitrarily assigned as sponsors, nor should people be coerced into composing for publication. Composition should be a natural and frequent curricular activity, and publication should serve composition, not the other way around.

School and other "homegrown" publications of beginning writers have a purpose and dignity all their own. There is much that is beautiful and worthwhile in original drawings, poems, and other compositions. It is a great mistake to make all school publications look like small editions of high school or college productions. They should have a style and format that are natural and appropriate to the composers' levels of maturity. Although these publications should be as attractive as possible, beginning writers need not be deprived of publication because of meager resources. Local publishers can often be helpful. Contact the high school typing, journalism, and printing classes for student helpers. Parents, friends, and volunteers of all kinds are all around us. Give them an opportunity to be of service.

Older composers will probably be able to handle many production matters, like typing, on their own. Jack Tohtz and John Marsh use this purposeful approach to writing with their students at Edinboro State College in Pennsylvania. Students act as staff writers and teachers as editors for a biweekly publication focusing on the community surrounding the college.

This plan is used by teachers in several schools to produce a monthly newspaper. The paper is part of the daily curriculum, not an extra. Teachers and students work cooperatively. Students are responsible for articles, letters, and advertising. One teacher is the publisher, to whom each department manager is responsible. Other jobs are changed every three months. The newspaper's departments and their functions are as follows:

The *news department* consists of several students responsible for obtaining information and writing news and feature stories.

The *editor* writes headlines and edits stories from the news department for content, grammar, and punctuation.

The *art department* draws cartoons, comics, graphics, and takes, develops, prints, and enlarges photographs.

The *composing department* lays out pages.

The *printing department* prepares and runs a stencil or makes copies.

The *circulation department* distributes the finished paper.

The *science department* covers science projects and scientific news, including weather.

The *advertising department* is responsible for selling and compiling classified advertisements; a separate group may be responsible for display ads. Advertising may be sold to friends, clubs, teams, and local businesses.

The *editorial page* can stimulate classroom discussion and respond to important issues; it includes letters to the editor.

The *entertainment page* considers plays, movies, concerts, and television.

Aunt Blabby answers letters about personal matters.

Kitchen Survival includes recipes and advice about nutrition.

Dr. Jekyll writes about health matters.

The *Locker Room* covers sports.

The *Library Corner* contains information about books, magazines, storytelling events, and reviews.

The *Personal Announcements* cover birthdays, awards, and obituaries.

The *Holiday Time* covers all holidays: national, state, community, and religious.

One issue each spring is planned to coordinate with a subject covered in social studies classes — for example, there may be a Revolutionary War or a Civil War issue. This is a project for the whole school. Each teacher takes responsibility to see that articles are submitted related to the subject he or she teaches.

Composing sheets, or layout sheets, are used to plan each page of a newspaper (figures 11.2 and 11.3). The editor decides how to use the available

Newsroom: 792-1231
Advertising: 792-2399
Circulation: 4,000

THE ECHO

Western
Connecticut
State College,
Danbury

Vol. 17, No. 8, November 10, 1981

Legislators assess both campuses

by Lynne Clarke

Comfortable shoes were a must for Connecticut state legislators on the Committee for Higher Education who visited WestConn's campus last week.

Senators M. Adela Eads of Kent, a Republican, Cornelius O'Leary a Windsor Locks Democrat and Representative York Allen, Jr. a Republican for New Canaan held a press conference in the Iron Door Room of the College Union at 2:45 last Monday, in between the touring of both the Westside and Midtown campuses.

The tour of the Midtown campus, which came after the conference, included Higgins Hall, the gym and locker rooms in Berkshire Hall and the Ruth A. Haas Library. The visitors were appalled at the appearance of Higgins and of the gym area. While in the gym, Eads remarked "We have more facilities and room at our high school."

Eads said it was a "shame" and that such poor facilities certainly couldn't do much for team morale or school spirit, let alone team turnouts.

A member of the entourage remarked, "Let's take care of what we already have ... and beautify this building." (Higgins) The legislators earlier mentioned in their press conference that maintenance and upkeep was a problem which definitely had to be dealt with.

The legislators were impressed by the library, commenting on how well it is built and how attractive it is. They also noted the extreme heat of the building, however. Eads asked, "Is it always like this?" and "Does it make studying difficult?".

President Dr. Stephen Feldman guided a tour of the campus last week for Connecticut State Senators Cornelius O'Leary (left) and Adelle Eads and Representative Yorke Allen (not shown), members on a committee for higher education in Connecticut.

Photo by Lee Bossuet

When asked for impressions of WestConn's campus as compared to the schools already visited, O'Leary said "Sports facilities are not typical of other colleges – of course Central is larger, but the new facilities at WestConn are going to be extremely attractive."

O'Leary said he expects that WestConn's staff has "as high a level of staff morale as the staffs at other schools."

He added that he already knew that WestConn most definitely has a "very enthusiastic administration ... doing the best they can with limited resources."

In response to a question on possible problems which the colleges may face in the future, the legislators mentioned enrollment first.

According to O'Leary, enrollment is a major concern because

continued on pg. 9

Big gain in enrollment

by John Fusto

Since 1962, WestConn's total enrollment figures have made a 500 percent jump, according to Assistant Registrar Henry Tritter.

In 1962, total enrollment, which includes part and full time, graduate and undergraduate students, was 1,501. Last week, enrollment for WestConn's 1981 Fall semester totaled 5,798, according to Tritter.

However, the greatest leap in enrollment occurred from 1962 to 1972, when enrollment was 4,529. Tritter attributed this to "the stupendous growth in higher education" during the 1960's. Since 1972, enrollment at WestConn has leveled off, Tritter said.

This year, WestConn's enrollment showed a 2.5 percent increase over last Fall. Full-time undergraduate enrollment showed an increase of four percent over last Fall.

The WestConn registrar said he believes that there are a number of factors which caused the steady growth of the college, citing the rapid growth of the Danbury area, "reasonable" tuition costs, and the popularity of the college's programs.

In addition, an increasing number of WestConn students are reported to come from the Danbury area. Registrar Robert Drobish attributed this to raising gasoline prices and high tuition costs.

Observers feel that tuition costs at private colleges may have driven students to WestConn. Drobish believes that financial pressure may have accounted for the steady growth at WestConn.

Specifically, female students outnumber male students at WestConn, comprising 57 percent of the 2,915 full-time students and 60 percent of the college's 2,883 part-time students.

It is believed that women are more numerous among WestConn students due to the college's emphasis on programs traditionally filled by women, such as elementary education and nursing.

SGA elections have boiled over

by Marsha Thesen

The controversy surrounding last month's election of a Student Government Association senator last week exploded in controversy.

Marylou Sanders, a WestConn senior, last week charged SGA members used "the system" against her in her attempts to invalidate what she felt was an unfair election.

At the center of the controversy was SGA Senator Cindy Gurski, a senior write-in candidate who won the election with 23 votes.

According to Sanders, she wanted Chuck Hutchins, the only candidate listed on the ballot, to win. When she got her ballot, she said she saw Hutchins name, as well as two spaces for write-in candidates. Sanders said the ballot said vote for three, but listed no other instructions.

Gurski, Sanders said, was standing near the ballot box, and told Sanders to vote for her when she expressed confusion over the write-in candidates. This Sanders said she did because the wording

of the ballot led her to believe both Hutchins and Gurski would win. In reality, the ballot was written to vote for one senator and two alternates.

Sanders said she approached the SGA with several complaints the day after the election. First, she said the ballot was unclearly written, and second, she charged Gurski with violating election guidelines by campaigning within 25 feet of the polling place. However, it was explained to her by the SGA that Gurski had not actually violated the guideline because it does not apply to write-in candidates.

SGA vice-president Mark Block asked Sanders if she wanted to lodge an official complaint. Sanders said she told him "no" when he said he would investigate the matter and get back to her. This, she added, he never did.

Two days after the election, Sanders went to the SGA advisor to officially write her complaint. Here, she said she ran into SGA President Joni Gomes, who said she would speak with Mary Souchuns, chairman of the electoral committee, and further promised that Gurski would not be installed. In light of this promise, Sanders said she cancelled her appointment with the advisor.

Gurski was installed at the Monday meeting of the SGA, but the matter was referred to the student court for consideration. Angered, Sanders said she approached the SGA that Wednesday and was told that the matter had been debated for two hours, but that Gurski had been installed under the premise that if she wasn't, no one could be. Gomes, she said she later learned, was the only one that tried to prevent the installment.

Sanders added that she was further angered because she had not been informed of her right to speak at the meeting.

According to Gomes, the SGA has never had a problem with write-in candidates before. She added that the SGA will revise election guidelines and review the SGA constitution.

"In my eyes, write-ins should follow the guidelines," Gomes said.

Sanders is concerned about the follow up, for as far as she knows the court has not met to decide the issue. "I have heard that with 25 signatures I can petition the court as a student," Sanders said, "and if I can't get them to meet any other way I will do this."

Their day: servers of the colors

by Joan E. Boggs

Veterans Day, the day set aside to honor those men and women who served in the United States armed forces and especially the 2,800,000 killed or wounded in American wars from the Revolutionary War through the Vietnam War, will be observed on Nov. 11.

It was first proclaimed on Nov. 11, 1919 as Armistice Day to commemorate the signing of the armistice on the 11th hour of the 11th day of the 11th month in 1918 which ended World War I, the "war to end all wars." World War I was soon followed by World War II, the Korean War and later the Vietnam War.

On June 2, 1954, President Dwight D. Eisenhower signed an Act of Congress, "to honor veterans on the 11th day of November of each year ... a day dedicated to world peace." Thus Veterans Day came into being with suitable observances taking place annually throughout the country and at Arlington National Cemetery outside Washington, D.C.

WestConn has no observance plans other than cancellation of classes. There will be a ceremony at 11 a.m. Wednesday in front of the Danbury Post Office.

When asked in a recent interview about changing attitudes towards Veterans Day, Dr. Kenneth Young, Professor of History, said that in the post-Vietnam era Veterans Day was downplayed because veterans were equated with that unpopular war and because in some circles patriotism was considered naive.

He said that in this era of renewed patriotism and desire for increased military strength, the Vietnam veterans have been "returned to the fold." In 1980

New business dean calls for interaction between the schools

by Carole Johannsen

Dr. Constantine Kalogeras, new Business Dean.

In an exclusive interview last week, the newly-appointed dean of the business school said interaction is essential between the business school and the community and with the other

schools of the college.

Dr. Constantine Kalogeras, 39, approved last Friday by the Board of Trustees, will take over his new post in January 1982, when the new Ancell School of Business building opens on the Westside campus.

He discussed the coordination of courses between the Business School and the School of Arts and Sciences and said, "You can't have a business school all by itself. A business student who doesn't know about arts and sciences isn't worth anything. We would be remiss if we let that happen."

Future plans for the school will revolve around a consensus, said the new dean. "I'm sure Dr. Feldman has ideas, the business community knows what it wants to see come out of it and the faculty has opinions as well," he said.

"Certain things have to be done," he said to digest the recent grants to the business school. The Ancell building, the Perkin-Elmer computer facility and the library, because of their proximity, will have to be in-

continued on page 4

Half-Mast

The flag displayed at Robert's Avenue Elementary School, across from the college, was at half-mast last Monday and Tuesday.

The secretary in the main office reported that the flag was set at half-mast to honor the death of Jack Schmidt, a local auxiliary police officer. Schmidt suffered a heart attack while working at a football game in New Fairfield.

Funeral services took place last Tuesday. The flag was returned to its normal position on Wednesday.

FIGURE 11.2. Front page

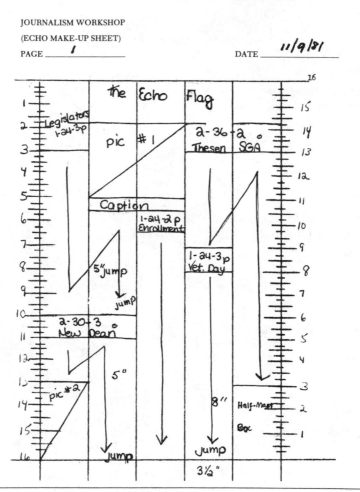

JOURNALISM WORKSHOP
(ECHO MAKE-UP SHEET)
PAGE _____*1*_____   DATE _____*11/9/81*_____

FIGURE 11.3.   Layout sheet for front page

materials — advertisements, stories, articles, and pictures. Each item is measured; a picture may be two columns wide and six inches long; a story may fill eight inches of a single column. The page arrangement is sketched on the layout sheet and sent to the paste-up person.

The paste-up sheet has blue guide lines (blue does not photograph) that enable the paste-up person to get every item perfectly straight. The lines divide the page into two-inch columns with an eighth of an inch space between columns. The pasted-up sheet can be photocopied directly or reduced in size and then copied.

Communication for Real

By the time a youngster graduates from high school he or she should have experimented with a variety of roles in the communication industry. Every student should have done some work on radio, on television, on a newspaper, and in the theater.

Writing and speaking should be for real — not for the teacher or the test or next year's teachers or college or some nebulous future. Communication in school should involve roles actually filled by adults in the communication industry. Schools should be organized to facilitate cooperative ventures in the theater, radio, and television. We have already discussed school newspapers and book publishing, and many schools have such programs. Some have drama programs for a few students. But a few classes or clubs are not enough. Radio and television are a fact of life outside and on the way to and from school. They should be part of the daily curriculum too. Students are entitled to learn not just how to listen, but how to produce. Give students the power of the press and the electronic media as a way of developing citizens who care.

SHARING COMPOSITIONS AS GIFTS

People of all ages often receive gifts from their friends. Sometimes when children gather their lunch, pencils, eyeglasses, milk money, and notebook before setting off for school, they add something to give a friend: a hand-drawn picture, a baseball card, or an extra cookie. These gifts may also include more personally composed material as people and compositions mature (figure 11.4).

Compositions can be delightful gifts. Greeting cards for seasons, holidays, or anniversaries, for family, friends, pen pals, soldiers, or institutionalized patients may be perfect gifts from a writer. If each person in a class or other group composed and designed just one, and made enough copies for all his or her friends, the group could have an interesting assortment for each season, holiday, or special purpose. Writers should be made aware that in composing their serious work they may be creating gifts of value.

With imagination and skill, cards, notes, and letters can be transformed into keepsakes, like those in figures 11.5–10. The card in figure 11.5 was changed by a little painting and the pasting of one card onto another. The note in figure 11.6 was enhanced by a design. The letter in figure 11.7 is decorated with a variety of vertical rainbow-colored stripes. The letter in figure 11.8 began as a watercolor picture, and the message in figure 11.9 will become a mobile. Figure 11.10 arrived on pieces of cardboard. Each part was read and attached to another. The end of the letter became the

FIGURE 11.4.   A composition as a gift

bottom of the box. Each shows creativity and shouts, "I care about you and want you to care about me."

One graduate student, a teacher, confided to her class that she had been worried all her life about what she could do to show her appreciation to her beloved foster father. The class assignment, to interview her father and compile his life story, at last satisfied her need. She amassed a collection of interviews of him and his friends; she used old family photographs, newspaper clippings, and copies of legal documents and alternated these with chapters or passages about his life and concurrent events in world and local history. She had created not only a gift but an heirloom.

Another student found his great-grandmother a font of stories that she had once told her children and grandchildren. Slides of the interview, tape recordings, typed story texts, and the written interview itself became a multimedia production. Copies have been requested by relatives in several countries who wish to share Grandma and Grandma's stories with their own children.

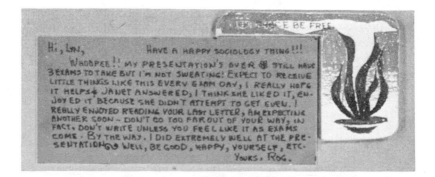

FIGURE 11.5. Decorated card

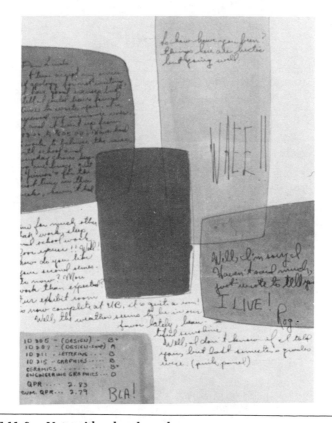

FIGURE 11.6. Note with colored overlay

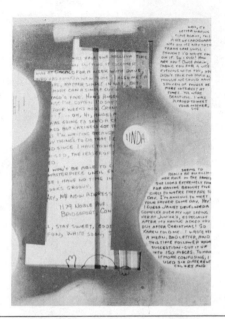

FIGURE 11.7. Letter with cutout and colored stripes

RE 11.8.   Watercolor picture combined with letter

FIGURE 11.9.   Letter-mobile

FIGURE 11.10.   Letter-box

There is so little time to be alive. A sensitivity to real feelings expressed in appropriate and original language is vital to every person's growth. It may begin at any age. It may take longer to nurture the ability to run, to skip, to dance with words in those long deprived of the opportunity. No matter how rich the community, how beautiful the school or center, how efficient the teachers, how loving the parents or children, how tidy their handwriting and spelling, people deprived of a composer's attitude are disadvantaged. Seek them. Find them. Hear them. Help them. Hug Them. They are all around us.

SUGGESTED READING

Arnold, Edmund C., and Krieghbaum, Hillier. *The Student Journalist: A Handbook for Staff and Advisor*. New York: New York University Press, 1963.

Brohaugh, William, ed. *Writer's Market*. Annual Publication. Cincinnati: Writer's Digest.

Burack, A. S., ed. *The Writer's Handbook*. Boston: The Writer, 1980.

Day, Robert, ed., and Weaver, Gail Cohen, assoc. ed. *Creative Writing in the Classroom: An Annotated Bibliography of Selected Resources (K–12)*. Urbana, Ill.: National Council of Teachers of English, 1978.

How To Plan and Publish a Mimeographed Newspaper. Chicago: A. B. Dick Co., n.d.

Jefferson, Blanche. *Teaching Art to Children: The Values of Creative Expression*. Boston: Allyn and Bacon, 1959.

Kinnick, B. Jo, ed. *The School Literary Magazine*. Urbana, Ill.: National Council of Teachers of English, 1966.

Lewis, Richard, ed. *Miracles: Poems by Children of the English-Speaking World*. New York: Simon and Schuster, 1966.

National Council of Teachers of English. *The English Language Arts*. Curriculum Series, vol. 1. New York: Appleton Century Crofts, 1952.

Tohtz, Jack E., and Marsh, John L. "Student as Staff Writer, Instructor as Editor: A Situational Context for Teaching Writing." *College Composition and Communication* 32 (1981): 327–29.

Wyckoff, Edith Hay. *Editing and Producing the Small Publication*. New York: Van Nostrand, 1956.

Appendices
FURTHERING
COMMUNICATION

The origin of writing, cloaked in mystery, has often been thought to be divine or magical. We now know that composition is the artful control of language, a skill that permits a person to look at life from different perspectives and think about it objectively. With composition, as with memories, roses are always available in December. To arrange and rearrange experiences, feelings, language, and forms is an art—there is no one way to do it. Like Japanese flower arrangers, we must strive to become one with these elements—to make them extensions of ourselves. Composition, then, is the ability to use language artfully and expediently to help represent and validate old experiences and make room for new ones. Appendix A is designed to help teachers and others recognize the nature of composition—the heart of communication.

Composition reflects the warmth of the inner light flickering in each of us. It thrives with care. Appendix B demonstrates how the values we cherish in composition are related to freedom of speech and other humanistic concerns.

Jefferson warned that "the price of liberty is eternal vigilance." Composition has only recently become part of the universal curriculum. In many civilizations, it was reserved for priests, scribes, and royalty. To control who can speak or write is easier than to control what is said or written. The danger of such control is real again. Great numbers of our citizens—intelligent, sensitive potential contributors to our hopes and dreams—are not using language effectively in oral or written form. Their effectiveness is diminished. Some educational errors that have contributed to this situation are noted in appendix C. Attempts to change any of these aspects of teaching writing often meet resistance. This must be faced and overcome.

The Nature
of Composition

Composition involves the disciplined ordering of personal experience into language in an appropriate form. Feelings must be converted into language that is coiled, springlike, capable of evoking feelings in the reader and listener. As Leland Jacobs points out in his lectures, composition has five distinct facets: art, force, formulation, process, and product. Each has value and deserves a place in the composition program. People unwilling or unable to stimulate, recognize, appreciate, or dignify the compositions of others have deprived themselves and beginning writers of some of the great joys of teaching and learning the arts of language.

ART

The arts of language — poetry, drama, and prose fiction — are often familiar to children before they come to school. They are not to be confused with such forms and functions of language as spelling, handwriting, and the common uses of language for social and business discourse.

The expedient use of language signs and signals in essays, letters, and reports usually requires attention to literal truth, logic, and syntax. These forms can be combined with greater or lesser amounts of artistic elements. There is, however, another use of language that Susanne Langer calls "nondiscursive." Nondiscursive language is a medium for representing feelings and insights in dreams, drama, fiction, and poetry. The artistic composer uses heightened language to create forms symbolic of human feeling.

All the arts of language are capable of creating new life, or at least new symbols. With nondiscursive language, a child may invent a toy and help someone celebrate a nonexistent birthday. He may create an imaginary grandfather or recreate one who is dead. The arts of language, then, help to recreate experiences, provide meaning, and symbolize feelings with honesty and empathy. By carefully organizing the elements of language, the author creates a balanced synthesis of symbols and emotion — a new life through artistic production.

FORCE

Composition involves force. Since earliest times, artistic forces have mesmerized and stimulated people and made them feel secure, valued, loved, and a part of something bigger — a cause, a movement, a church, a people, a country. This created force, generated by the recurring use of imagery, meter, line, heightened language, and rhyme, is one of the major distinctions between common and artistic language.

Artistic forces may appear magical because they are able to elevate one to a supernatural world. For the moment there is a total suspension of disbelief, a willingness to be transported to faraway places. Verbal magic is not so different from the primitive magical beliefs of childhood — in fact, it may be a remnant of them. A composer's thoughts are more primitive and less self-conscious than most adult thoughts. Because of this magic, language has the power to generate and synthesize sound, sense, thought, emotions, images, and ideals.

The artistic forces we have been discussing begin within the composer. New experiences are woven into stored experiences. Like yeast, recollections and energies begin to ferment and rise, building up pressure. Seeking release, the internal forces increase in ebullience until there is an explosion. The transformation of experience into new thought, fashioned artistically by the composer, produces a language form capable of evoking further experiences and forces within others.

Composition may also create a sense of fulfillment in the composer. During composition, excitement and tension are generated. When the work is completed, feelings of release and satisfaction predominate. Whatever its content, in this sense artistic composition is a force for personal freedom — the force needed by some to reach fulfillment.

Artistic power sometimes springs from a bold style ornamented with colorful figures of speech, and sometimes from ideas vital to the composer and generated by genuine feelings. Whatever their origin or classification, artistic forces move us to action. They bind people to people, people to their gods, and both to eternity. Conductors of artistic forces are available to us. They remain tethered, waiting to be released, loaded with connotations and denotations, packed with associations and emotions. They can be harnessed and put to work.

FORMULATION

Composition is an experience in creating a new life from the speaker's or writer's personal perceptions, thoughts, and feelings. This offspring is an independent formulation of personal seed and labor. The writer-speaker organizes experience and gives it a representational life of its own. The composer then becomes a compositional creator.

Formulations may evolve from a flash of understanding or a nonrational identification or articulation of feelings. These are developed and shared through the use of language. Like photographers, authors may make them crystal clear by filtering out extraneous reality or using a variety of intellectual lenses. Photographers heighten sensitivity with selective focusing, special film, paper, and filters. Artistic formulations use three varieties of filters: playful, behavioral, and spiritual. Each may serve the composer's particular purpose. They may also be used in combination.

The Playful Filter

Some compositions exemplify special ways of using and enjoying the pleasures of language. Their primary effect is achieved through playful intervention. For example:

> Why do bees buzz?
> Who tickles their fuzz?
> — *Robert, grade 6*

Riddles are a kind of word game.

> Riddle, riddle ree
> What color do I see?
> It starts with an "r"
> And ends with a "d."
> — *Liz, grade 5*

Lilian had fun with letters that sound like words. She put together a make-believe dialogue with her friend Abie.

> A B C D froggies?
> M N   no froggies.
> O S M R 2 froggies.
>   M R B's!
> — *Lilian, grade 6*

There are other inventive ways of playing with language to form a new picture.

THE PIED PIPER

Inside the mountain, oh you should have seen,
Bats that were red and bees that were green.
Animals of various sizes and shapes,
Overgrown ants and pint-sized apes.

The interior was of the finest of textures,
Although if you lived there it would not be a pleasure.
For everywhere it was damp and soggy,
You might even think it seemed a bit foggy.

But the children who were very enchanted,
Didn't notice the walls or the soggy embranched.
They weren't really bothered by hanging red bats.
Nor were they bothered by hat-snatching cats.

By an underground passage they skipped along,
While the piper kept playing his very gay song.
Then, as if by some magic, the bright cave turned dull,
And within a few moments they were flying like gulls.

Over the clouds and the colourful rainbow,
They flew as if it seemed just a bit painful.
Then all of a sudden they just disappeared,
And never again will we see them I fear.

—Janis, grade 6

The Behavioral Filter

Some compositions provide a shortcut to action or a response to action or the lack of it. Such products offer a practical way of "feeling into" a critical moment or experience. The following selection concerns the composer's memory of her brother. It can be shared with those who never knew him.

Roy was three years old.
He used to play with his toys.
They stand dust covered.
—Stephanie, grade 6

The feelings of aloneness and being unloved are known by many.

Alone in the dark
No place to go for loving
He walked sadly by.
—Debbie, grade 5

Gary used a behavioral filter to share the excitement of a game.

THE HOCKEY GAME

The flashing blades, the flying spray,
The action getting hot,
A flying check, a breakaway,
The goalie stops a shot.

The visitors are winning,
The score is five to four,
The center has scored one goal,
He's trying to get one more.

The game has almost ended,
But the action doesn't cease,
The goal is scored, it's disallowed,
A man was in the crease.

A penalty is given,
The home team gets a chance.
The center starts to stickhandle,
The goalie's in a trance.

But now the game is over,
All the work's been done,
The visitors were winning,
The visitors have won.

— Gary, grade 6

The Spiritual Filter

Other creative formulations combine refined language with insights that seem to be inspired by an exalted attitude or perspective. These compositions may be called contemplative or spiritual.

Helen expressed her flight of fancy as a universal, spiritual question.

WHERE WOULD YOU GO?

If you were to fly, higher than the low whistling wind,
Beyond the feathery fingers of the highest trees,
On and on, past a haven of clouds; and even farther,
Where would you go?

Through valleys of stars with eerie whispering tones?
Pausing, perhaps, to pluck a star from the darkly woven skies,
Or explore dark worlds with faith to guide and stars to see by?
Where would you go?

— Helen, grade 6

Wendy caught the spirit of the illusive mist with her contemplative filter.

THE MIST

Catches you,
        like wisps of white chiffon;
Entrances you,
Pounces on you in an unsuspecting moment.
Springs from tree to tree
Like a nearly transparent ballet dancer;
hides everything,
        in a snowy white veil;
Startles you,
Like the "Surprise Symphony,"
Leaves quietly . . . on tiptoe.
                    — *Wendy, grade 6*

The ugliest of subjects can be presented contemplatively and with dignity.

THE JUNKIE

An evil wind
    blows down the street
    past the garbage
Through the schoolyard fence.
                — *Luís, grade 7*

Roger described a wall as an immutable camera's eye. Advancing age, a noble past, and the uncertain future are pictured here more succinctly than an album of photographs or a Hollywood film.

THE WALL

Grey granite wall, tall, with an air of importance,
Looks down on the lesser buildings scornfully.
Cannons once took refuge behind its sturdy stones;
It had felt bleeding soldiers
Gasp out their lives on its ramparts.

It had seen sweating soldiers
Scurry into tunnels to escape bursting shells,
Moments when blood was valued less than an advancement
Yet always, there had been a time when even rows of men

In dazzling scarlet uniforms
Were decorated with dancing medals.

Today, curious, ignorant footsteps echo
Within its sheltering expanse.
People abuse the graves of heroic bodies,
Unaware that they tread on the creators
Of their way of life.

                            — *Roger, grade 7*

The study of Greek history, art, and architecture has moved many a child to painting or dramatics. Gordon composed the following selection:

AN ANCIENT TEMPLE

Searching and lonely
Black corners and flying shadows
    Standing apart.

Reaching for support
Among ones that cringe
Glowing light — once
Silent darkness — now.
          — Gordon, grade 6

John brings to the reader the grandeur of a lone tree filtered out from the background.

THE LONE TREE

There is a tree that swings,
Lonely and far. Along the ancient forest
The tree's fingers play faintly on the strings
Of that rare violin, the night wind,
And it whispers a long, lonely key
To the only friend it has, me.
          — John, grade 7

Literary filters can provide greater detail than the human eye alone can take in. The composer may combine obvious or subtle elements to concentrate and heighten sensory experience and form a new entity. Obvious elements include real or imagined experiences, sincere feelings, classic forms, end rhyme, strong meter, and vivid imagery. Subtle artistic elements include symbolic language, suggestion, near and internal rhyme, varied rhythm, simple diction, synthesized feelings, and unified but varied forms. Artistic composers pass along the same paths we do; they see and feel and try to capture and project the experience of those paths, the going on them, or "the road not taken." They can also create new roads.

PROCESS

Turning Off and Turning On

Artistic composition is a process of turning off extraneous distractions in order to turn on sensory perception. It invites a fresher, less hackneyed view of existence. The writer, like the artist or a person who is hard of hearing, relies on selective attention. The artist may intentionally blur the background to focus more intently on the subject. The hard of hearing are sometimes the only people able to follow conversations in noisy subways, airplanes, and factories. Not bothered by background noises they cannot hear, they become skilled in attending to other sensory clues, reading lips, facial expressions, and body gestures.

Composers turn off distractions in order to turn on their insight. Turning off distractions often brings into sudden focus experiences, ideas, or feelings. Concentrating on one of them may lead to a crystallization of ideas and a frenzy of writing.

At the moment of greatest clarity and interest, photographers frantically take pictures; painters and writers sketch and scribble rapidly to capture fleeting images. No wonder the onlooker is confounded by the composer's sudden flurry of activity. He or she is struggling to preserve the moment at hand. It is understandable that people once believed writers were obsessed or insane. The turning off–turning on process is not, however, a communication with supernatural beings or one's personal mania, as conceived by Socrates and perpetuated by Plato, but a communion of the spirit between composers as persons and their creative selves.

The process of tapping and maintaining the composer's wellspring of ideas is the heart of composition. After the flow has begun, the water may vary in purity. It can be cleared later; the flow is of paramount importance. In composition, attention is turned toward opening the dam and away from anything that dams the flow.

Turning Away and Turning Toward

As we have just noted, the composing process requires a turning away and a turning toward: one turns away from some habits of language and personal behavior associated with the mere communication of literal meanings, and toward the expression of feelings about experiences and ideas in appropriate and unified forms.

There is no one way to artistic composition. Some composers turn toward their own experiences and write out of them. Others turn toward representations of experiences. Thus, a lightning bug may represent summer nights in general or be reminiscent of one particular summer night. Some composers begin with an idea, a word, a phrase, or a sense impression. They allow themselves to travel cyclically like soaring birds, or they meander like streams through the woods. And there is another way — by stimulating language, images, and the senses through a kind of free association or brainstorming similar to a pinball game in which the ball is allowed to bounce randomly. This kind of composition can also be compared to group decision making, a merging of elements from different experiences that produces unanticipated results.

Artistic composers turn away from literalness, linearity, sentimentality, the hackneyed, the practical, the commonplace, the expected. In school, composition can help youngsters turn away from the habit of trying to anticipate the desires and reactions of their teachers. They can turn away, at least for a little while, from bitter competition with their peers in routinized activites. Composing without inner satisfaction has led many people to enjoy only the moment of completing the assignment rather than the whole process of composing. In artistic composition, teachers and students turn away from standardized expectations, premature or hypercritical appraisals, and preconceptions regarding subject matter and language. Artistic composition is a turning away from the habit of marching down streets called conventional logic or reasoning or dispatching squads of words in boxlike truck convoys along boulevards called paragraphs. The artistic process of using words need not be straightforward and literal. Its purpose is not to convey facts but to evoke feelings or thoughts. The artistic process allows the expression of things that cannot be expressed as well literally.

PRODUCT

Artistic composition is a product of personal energy. After synthesizing emotions and language into what seems to them to be a meaningful balance, composers step back to look at their artistic product. This potent force, this composite formulation of their artistic existence, this process of searching, has resulted in a newly unified product.

Artistic products may be prized by both children and adults. There must, however, be a readiness to enjoy the range of experience the new products make available. The reader must be free to approach them as a child approaches a new jack-in-the-box or kaleidoscope. Artistic compositions are waiting to spring up and surprise those ready for surprises. They cause the most ordinary environment to be viewed in surprising ways. They are waiting, available but compressed, to serve the reader who allows the composition to be a finished product.

Artistic products do not lend themselves to a simple explanation, but the varieties may be categorized or described. Artistic products may be short or long, narrative or lyric, metered or unmetered, rhymed or unrhymed. They usually employ one or more artistic devices. Every artistic product, in other words, has a style.

The present age has outproduced all others in the variety of artistic styles. Today's compositions are dressed in both formal wear and sports clothes. Some use classic forms and eloquent language. Others use the idiom of the common people. Language today is influenced by the playful alliteration of advertising and the verbal economy of headlines. Each style has followers. All have value.

Artistic products speak to the senses rather than to the intellect. Usually they are meant not to communicate literal meanings or to be logical or verifiable, but to be believable. An analysis of style may help readers appreciate the composer's intention, which may range from sheer fun to spiritual inspiration. All artistic products, however, are generated from feelings, colored with langauge, and fashioned with energy. Separating the elements of composition may be like separating water into hydrogen and oxygen. It can be done, but the water will disappear. The individually explosive elements, when synthesized correctly, produce the liquid that quenches our thirst on a hot day and stretches the soup when unexpected company arrives.

Artistic products, too, are greater than the sum of their parts. The difference between the totality we call a poem, a story, or a play and its constituent parts depends upon the changes and connections that take place among the components during their synthesis. In a poem, as in an orchestra, each element has its sound. Together they become more a fusion than a mixture of individual sounds.

Nevertheless, each artistic element may sometimes be appreciated alone as part of the artistic whole. In the elementary school, a composition may be merely a clear image filled with the honesty, enthusiasm, and scuffling of childhood. Artistic fragments, like sticky fingers not ready for company, still serve well in getting to the literary itch. Whether fragments or complete works, artistic products require sorting to identify those designed for pleasure, for work, and for sheer beauty. One who knows the beauty of diamonds and art appreciates their facets.

We have surveyed the five facets of composition: art, force, formulation, process, and product. Composition need not be taught as if all the students will become professional writers. People should be taught composition so that their language will contain a poetic essence and they will see themselves and others as capable of artistic expression. Poetic essence is the seasoning of language.

Artistic composition as an educational resource provides a way of nurturing the composer's sense of personal freedom. To protect and perpetuate this sense is the goal of teachers, parents, or friends, and for this reason alone artistic composition surely should be encouraged at home, in school, and throughout life.

SUGGESTED READING

Brooks, Cleanth, and Warren, Robert Penn. *Understanding Poetry*. 3d ed. New York: Holt, Rinehart and Winston, 1960.

Deutsch, Babette. *Poetry in Our Time*. New York: Holt, 1952.

Dewey, John. *Art as Experience*. New York: Minton, Balch, 1934.

Langer Susanne K. *Feeling and Form*. New York: Scribner, 1952.

_____. *Philosophy in a New Key*. Cambridge: Harvard University Press, 1942.

_____. *Problems of Art*. New York: Scribner, 1957.

Lewis, Claudia Day. *Enjoying Poetry: A Reader's Guide*. 3d ed. Cambridge: National Book League, at the University Press, 1956.

Wolchonok, Louis. *Lessons in Pictorial Composition*. New York: Dover, 1969.

The Value of Composition

The Wolsch communication program is organized into three stages: evoking visions, fashioning revisions, and sharing visions. It stresses speaking first, then writing, and finally reading. The first stage helps people to perceive themselves as creative thinkers and composers; the second helps them to make their language precise as well as vital; and the third helps them to share and appreciate their own compositions and those of others. Composition helps people of all ages develop their potential. It is a disciplined art that also helps nurture the confidence and the desire to reach out to others peacefully. In this appendix, therefore, we emphasize the social values of composition.

POSITIVE SELF-AWARENESS

Some children think and act intuitively and spontaneously. They combine interest and awe when struggling to face life's problems. Their play, including their teasing, tugging, and taunting, is charged with elements based on reality. Their reactions to most things are like a nature lover's response to the first robin or crocus of spring. Their curiosity, astonishment, and wonder seem endless. Their bodies and minds react totally to their world. They are naturally rhythmic, perceptive, and creative. Many adults are too.

Composition helps people heighten their awareness and appreciation of spontaneous feelings and reactions. It helps them to recognize that they are indeed capable of thinking and acting imaginatively. It serves to connect them to the world and people around them before, during, and after their school and work years. It helps them to develop pride in their language, to express their ideas vigorously and concisely, and to nurture their empathic qualities by sharing their thoughts with others.

Composition lends direction and dignity to innate wit as well as acquired abilities. There is a marked difference between learning a skill and accumulating information, just as talking and reading about a subject are different from actual experience. There is, for example, a difference between learning about skating and learning how to skate. One can feel the difference in one's seat and knees.

Healthy preschool children know a great deal about how to learn. They touch a flower, smell it, shake it, taste it, and try to bounce it. They learn at leisure and have the time to relate new knowledge to their previous feelings, experiences, and ways of learning. They often learn about the world in an analogical, connotative way—the nonverbal way familiar to children everywhere. To learn about a flower is to attempt to become like a flower, to study its textures, to try to perceive as a flower might. To know a flower is to better know the difference between the flower and oneself. This is one way of better knowing other persons and other things. A child's way to knowledge is an empathic, humane way—a creative way.

Children and artistically involved adults present things spontaneously, nonjudgmentally—like unretouched photographs. Their spontaneous reactions are unclouded by social graces, hesitation, fear of reprisal, and linear logic.

It was a child who saw the real, unclothed emperor in Hans Christian Andersen's story. Composition keeps the door open for a variety of ways of thinking, no matter what one's age. Children know ambivalence from their most direct, most intimate experiences. They love their parents but hate them when they are spanked; they love the snow but hate to put on their boots; they are both attracted to and repelled by certain aspects of fictional monsters, animals, relatives, and school. They may be confused, however, when confronted by situations that allow for only one way of thinking and exclude the middle ground and paradox.

So-called adult thinking—logical thinking—has its dangers for adults as well as children. It may be frozen into unfeeling, rigid, digital thought patterns. While it will not protect a mind from domination by cliches and stereotypes, it can cause it to ignore alternatives and deny the existence of intermediate positions, as suggested in Aristotle's law of the excluded middle. Must people be all wrong or all right? Are things all black or all white? Must all writing and speaking be like a business letter?

People can be logical without being limited in this way. Teaching people to use only one mode of thinking may make them suspicious of other ways to think and know. For some children, step-by-step analytical learning requires an abrupt change from nonverbal, nonrational, timeless, intuitive preschool ways of thinking. To require them to adopt new ways too soon may cause them to doubt and exclude their old ways. This has already happened to many adults, who are now unable to speak or write, or at least are reluctant to try.

Composition using analogic thinking helps people relate what they do not know to what they do know. Once their ideas have been written down, they are more likely to see the need for digital thinking, further distinctions, and new points of reference. This is learning by analogy. Some analogies require conscious effort; some do not. Some require logic; some develop prelogically. The analogous route to knowing, familiar to young children but different from step-by-step analysis, is available to adults through creative composition.

People of all ages can find value in their own nonrational or prelogical ways of knowing. Intuitive, mythical, analogous, symbolic knowledge may add another dimension to the process of learning. Helping people draw upon it may introduce them to a new relationship to nature, to others, and to their own existence.

The ways of children are special. Some call them spiritual; others, creative. The admonition to humble oneself and be like a little child is sometimes interpreted as a prescription for meekness. It may also mean that one should become open to the ways of childhood, when the creative spark lying ing dormant within each person is active. Nurturing that spark may help it illuminate the paths of all of us.

As is true of the other arts, composition may stimulate and satisfy the drive to create. It provides an alternative to the ready-made, the prepackaged, the coloring in, the turning on, and the tuning out of irresponsible, passive, anticreative experiences. It provides opportunities for recognizing that both the composition and the composer are capable of change, and this insight can lead to self-improvement. The act of creation itself raises aspiration levels.

Composition provides a way to maintain creative abilities at a level equal to or above preschool performance. Some researchers urge teachers and parents to keep preschool fantasy alive at least until the child's intellectual development permits him or her to engage in other types of creative activity. Some voices plead that creative thinkers be given equal recognition and equal status with those who are more logically oriented, arguing that it is the combination of creative and retentive, divergent and convergent, closed and open-ended, left-brain and right-brain practices that equips people for what they are to become.

Composition can help build a continuous bridge between the modes of communication people develop before, during, and after their school years. It may be a way of preventing the dramatic loss of creative vigor ex-

perienced by children upon entering or leaving school and adults upon beginning work or retiring. Providing opportunities for familiar types of
creative expression is a way of showing respect for people, their feelings,
their experiences, their customs, and their future.

Realizing one's potential is a birthright. The potential of its people is a
country's greatest resource. Freedom to discover and to value its citizens'
abilities is the nation's heritage. Composition is one way of tapping this potential wealth. It provides citizens — junior and senior — with a way of
thinking beyond the boredom of their everyday world. It helps to maintain
and reinforce their innate talent. Writers and speakers can reach new levels
of personal and social awareness. The value of keeping creativity alive is indeed great.

LANGUAGE DEVELOPMENT

The adventure of shaping ideas and feelings in a skillful fashion brings
vitality to the study of language. The precision needed to produce word
paintings brings pleasure and justifiable pride.

Precise language helps develop self-knowledge by enabling people to organize their thoughts and feelings. Once ideas are written down, people
can examine the way their thinking, plans, or alternatives are ordered. Expressing themselves in precise form brings people closer to their inner
selves.

Composition provides a warm, nonrational, "let's take a chance" environment. Once people learn to catch their visions and preserve them with
language, they also learn that they can arrange and rearrange language to
try out new ways of dealing with past, future, and hypothetical experiences. They may then create their own order out of the chaos around them.

Composition is a valuable tool. As survivors of the Depression learned to
appreciate more by making do with less, so too a composer learns to appreciate subtlety and use words economically. Whittling language develops
skill in sensing the right word, the right rhythm of the phrase, a feeling for
language balance, and a distaste for verbal clutter in *all* kinds of writing
and speaking. Composition, therefore, is appropriate as the heart of the
communication program.

REACHING OUT TO OTHERS

A program of composition can be expected to produce individuals of
character. Fashioning compositions with personal insight and precision re-

inforces appreciation and sensitivity — empathic alternatives to some of the brutalizing forces prevalent in today' society.

Empathy is the kind of vicarious imagination needed to anticipate and understand the feelings of another. Successful teachers are often exemplars of this quality; their students learn to observe and anticipate the feelings of others. Composition affords opportunities for such learning through composing itself and through reading or listening to the compositions of others.

Last year we participated in a marriage enrichment weekend. We went seeking new ways to enrich our lives and the lives of our children. We learned about the value of writing to someone you love by writing to each other every few hours. Then we each read what the other had written, and discussion followed. An opportunity for private writing that will receive the total attention of the reader is rare in this hectic, me-first world. To delay discussion until the other person had had a lengthy opportunity to read, reread, and make notes was an exercise in respect. Respect is certainly a requirement for love.

The marriage enrichment weekend reminded us of the youngster who wrote the three-line biblical episodes printed in chapter 4. He had a serious voice problem and was entrusted to a speech and voice consultant. He arrived in the consultant's office but would not speak. Silence is the loudest type of nonverbal communication. He did accept another way to communicate — writing — in a form that challenged his intellect: three lines, seventeen syllables. The experience was similar to the marriage enrichment weekend. The consultant communicated respect for the boy's silence, his writing, and the boy himself. He eventually spoke to the consultant and took his advice about improving his voice.

Sitting alone with a child on the school stairway or by a desk demonstrates — like the letter writing of the marriage enrichment weekend — that that person and his or her composition is getting all the teacher's attention. This is a vital ingredient for beginning speakers and writers — the knowledge that someone they trust will spend time with them and their oral and written language, and treat both respectfully.

There will, of course, be others who may not understand or appreciate one's work. The ways of critics are diverse. Artists have an opportunity to learn that people sometimes agree with their decisions and their creation and sometimes do not. There is great value in learning that someone may not be pleased with the product but may still be pleased with the producer.

With composition people may hold on to their outer and inner experiences, add dignity to their wonder, see the beauty, vigor, and usefulness of their own language. They may recall the evils of the past, share their present experiences with others, and draw their own blueprints for the future.

With this knowledge, they may bring their whole selves to school or work or retirement.

To help speakers and writers feel and react like composers is to help them learn to use language to reach out to others with dignity during times of pleasure or pain. Even in the loneliness of a megacity, people may do more than stamp their feet, play truant, or throw bricks through windows. They may see a touch of beauty in the surrounding squalor. They may write down their strong feelings to hold on to moments of ecstacy or to ease the pain.

What could one do after the senseless killing of John Lennon? Many observed the two minutes of silence requested by his wife, Yoko Ono. Others pressed for the control of handguns. David Spangler, a Westchester County high school teacher, spontaneously produced a poem.

> What hate breeds those murky men
> Whose shadowy deeds sap the spark
> Of our most brilliant companions
> Allowing only the aftertrail
> Of those shot stars
> To illuminate our otherwise
> Dark passage into the
> Cavernous recesses of space and time.

"The poem," he explained, "is in its first form and much revision would have to be done before I would previously have shared it. For so long, I viewed writing as an obligation, not as an opportunity. I've learned to value writing as an agent for expressing my feelings and as a means to understand myself."

People who have learned to respect and draw upon their own environment, language, and experiences in composition have learned to reach out to others in a humane way. Communicating orally and in writing is important and stimulating work; the writer or speaker is important and stimulating too. Communication provides us with another way of knowing. Some explore their own thoughts; others fashion new ideas. Both can learn to control the elements of language and discover new and effective ways of reaching out to friends and strangers.

Composition is of value not only for its beauty but, like other arts, because it helps the composer achieve his or her potential. It is a way of synthesizing the past and present resources of people, their knowledge, their intelligence, their experiences, their emotions, and their language. It is basic to the development of deeper communication at any age. In this way composition helps build the ultimate community of people.

SUGGESTED READING

Behn, Harry. *Chrysalis: Concerning Children and Poetry.* New York: Harcourt, Brace and World, 1968.

Bruner, Jerome S. *On Knowing: Essays for the Left Hand.* New York: Atheneum, 1965.

———. *The Process of Education.* Cambridge: Harvard University Press, 1961.

Chukovsky, Kornei. *From Two to Five.* Translated and edited by Miriam Morton. Berkeley: University of California Press, 1963.

Edwards, Betty. *Drawing on the Right Side of the Brain.* Los Angeles: J. P. Tarcher, 1979.

Hailey, Jack. *Teaching Writing, K–8.* Berkeley: Instructional Laboratory, University of California, 1978.

Hourd, Marjorie. *The Education of the Poetic Spirit.* London: William Heinemann, 1954.

James, William. *The Varieties of Religious Experience.* New York: Longmans, Green, 1902.

Overcoming Blocks to Composition and Communication

If people were taught to speak as they are often taught to read and write, stuttering would be commonplace. Approximately one persent of school age children stutter. Most, however, learn to speak rhythmically, noncompetitively, and grammatically by listening, feelings, and reacting. Compare that to the way we learn other basic skills. Reading and writing are often taught competitively, unrhythmically, judgmentally, and humorlessly by teachers using a foreign, formal language and stressing mechanical skills rather than communication. Too many schools promote stuttering in reading and writing.

How many eyes and hands approach communication through reading and writing and then avoid completing the act because of a learned anticipatory-avoidance reaction? This reaction is learned when people are invited to communicate and then experience rejection. They afterwards fear the repetition of this unhappy interaction. Here is one reason eyes dart back and forth when the time comes for reading and hands clutching pencils freeze, leaving an empty page instead of their writing.

The Wolsch stuttering-prevention approach to communication has three principles: first, speaking, writing, and reading develop in that order and should be taught in that order; second, communication skills depend upon memories of success and "can do" feelings and behavior; third, communication skills, to become part of life, require practice in real life situations. To approach basic skills otherwise is to invite hesitancy, repetition, and blocking — all signs of fear and avoidance of the communication act.

This appendix has two parts. The first parades the confusions that block speaking, listening, writing, and reading. The second part provides three alternatives to these confusions. We can unblock beginning speakers, writers, and readers by helping them to develop a positive attitude toward their personal communicative abilities, instilling a love of the arts of language, and improving educational programs for teachers and students.

THE CONFUSIONS

Confusing Language Tradition with Fact

Children know, but many adults forget, that it can be fun to work with words, to paint pictures with them, and to express feelings and thoughts interestingly, analogically, and artistically.

After we have led a teacher workshop on the natural progression from speaking to writing to reading, somebody usually whispers to us over coffee and doughnuts or at the water fountain, "I became a teacher to do those things with students. But I can't."

"Why can't you?" we whisper back.

"The administration won't let me." Or "There isn't enough time after the reading groups or grammar drills or spelling tests."

One teacher expressed concern to us about a second grader who did not complete the pages of grammar drills, and was therefore failing English. When asked why there were so many of these assignments, the teacher admitted their ineffectiveness. "But the principal wants us to go through the workbook."

The principal confessed his dislike for the exercises too but said they were requested by the district language arts coordinator. The coordinator smiled and admitted having doubts about the workbook but said it was prescribed by the assistant superintendent in charge of instruction, who also agreed that the material was not practical or appropriate, "But it was required by the Committee on Language Arts at the state capital."

"That's strange," we replied. "One of us was on that committee [established by the state Education Department to revise the forty-year-old state language arts syllabus], and we said 'Don't do that sort of exercise.' Furthermore, the old state syllabus said in effect, 'Don't waste time with technicalities of language. Use the time available to help your students communicate more effectively.' " It was a fine old syllabus, but this administrator in charge of the education of twenty thousand youngsters could not find a copy.

We contacted the seven largest districts in that county. Not one copy of the old language arts syllabus could be located. Many language arts programs are based on traditional myths about language rather than on the research and practical methods that have been described and debated in the professional literature for fifty years.

Confusing Parts of Language with Arts of Language

We know something is wrong when "the return to the basics" turns out to be a euphemism for spending time, year after year, in the naming, filling in, and drilling of questionable language parts and similar matters. That time should be spent teaching people to communicate in appropriate formats. The technicalities of language are for the teacher; they should not get in the way of the writer. This confusion of the parts with the whole does not result in improved communication.

Too often language is broken down into spelling, vocabulary, grammar, usage, handwriting, and reading skills. The relationship of one skill to the others, of expression to reception, of decoding to encoding, is never clarified. And where does thinking enter this process? Minds drilled in language parts may confuse remembering with thinking and writing with a pen with composing with words — also confusions of the part with the whole. Parts can be taken out of the whole for practice or improvement, but they must be put right back into a meaningful context.

Confusing Formal Language with Standard Language

Something is wrong when we listen to and speak one language but are expected to use only a foreign, formal language for writing and reciting. Everyone's language has at least seven levels: first, Anglo-Saxon profanity, short and direct, as spoken on street corners and in the bowels of ships and written on bathroom walls; second, colloquial, regional, neighborhood language; third, family language; fourth, informal, standard school talk; fifth, aesthetic, artistic, or spiritual language; sixth, professional language (legal or computer terminology, for example); and, finally, a seventh, a strict, contractionless, nineteenth-century, formal, term-paper style that is foreign to almost everyone. Each language has its place; each communicates. To expect formal language from fledgling speakers and writers is unrealistic. For many beginners, formal English is a major roadblock to communication.

Confusing Spelling Vocabularies with Speaking Vocabularies

We have four vocabularies. Each can be represented by the concentric circles of a bull's-eye target. The outermost circle — the largest one — represents our listening vocabulary; we understand more than we say. The second large circle represents our speaking vocabulary; the third, our reading vocabulary; and the smallest our spelling vocabulary. Successful writers and executives use their speaking vocabulary for dictation. Their secretaries worry about spelling. Too many beginning speakers and writers assume that they must use their spelling vocabulary for first drafts. This shows a misunderstanding of the composing process. Starting with overprecision stops the flow; each step produces anxiety, and writing becomes a chore to be avoided.

Confusing Phonics with Phonetics

Something is wrong when people idealize phonics — a Swiss cheese system with "wholly" exceptions — confusing it with phonetics. Phonetics involves the use of the International Phonetic Alphabet, which has more than forty-five symbols for the phonemes of American English. This alphabet uses one symbol for each sound; there are no exceptions. Phonics, on the other hand, depends on the twenty-six letters of the English alphabet.

"Sounding out" words is useful to beginning readers, and we applaud the effort. But when a person phonetically (or phonically) tries to apply the same logic to writing and spelling, he or she is faced with rejection and frustration. Our spelling is not phonetic. Too many people become demoralized when the logical, phonetic spelling of their early drafts is rejected.

Language is constantly changing, but powerful forces are ranged against the movement to simplify English spelling. Teddy Roosevelt was threatened with impeachment for asking Congress to authorize simplified spelling. George Bernard Shaw, a lifelong student and master of the English language, decided that the budget of the English-speaking world could be balanced by using simplified spelling and was declared incompetent by the London Probate Court. Why? Because he willed his estate to the Simplified English Spelling Association, thereby antagonizing spelling traditionalists.

Someone who grew up in a Spanish- or German-speaking country, where spelling is consistent with pronunciation, will confirm that such countries have no spelling books, no spelling tests, and few spelling mistakes by secretaries. We, on the other hand, waste time, paper, books, mountains of money, and generations of potential authors because we have only twenty-six letters for forty-five sounds — a gift from the Romans and present-day opponents of spelling reform.

Confusing the Phrase with the Sentence as a Unit of Thought

The phrase — not the word, not the sentence — is the basic unit of thought in speaking and in written composition as well. How does one recognize a phrase? A phrase is a word or group of words surrounded by pauses that are used to take a breath or add emphasis. There is no one way to use pauses: today we may say something one way; tomorrow we may change our phrasing. Writers and readers use pauses and phrases when imitating speech in plays, poetry, and stories. The phrase should have the status we have given the sentence. If reading materials and compositions were set up in a phrase-a-line format rather than in paragraphs, reading and writing skills would soar.

Confusing Rightness with Correctness

Judgments of good and evil are influenced by language. Right-handed people have often been considered superior to left-handed people because of language and custom, and at one time parents and teachers forced youngsters to use the right hand — the correct or straight or just hand. All this from language — the influence of words like the Anglo-Saxon "*recht.*" "*Lyft*" meant weak or worthless; it was used to refer not only to weak left hands, but also to the woman's place on the side of her husband. The Latin word for the left hand — "*sinister*" — had similar connotations. Left-handed compliments still carry little value. In politics, the right is conservative and admiring of national power; the left usually promotes change and is sometimes associated with radicalism.

Oddly, it is the left side of the brain that is thought to control the conventional "basic" skills, including writing. Old attitudes as irrational as the bias against left-handedness lead some to consider the right-brain skills like artistic thinking and writing less important than the "basic" ones. Must people, in the use of their hands, brain lobes, or skills, be all right or all wrong?

Confusing Discursive with Nondiscursive Writing

Too often teachers treat an excellent nondiscursive composition as an inadequate discursive one. Rational, literal prose is only one way to use the language. Too much emphasis on it may lead to rigid, digital thinking and writing. Nondiscursive composition, the artistic, meandering, personal use of language, is another honorable way to communicate the truth as one sees it. It should be readily available to all. Aristotle's law of the excluded middle has dominated Western thought for too long. Eastern philosophers have long taught another way. Must we continue thinking that if you are not for me you must be against me? Is everything either black or white? Must we all believe in the same things? Must we all write in the same ways?

Confusing Analytical with Analogical Thinking

Analogical thinking and writing help relate what people do not know to what they do know. Once their ideas have been written down, they are more likely to see the need for further distinctions and new points of reference. This is thinking by analogy. It is common to children, artists, poets, inventors, storytellers, and writers. "Left-handed," analogical, nondiscursive, metaphoric language adds another dimension to speaking and writing and deserves at least equal status with all-or-nothing thinking and linear discourse.

Confusing Prescriptive Grammar with Descriptive Grammar

Idealizing prescriptive Latinate grammar and phonics is like forcing an elephant into a girdle. Neatness and grace are intended, but about 40 percent spills over.

Latin was for centuries the language of priests and scholars. Their students, who became teachers in their turn, required it of their students at all levels, down to Latin grammar schools. As schooling became universal in the United States, Latin was eliminated as a universal requirement. Prescriptive Latinate grammar remains, however, traditionally girdling English in many classrooms. Some people still refer to elementary schools as grammar schools.

But English — unlike French, Italian, and Spanish — did not grow directly out of Latin. English descended from the dialects spoken by the Germanic Angles and Saxons, with some Scandinavian and Greek influence. It was not until 1066 that the Normans invaded England and flavored the language with their Latin-derived French. By that time the English language cake was already baking in the oven. Anglo-Saxon provided the substance — the flour and eggs; the Scandinavians provided the baking power and butter; French provided the sugar and icing, and the Greeks added the cherry on top.

Grammar is more than the study of how words are formed, compounded, and arranged in sentences. Grammar may also include the study of speech sounds and the history of sound changes, versification, spelling, pronunciation, language forms, and word meaning; in some cases it encompasses punctuation and usage. It may be descriptive or prescriptive. To some, descriptive grammar may be a cathedral, and prescriptive grammar may be a jail.

Drilling in the parts of speech and the technicalities of diagraming sentences before high school has been proven to be no more useful in improving speaking and writing than learning geometry or practicing basketball foul shots. Why is so much school time still wasted this way? Grammar can be learned through the skillful use of the language — listening to it and trying it on orally and in written form in order to appreciate it.

Confusing Decoding with Communication

Something is wrong when so much money and effort are devoted to reading skills and so little to the enjoyment of reading, oral and written composition, and the interrelationship of encoding, decoding, feeling, and thinking. *Reading Is Only the Tiger's Tail* — the name of a book and a program developed by Robert and Marlene McCracken — is true! Reading — that is, decoding — should not be the whole focus of the language program. "Language arts" is a broad term meant to suggest the intended interaction of the parts of language with the subject matter and other concerns of the learner. Unfortunately, in many schools the language arts program merely covers reading and some language drilling. Because of this change of meaning, we now use the term "communication arts" to convey the integration of listening, speaking, writing, and reading with art, music, dramatics, movement, audiovisual aids, and meaningful subject matter. The writing moment is also a moment of reading. The insights derived from studying the communication arts together are much greater than those derived from concentrating on one at a time.

Confusing Reading Level with Comprehension and Communication

Will decoding on the appropriate grade level result in the ability to speak and write effectively? Perhaps. On the other hand, nurturing the composition of narrative patterns based on a logical order of exposition may provide a valid supplement or alternative to the conventional concern with reading levels. People with the same decoding ability may vary greatly in comprehension because some are more able than others to relate to the theme, the characters, the cultural view, or the narrative conventions. Some people are able to comprehend written material in spite of their relatively low reading level because of their compositional or rhetorical skills. Teaching rhetoric — that is, oral and written composition — is at least as important as manipulating readability formulas in developing language comprehension and general cognitive abilities.

Confusing Hypercriticism with Criticism

Criticism includes praise as well as blame: theater and book critics often recommend the play or the book under consideration. Some people of all ages and backgrounds fall victim to hypercriticism, or fault finding. It is intimidating to find fault with another person or his or her work. Fear of red and blue pencil marks or verbal interruptions has inhibited too many writers and speakers. Attempting to be fair, teachers distribute their hypercriticism in equal amounts to everyone. This is a mistake with beginning speakers and writers.

One dedicated professor was so critical of the attempts of her students and her own work that she was never able to put down on paper a lifetime of scholarship. What a loss for her and for the generations who will never read her written work! A student asked, "Isn't there anything here of worth?" It did not matter — she was programed to find fault rather than worth. People like that mark all the errors on a paper, but not the beauty and values. It's appropriate to heckle opposing pitchers and batters to rattle their confidence, but why do it to beginning writers and speakers?

Confusing Lack of Recognition with Lack of Ability

Few of the potential writers around us have tasted recognition or success. Too many come to believe they have no talent. One should never dismiss a composition because of mechanical irregularities. For example, one high school composition rated a zero because the heading of the page did not include the writer's name, surname first, and the writer failed to maintain a margin of an inch and a half. What a lesson for the student and his teacher when the same composition was later published in the school's literary journal and, years later, in its collection of the ten best pieces of the World War II years.

Another form-first college teacher failed a young man in freshman composition. Three years later, out of the Navy, the young man submitted the same freshman themes to a different teacher and received an A. Now we ask our graduate students to rank the five compositions by fourth graders printed in chapter 1. In nine years, no group of certified teachers in this class has come close to any agreement on ranking these compositions. Still, many of them go back to their classrooms and grade their students' writings the next day. But some learn not to; they hide their bloody red pencils and encourage communication.

Confusing Teacher Graduation with Teacher Qualification

Would you want a brand new premedical graduate to be in charge of the hospital emergency room? To set your broken leg? To operate on you? Would you engage a physician with a bachelor's degree and limited experience, but extensive political connections? Can you imagine not giving a physician credit for excellent work he or she performed in the next state?

Would you feel confident if the hospital administrator made the decisions about the operations to be performed? This is what is happening in school districts all around the country. Teachers are hired right out of undergraduate programs, preferably on the bottom of the salary schedule. Residents of the school district are given preference. Inexperienced people with minimal training are entrusted with the most vital aspect of education — the language arts or communication program. To make matters worse, there is little in-service education available for these teachers. Because of the teachers' inexperience, administrators are making curricular decisions, and few of them are language arts or communication specialists. The blind are often leading the blind.

Graduates of teacher preparation institutions are certified by the state education department; it is therefore generally believed that they must be prepared. Not so. Many, many teachers have gone through teacher-training programs — often for six years, long enough to acquire a master's degree — without sufficient preparation in the language arts, the major concern of the schools. Many have had only one course in freshman composition, an interpersonal speech course, a literature course, a children's literature course, and one or two courses in the teaching of reading. Many do not speak or write effectively or know much about the language. Their language arts background is primarily in the teaching of reading skills. Memories of what was done to them in composition classes guide them in what they do with their pupils. And the in-service budget is cut each year.

Confusing English Teachers with Composition Teachers

A number of teachers are magnificent, most are dedicated, and all are overworked. Not all English teachers or reading teachers are equipped to teach composition. English teachers who are literary scholars enjoy teaching literature. Some enjoy teaching writing. Many do not. Sometimes reading teachers are also assigned to supervise the elementary school language arts program. Few of these teachers have had training and experience in teaching composition, speech, or literature.

An English professor friend was asked during dinner about his freshman composition class. "Analogous to the thumb-screw" was the reply. His Ph.D. preparation had included no courses dealing with the teaching of composition or speech. He tolerated freshman themes but looked forward to the teaching of literature. He used works of literature as models for his writing students to emulate; they seldom had any effect, but he persisted.

The following incident occurred during an interview for a job teaching communication to college students with little preparation in writing and study skills. Many were poor and from the inner city. "What type of writing assignments would you include?" was the lead question from the chairman of the committee, a British scholar whose field was sixteenth-century English literature. The applicant outlined the program covered in this book and added that he would ask students to compose a letter of protest to a landlord. It is impossible to forget the British accent or the incredulous tone in which he repeated, as if questioning his own hearing, "A protest letter to a landlord?" We wonder what happened to those youngsters, that writing program, and the government grant that funded it, and who they hired.

Who then should teach composition? Certainly it should be those who have something to offer and want to teach, but the preservice and in-service education of teachers must ensure that communication — including speaking, listening, composition, and the reading of literature — is taught by people with an appropriate knowledge of American English, proficiency in using the language, and the flexibility and imagination to develop new ways of teaching. Teacher interviews should include questions about the teaching of language and ways of communicating with words. And it should not come as a surprise if the composition teacher includes a protest letter to a landlord in his or her syllabus.

Confusing Permanence with Excellence

Our Connecticut home base is eight miles from New York State; half our college students are residents of New York. Public school teachers can teach in either state because of generally reciprocal licensing agreements, but they cannot bring in equal retirement credit for teaching experience in the other state.

What difference does that make to the teaching of composition or anything else? Plenty. One department chairman tried to entice experienced and expert teachers from another state to join his staff. Most would not. They were perfect for the position offered, for the students, staff, community, and administration. That was how it had been for them fifteen or twenty years before when they accepted their present positions, but everything about their work had changed. Yet they refused to leave if it meant crossing the state retirement line. "Why should I give up so many years of retirement credit?" they asked, and no answer made monetary sense. So they remain in positions that might be better filled by someone more in tune with that community or student body. No longer deriving satisfaction from their work, they seek personal benefits — salary, hours, working conditions, retirement benefits. It is all understandable, but it is unfortunate for the schools and the students.

Canada has a single teacher retirement system; teachers can move around without losing benefits. Private school and college teachers in the

United States have the Teachers' Insurance and Annuity Association because the Carnegie foundation knew that mobility is important. But our Congress has let a bill that would extend this right to public school teachers, the Mobile Teachers Retirement Assistance Act (HR 2504), mildew in committee for many years. The hidden costs of attaching teachers and supervisors to one district for life are enormous. Some of the best teachers for your composition program are stuck in another state, tied to a retirement system. If they joined your staff, they would face teaching too many additional years after reaching retirement age. In effect, they would give up years of their retirement credit to the general fund of the state they had left. So they do not leave, though often they would like to. You find someone else from the small pool of candidates in your area, often someone without experience. And then we go about our business and forget what it might have been like to have the best person in that teaching position.

Teacher retirement systems are designed to reward teachers who remain within the system and penalize teachers who leave. To leave is to sacrifice a secure old age. What we need is a great letter of protest to Congress, not forgetting to include a clause about the older teachers who may be just the right persons to inspire a love of langauge.

Confusing Administration with Ministration

Something is wrong when supervisors cannot help teachers, particularly inexperienced teachers, who often do not know where to go for assistance. In many districts there are no language arts supervisors. In others, there is a secondary English teacher or ex-chairperson of the high school English department or a reading teacher whose duties have been expanded to include the language arts — provided this person has an administrator's license.

An administrator's license can be obtained by applicants with meager backgrounds in language arts other than reading. Administrators are seldom specialists in teaching composition. The purpose of supervision is to help or advise, and it must be said that help for teachers of communication — particularly composition — is unavailable in many schools. It should also be said that there are helpful administrators. Some are both excellent communicators and charismatic individuals. Others recognize and lend support to successful teachers by providing in-service opportunities, hiring consultants, and building interdisciplinary teams that include classroom teachers and art, music, drama, movement, and audiovisual specialists.

We have briefly viewed an array of problems confronting students and teachers. These problems appear at a time when the beginner's attitude toward communication is forming. Impressions created at this time often persist and cause different kinds of compositional stutter — hesitation, racing through, avoidance, perseveration — that block composition and the progress of would-be composers and their would-be helpers. Having seen how this parade of problems contributes to the difficulties of beginning speakers and writers, we will now consider what we can do to set the communication cycle moving in a positive direction.

WHAT TO DO

Speakers and writers need to acquire a positive attitude about their own ability to communicate, develop a love of the language, and aim for a way of life in which they can use and improve their communication skills. Parents, teachers, or friends may help them to attain these goals. Few speakers and writers can do it alone.

Developing a Positive Attitude

To gain confidence in their ability to communicate effectively, beginners need more than a strong will. They need positive experiences — early in life, and reinforced throughout their lives. One way to develop a positive attitude is to pull oneself up by the bootstraps through hard work and perseverence. Another way is to have a parent or teacher model, a charismatic coach expert in various aspects of communication. A third way is to have several coaches, each with a specialty — drama, speech, composition, speech making, oral reading, radio and television production, photo journalism, or graphics. Many of these specialists are present in the schools but available only to a selected few in their classes.

The schools could provide time, space, materials, and consultants and in-service educators to help more students. Changes could be made in teacher education, teacher selection, and scheduling. Consultants could work with teams that include classroom teachers and students. Teachers on all levels will have to be viewed more as part of a team. All should see themselves as teachers of the arts of communication. All should be role models and coaches sensitive to strengths in students.

The positive attitudes of students often depend on the reflection of positive opinions from important others — parents, teachers, friends. Testing and strengthening this cycle of positive communication requires a commitment by everyone concerned to an open, experimental attitude.

This goal of a positive attitude for student communication can also enhance the teacher's effectiveness and self-image. Too many teachers feel isolated, overworked, ineffective, and unappreciated, fair game for critics from every segment of society. Being part of a school, district, or professional team dedicated to mutual support, in a massive movement to improve the communication effectiveness of our citizens, could inspire such teachers. This movement could bring together all those interested in American education.

One way of moving in this direction is represented by a program developed cooperatively between the public schools of Bethel, Connecticut, and Western Connecticut State College. Faculty members from our department of Speech Communication and Theatre Arts acted as guest lecturers to one session of a graduate course entitled "Speech Arts in the Classroom." Each professor spoke about his or her specialty. Subjects covered included dramatics, public speaking, group discussion, voice and diction, nonverbal communication, language development, oral interpretation, and the relationship of speech to writing and reading.

The graduate students, mostly experienced teachers from a variety of school districts, worked with each professor, suggesting ways to further apply the concepts to youngsters in the schools. The following week, armed with greater insights into the needs of teachers in the schools, the same professors became guest lecturers at an in-service program in the Bethel public schools. In addition, teachers from the graduate class visited Bethel classrooms to work on communication assignments with the students of the teachers in the in-service class.

Teachers on all levels — college teachers and public school teachers — worked together to help one another and the children. Teachers from one district helped teachers and students from another district. We referred to this project as a mobile teacher center. It certainly helped improve self-images, communication abilities, and attitudes toward the teaching profession.

Learning to Love Language

Love also develops out of positive experiences. We need a language environment filled with positive sounds, rhythms, images, hues, meanings, double-meanings, emotional tones, and bright ideas. People who love language collect words, phrases, and images. They are alert to new, old, and unusual words. They savor how a word feels on the lips; enjoy the reactions of friends and enemies; study how it looks on paper, in books, on packages, trucks, shirts, or balloons. These "word people" collect language pictures; they find that words can protect them, give them social status, provide sensory pleasures, be valued possessions, and help them become part of something bigger.

A love of language can also come from a relationship with someone who finds language exciting and who uses language excitingly. This person could be a parent, teacher, or friend. Teacher education programs can be retooled to foster a love of language.

Living with Our Craft

Active communicative lifestyles are enjoyed by people who can effectively speak, write, and share their work in and out of school. They are helped by education programs that produce teacher-students who prize their own communication skills and those of others. We need education programs that promote life goals rather than busywork. We need programs that take time to promote the communication goals already established rather than wasting time arguing over new goals again and again.

Something is wrong when the people who are most knowledgeable about educational problems refuse to share their professional opinions because of fear of reprisals. Everyone has ideas about language and how it should be taught, and most of these ideas are familiar ones because of the long tradition of some language-teaching practices. To suggest change is to risk being considered disloyal. To suggest radical changes is to risk being considered a radical.

The Initial Teaching Alphabet (a phonetic system similar to the International Phonetic Alphabet) and the Language Experience Method (wherein students produce their own reading materials out of their own experiences and language) have been used successfully for years in schools in English-speaking countries around the world. Why is it not generally known that students taught through these methods usually soar in writing, speaking, and reading ability compared to students taught through traditional books and methods? These nontraditional systems never caught on in the United States. Why?

President Eisenhower, in his last speech before leaving the presidency, warned the nation to beware of the military-industrial complex. Shouldn't we beware also of the established, multimillion dollar reading and publishing complex? Students who produced their own reading materials probably would not need as many traditional readers. Phonetic spellers would not need spelling books and spelling tests. There would be less business for traditional textbook publishers and producers of reproducible "busy work" sheets of drills, fill-ins, and tests.

The effort to teach speaking, writing, and reading for communication requires curriculum changes in the schools on every level — from preschool through high school to the preservice and in-service education of teachers. Real speakers and writers and readers should be brought into the schools to work with children and teachers. Real speaking and writing and reading should be considered a vital part of the education of teachers. We should use the student's own speaking language for writing and reading and avoid dull workbooks, readers, spellers, and the rest of the costly busy work advocated by the reading-publishing complex.

Painting with words, like good nutrition or regular exercise, can begin at any age, but it is more likely to become part of one's life when started early. We need to make sure that communication programs for teachers as well as students include the advice of recognized experts rather than a consensus of the uninformed but vocal.

The following Goals of Communication Instruction were developed while Bob was communication arts consultant to teachers in Yorktown Heights, New York. It exemplifies the broadened scope that comes from having representatives of all of the arts as contributing members of a school committee on communication arts.

GOALS OF COMMUNICATION INSTRUCTION

I. The student demonstrates, through works presented, an understanding that communication requires thinking, perceiving, and empathizing with others.

II. The student demonstrates a balance of skills in the receptive and expressive aspects of communication (listening, observing, speaking, writing, and reading).

III. The student participates in a balanced program of literature relating to his personal experience, expanding his ideas, and stimulating his reading appetite and his imagination.

IV. The student is able to use spoken words and written symbols interchangeably to communicate the same idea: every experience in one aspect of communication may be applied to another.

V. The student demonstrates knowledge and appreciation of the flexibility and growth of our language.

VI. The student expresses and shares feelings, impressions, and ideas in varied interesting and productive ways.

VII. The student communicates in varied media including movement, art, and music.

VIII. The student gives evidence of understanding that appropriate choices of media, mode, and manner of communication are necessary to achieve a desired effect on others.

IX. The student expresses delight, pride, and confidence in developing craftsmanship in all modes of communication.

X. The student applies all forms of communication arts, techniques, and concepts to all parts of the curriculum.

XI. The student develops criteria for evaluating all forms of communication.

XII. The student uses his/her maturing interests and learned communication skills to participate in the school and community and to develop a personal lifestyle.

These goals reflect the desire of the committee members that this program
prepare students for a lifetime of active communication.

Traditional organizational arrangements—departments, disciplines,
facilities, responsibilities, and perhaps teacher certifications—should be
reconsidered. For example, music teachers know a great deal about listening, composing, and sharing with audiences. These specialized teachers
have much information and experience to share with in-service language
arts committees and much to contribute to the preparation of teachers of
language arts. The insights of art teachers are needed for teaching composition and handwriting. Dance and movement teachers can help with listening, composition, and sharing by performance. Theater teachers, general
speech teachers, and remedial speech teachers are needed for their insights
into the speech and language development process. Filmmakers, photographers, graphics specialists, journalists, playwrights, librarians—all are
needed in the language arts program, and particularly in teacher education
programs and on in-service committees. Too long have nonspecialists controlled the teaching of communication. Too long have artist-teachers been
excluded from the language arts program. Too long have college communication arts departments remained aloof from the problems of their colleagues in departments of education. Too long have professional associations, disciplines, and departments staked out claims to narrow areas of
communication without cooperating with people in the front lines of the
war on illiteracy. Oral and written communication is too important to be
considered the responsibility of only classroom teachers or English teachers
or reading teachers or speech teachers.

Under present college and teacher certification rules, teachers are not
required to be proficient in the arts of communication. This presents difficulties, since teachers of communication teach a great deal by example,
whether or not they are aware of it. Some move from an authoritarian style
of teaching to a democratic one to a laissez faire one, depending upon the
makeup of the class and its receptiveness to particular leadership modes.
Whatever the teacher's leadership style, the effectiveness of teaching is enhanced when students perceive the teacher's communicative abilities as
worth emulating. Successful teachers, administrators, and coaches project
a certain charisma through themselves and the material they teach. They
seldom work alone. They enlist the aid of art, music, and drama specialists
and other communication leaders, and they know the value of working as a
team. Great teaching teams are a prerequisite for successful programs on
all levels of education, from preschool through graduate school.

Effective communication should be the first goal of our schools. Reading skills alone are not enough for youngsters today and will certainly not be enough to guarantee effective communication in the twenty-first century. Teachers equipped only to teach reading skills are like automobile salespeople with only eight-cylinder four-door models available. The communication arts are developing at least as rapidly as the automobile industry. Today, cars are used for more than Sunday family outings. Communication arts involve more than simple reading skills and writing mechanics. Retooling our communication arts industry is critical. We must all enlist or be drafted.

Dr. Elizabeth Lynn describes the Graduate Communication Arts program for teachers at Western Connecticut State College as an exemplary program with precisely this goal.* There the communication arts are considered basic. Teachers who complete the program radiate the love of language. They are equipped to lead programs in this specialty. In this interdisciplinary program, as in the pages of this book, it is assumed that everyone is capable of creative communication. Like children who learn to construct model planes that fly as the young designers want them to, speakers and writers learn their craft from fearlessly taking every opportunity to test their verbal flights of fancy.

Curriculum development, the improvement of what actually happens under the jurisdiction of the school, depends not upon texts, courses of study, or the latest machines and boxes of lessons, but upon the preservice and inservice education of teachers and supervisors. Programs on all levels must nurture the three stages of teaching described in this took.

In summary, to unlock beginning writers and speakers and readers we must believe in them. Word-painters are all around us. Their numbers depend upon how we care for the language environment.

Whenever we come upon an environment that includes a polluted lake or a row of abandoned buildings, we wonder what was considered basic in that environment. We may also think about the following appeal composed by an anonymous ninth grader and wonder about his language environment and what it will be like for his children.

    BLACK STUCK IN SCHOOL
    Teacher help me.
    I am Black.
    I live in the slums.

---

*Elizabeth Meagher Lynn, "A National Survey of Graduate Courses in Clasroom Communication Theory and Skills Available to Practicing Elementary and Secondary Teachers" (Ph.D. diss., Indiana University, 1974). See also her article "In-Service Teacher Education in Classroom Communication," *Communication Education* 26 (1977).

Teacher help me.
I cannot read good.
Not good enough.
So if I can't read
I can't spell too good.

Teacher help me.
Pollution, poverty,
Unemployment.

Teacher will you help me?
I just burned
    part of a school
    to get a center.
I go to court Monday.

Oh teacher would you please
    help me?
This is it for school.

I am Black,
    sixteen years of age.
no more.
Teacher help me.

This youngster, like our own, is now an adult. His plea continues on be-
half of his own future children. Soon these young men will hold their own
babies in their arms, as we did, wanting to communicate. Are you a parent,
a grandparent, a nurse, a therapist, a guard, or a friend? Then you are also
a kind of teacher.

Will your communication program help him, his children, or his grandparents? There are so many potential wordsmiths all around us. Listen for
them. Appreciate them. Help them. Please help them communicate from
within. Say with this teacher

Your words will dazzle
Your voices are free
Dance   Sing   Paint
                            for me.
I'll be your tool
I'll be your pen
Laugh   Dance   Build
                            again . . . .

                            Draw for me
                            Speak to me

The world will see
>within your soul.
>Share with me
>Sing to me

The world will LOVE

>your world—
>i know

—*Marian DiFabbio, graduate student and teacher*

SUGGESTED READING

Cooper, Charles R., and Odell, Lee, eds. *Research on Composing*. Urbana, Ill.: National Council of Teachers of English, 1978.

Evertts, Eldona. *A Minimal Professional Reference Library on Language Arts for Elementary School Teachers*. Urbana, Ill.: National Council of Teachers of English, 1976.

Finegan, Edward. *Attitudes Toward English Usage: The History of a War of Words*. New York: Teachers College Press, 1980.

Lynn, Elizabeth Meagher. "A National Survey of Graduate Courses in Classroom Communication Theory and Skills Available to Practicing Elementary and Secondary Teachers." Ph.D. dissertation, Indiana University, 1974.

Martin, Nancy; D'Arcy, Pat; Newton, Bryan; and Parker, Robert. *Writing and Learning Across the Curriculum, 11–16*. London: Ward Lock Educational, distributed by Hayden Book Company, Rochelle Park, N.J., 1976.

McCracken, Robert, and McCracken, Marlene. *Reading Is Only the Tiger's Tail: A Language Arts Program*. San Rafael, Cal.; Leswing Press, 1972.

Moffett, James. *Teaching the Universe of Discourse*. Boston: Houghton Mifflin, 1968.

Smith, Eugene. *Teacher Preparation in Composition*. Urbana, Ill.: National Council of Teachers of English, 1969.

Westby, Carol E. "Children's Narrative Development: Cognitive and Linguistic Aspects." Paper presented at the Conference on Language, Learning, and Reading Disabilities: A New Decade, Graduate Center of the City University of New York, 22–23 May, 1980.

Wolsch, Robert. *Life Skills Educators Curriculum Manual*. Brooklyn: Training Resources for Youth, Inc., 1967.

_____. "Poetic Composition in the Elementary School: A Handbook for Teachers." Ed.D. dissertation, Columbia University, 1969.

Wolsch, Robert, and Wynn, Don. Report to the U.S. Government, Life Skills Curriculum Task Force: First Progress Report. Brooklyn: Training Resources for Youth, Inc., 1967.

Wright, Keith. *A Minimal Professional Library for Secondary School Teachers.* Urbana, Ill.: National Council of Teachers of English, 1975.

Index